Advance Praise for *The Year My Son and I Were Born*

"Kathryn Lynard Soper's *The Year My Son and I Were Born* takes on, with grace, honesty and candor, a difficult subject: what it means, in our culture of perfection, to become the mother of a disabled child. From her son's early, traumatic birth, to learning what it means to be the mother of a child with special needs, Soper's journey with Thomas will appeal to not only readers who share similar experiences, but also to any reader who has found life can often turn out not to be as expected, or predicted—in other words, all readers."

—Vicki Forman, winner of the Bakeless Literary Prize, author of *This Lovely Life: A Memoir of Premature Motherhood*

"Kathryn Lynard Soper's prose is spare and achingly honest. With her talent for to-the-bone expression, she has produced this remarkable memoir about the birth of her Down syndrome son and the inevitable life changes he brought to her family—and to her own life. It is at once heart-wrenching and redemptive, a memoir not just for someone dealing with a child's disabilities (whatever they might be), but for anyone coping with a hard surprise. Soper is candid about the difficulty of embracing the unexpected, and leads her readers through the transcendant process of recognizing and loving the gift at the core of the challenge. . . . This book . . . will be a guide and a comfort for any reader."

—Margaret Young, Creative Writing instructor, Brigham Young University

Your pain is the breaking of the shell which encloses your understanding.

—Kahlil Gibran

THE YEAR
MY SON AND I
WERE BORN

A Story of Down Syndrome, Motherhood, and Self-Discovery

KATHRYN LYNARD SOPER
Foreword by Patricia E. Bauer

life

Guilford, Connecticut

An imprint of The Globe Pequot Press

life

Copyright © 2009 by Kathryn Lynard Soper

GPP Life is an imprint of The Globe Pequot Press

Text design by Libby Kingsbury

Photo on page 328 by Maralise Peterson. All others courtesy Kathryn Soper.

Library of Congress Cataloging-in-Publication Data is available on file.

ISBN 978-0-7627-5061-0

Printed in the United States of America

10 9 8 7 6 5 4 3 2 1

For Thomas

Foreword

As I write this, in the fall of 2008, the media is full of photographs of an attractive, dark-haired woman; in her arms is an adorable baby with chubby cheeks and big eyes full of wonder. If you look very closely, you might notice that the boy's eyes are ever so slightly almond-shaped. He is Trig Palin, son of vice presidential candidate Sarah Palin, and he is for many Americans the first person with Down syndrome they have ever welcomed into their homes.

The arrival of Trig on the stage of the national Republican convention this fall, amid tumultuous applause, has prompted a national conversation about genetic disability the likes of which we've not heard before. These 400,000 Americans with Down syndrome, people are asking one another: Who exactly are they, and what kind of lives do they lead? What does an extra chromosome mean to a person and to a family?

For expectant and prospective parents, Trig's presence on the campaign trail is particularly poignant. His face carries some of the characteristics that they're worrying about as they navigate the modern era's medical maze, with its many offers of prenatal testing.

Doctors estimate that 90 percent of pregnancies in which Down syndrome is diagnosed these days end in termination, a fact that seems at the very least to reflect our society's profound ambivalence about disability. Expectant parents are being asked to decide for themselves whether they believe disability is something to be accepted or prevented, and to predict whether they could possibly have a happy, fulfilling life in the company of someone who may not be, in Garrison Keillor's wry words, "above average."

Is it possible, these parents wonder, to love a child who isn't "perfect"? What is the value of a life lived with a disability—a life that many in our society view as preventable?

In the pages ahead readers will meet a woman whose experiences may provoke fresh thinking about some of these important questions. Kathryn Soper isn't what you'd call typical in some ways—she's a Mormon and the mother of seven children—but in one very significant way she's just like the majority of Americans. For most of her life, she hadn't given any serious thought to the subject of disability. That all changed the day her son Thomas showed up with an unexpected extra chromosome.

Kathryn welcomes us on her journey through Thomas's tumultuous first year as she struggles to realign herself to her changed circumstances. In between the tales of sleepless nights and dirty dishes, the ferocious breast pump and the wayward hearing aids, we come to know the heart of a woman who is struggling to accept the loss of the child she thought she had, and yet is fiercely loyal to this new and endearing youngster. She worries: Can she discard her preconceived notions about disability and love Thomas for himself? Can she protect him from the world's disapproval? And can she be the mother Thomas deserves?

As Kathryn's story unfolds, she shares with her readers a rare combination of candor, wit, and reassurance. Fearlessly, she lays out for us her worries and self-doubts, and we rejoice with her when she moves beyond them in favor of celebrating her son's unique and irresistible self. To her great relief and ours, Kathryn comes to understand that Thomas is indeed a boy with gifts, charms, and possibilities, a valued and irreplaceable member of his family and community. And as Kathryn accepts Thomas with his imperfections, she also comes to accept her own.

An editor with a keen analytical eye, Kathryn first applied her newfound knowledge of parenting on the edge of disability by compiling a collection of essays written by mothers of children with Down syndrome. In *Gifts,* these mothers shared much-needed information and insight with women contemplating one of the most important decisions of their lives. Like all mothers' tales, theirs are full of joy and laughter, disappointment and resolve. A second volume, *Gifts II,* is in production.

Now, in writing the story of her journey with Thomas, Kathryn offers her own personal support to moms and dads whose children defy traditional norms. In doing so, she also issues to us all a timely summons to reexamine what we think we know about human difference. As she looks into her son's beautiful gray eyes, Kathryn sees what we all perhaps have been trained not to see: that different is not bad, it is only different; that everyone has something to contribute. She finds in Thomas a reminder of what really matters, and a small but important person who is worthy of her respect, admiration, and love.

A quarter of a century ago, my own daughter was born with Down syndrome. Kathryn's book takes me back to that year, back when I had many of the same doubts and worries. Early in that first year, a friend counseled me that Margaret was more like the other kids than she was different, and that she would teach me more than I could ever teach her. My friend was right on both counts. But don't take my word for it. Let Kathryn explain.

Patricia E. Bauer
Atlanta, Georgia

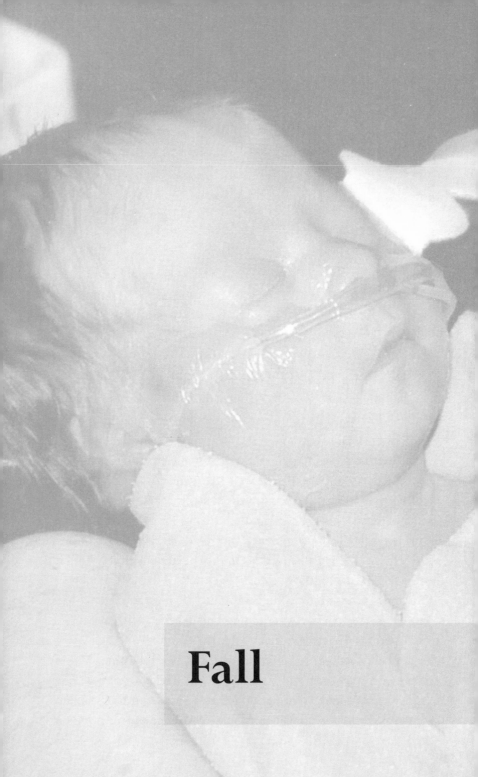

Fall

No. Oh, no.

My fingers froze on the laptop keyboard. A strange sensation welled up in my pelvis like a giant bubble. Slowly the bubble rolled downward and burst, soaking my maternity jeans and the woven hospital blanket.

The air stilled. I sat motionless, understanding what this meant, but not believing. It was 3 p.m. on my fourteenth day of hospital bed rest. The obstetrician stood at the nurses' station signing my discharge papers; my husband Reed waited at home for my call. I had just e-mailed friends to tell them I was on my way home. Home, where I'd lie on the couch for a month until it was safe for me to move again.

But as the amniotic fluid continued seeping out of me, I had to believe the truth. I wasn't going home. I was having a baby—ten weeks early.

Hand shaking, I reached for the nurse's call button. Within moments the room filled with the brisk energy of pending emergency. The resident performed a vaginal exam by speculum and flashlight, not daring to touch my cervix. She had me summon

Reed by telephone. My bed, transformed into a gurney, was pushed down the hall to Labor and Delivery. Two nurses helped me roll from one bed to the next, then began attaching all the high-risk accessories: blood pressure cuff, IV line, fetal monitor, heart and lung monitors for me. I turned my head to watch the paper readout uncurl from the contraction monitor: a flat black line at first, then a slight upward curve that peaked and dipped.

"Are you feeling that?" one of the nurses asked.

Yes. I was.

7 p.m. Reed stood by the delivery bed, holding my hand while I leaked tears and sweat into the sheets. The contractions had intensified from squeezing to wrenching. My bladder swelled with IV fluids, but I couldn't urinate when I tried. As the pressure in my pelvis mounted, I writhed on the bed in raw panic.

The nurse put her hand on my shoulder and asked if I'd like some pain relief before she inserted a catheter. "The urethra gets swollen during labor," she said. "It might be hard to get the tube in."

Twenty minutes later I bent over my bulging abdomen to receive a spinal needle. As I sat upright my head spun and my vision blurred. The nurse strapped an oxygen mask to my face. By the time my blood pressure stabilized and my bladder had been drained, the contractions had stopped, leaving me six centimeters dilated—a point of no return. The nurse hooked a bag of Pitocin to the IV pole and started a drip. Reed and I looked at each other in disbelief. After two weeks of doing everything possible to keep the baby in, he would be forced out.

Our son. We'd chosen his name already: Thomas Reed. In the ultrasound photos his face emerged in wrinkles of light and darkness, the landscape of humanity. He was due December 23. A Christmas baby. But this was early October, not even Halloween.

After the nurse left, Reed slumped in the armchair. I curled on my side, facing him. The wall behind Reed had a sliding window—*a drive-thru window,* he had joked earlier—which led to the NICU. The last place we wanted to be. Two years before, our newborn son Sam had spent three weeks in a different hospital's NICU, critically ill with lung failure, and I would never forget the grimness of that place. The doctors said Sam's illness was a freak occurrence and that if we wanted another baby, we had every reason to expect a healthy birth. My prenatal exams and ultrasounds for this new pregnancy had all been normal.

But nothing was normal about giving birth at thirty weeks gestation. I knew the statistics. Chance of respiratory failure: one in three. Chance of brain hemorrhage: one in five. Chance of death: one in ten.

Reed and I were quiet. There was nothing to say. The only sound was the *whoop whoop whoop* of the baby's heartbeat on the fetal monitor, a manic rhythm pushing all three of us into the future.

11 p.m. I jerked awake as pain seared the sides of my belly and gathered it into a tight fist, then rammed downward through my pelvis, pushing the bones apart. I cried out. Reed stood and reached for my hand as the pain came again, splitting me in two. I squeezed my eyes shut, my tears futile against the power of birth, which came in wave after wave, carrying me deep into a bare place far from reason, an altered state that ushered in life but felt like death.

After midnight the nurse's gloved fingers found ten centimeters of space: Dilation was complete. "I'll get the doctor," she said, turning on her heel. Another nurse uncurled my limbs and lifted my knees, telling me to hold them while I pushed. But within seconds my arms fell limp, my strength gone, my fear bursting out in sobs.

Hands lifted my feet into stirrups. The OB appeared at the foot of the bed, his glasses glinting in the overhead light. "Kathryn, I need to you to push now." His voice came over and over as I strained and cried. The baby was so small; they'd told me he would slip right out. They were wrong.

"Push!" the nurse barked.

"I *am*!" Every push dissolved into nothing, as if I were gunning a car engine stuck in neutral. "Please get it out. Please!"

The OB spoke in that calm voice doctors reserve for hysterical patients. "The baby is too small to use forceps safely, Kathryn." And I didn't care. I didn't care. The pain came with blind force, merciless. I thought it would kill me.

The next contraction hit, fast and hard. "Hold your breath and push!" the nurse ordered, and I gasped and heaved and felt a twisting within me, a little skull turning. My muscles took over, finally able to work, the pushing now a sweet relief.

"Here's the head," the doctor called as a sharp burning ripped my flesh.

"Just a bit of tearing," the nurse told me. I felt the head slip free, and then a shoulder and a small, wet body. Thomas. I heard a weak, gurgled cry before they whisked him through the window, and he was gone.

1 a.m. I couldn't stop crying. Dignity long gone, I wept with abandon, as if I were alone, as if I were curled up in my childhood bed, my lungs scraped raw by jagged breaths. Reed sat in the

armchair, head bowed, face in his hands. Behind him was the sliding window, spilling harsh light onto the floor in front of the wall. On the other side doctors were evaluating the condition of our child, the condition of our future.

A dozen possibilities loomed ahead: ventilators, rotting bowels, heart failure. Coils of oxygen tubing, scores of syringes. Needles. Beeping monitors. A home in tatters, relationships strained pale. Mental and physical and social delays. A funeral. A tombstone.

But I wasn't thinking about any of that. I wasn't thinking at all. Two words kept pounding through my mind, and there wasn't room for anything else. *Never again. Never again.* I would never bear a child again. I had endured six other births in the past, six episodes of keen pain and near-impossible demands. But nothing like this. I felt utterly empty, as if I'd delivered not only a baby, but some essential part of myself.

Without warning the window slid open and a nurse poked her head through. "I've got the scores," she said. Apgar scores.

Time froze.

"One-minute score was eight. Five-minute score was nine." She grinned through the open window. "He's breathing room air."

Reed and I gave each other trembling half smiles. Between sobs I choked out a laugh.

"You'll be able to see him before too long," the nurse promised. "The doctor will let you know when it's time."

A half hour passed. Slowly, my crying eased into the blank peace of a heart squeezed dry. Reed and I spoke softly, as if loud noise could break our spell of good luck, of blessings. Already I was making plans for the wind-up scenes of the crisis: a few days in the NICU, then we'd bring Thomas home and begin picking up the scattered pieces of our family life. Still daunting—but by comparison, doable.

Reed and I were still talking and smiling when two doctors

appeared at my bedside. They waited quietly until we turned to face them. An old man, a young woman.

Two doctors, not one. Two doctors with solemn eyes.

The woman cleared her throat, then paused. Silence pressed against my ears.

"Mr. and Mrs. Soper, we think your son has Down syndrome."

Nobody spoke.

"He has several of the physical characteristics," the woman continued. "We're nearly certain, but we'll do a blood test to confirm."

Nobody spoke.

I turned back toward Reed. A look passed between us. It lasted only a few seconds, but it held the weight of years. The weight of lifetimes.

2 a.m. The heavy wooden doors of the NICU swung open silently. Reed pushed my wheelchair through. I'd been there a few days before for a VIP tour of the facilities. I recognized the lavender paint on the walls and the flickering hum of fluorescent lights. Still, it felt like alien territory.

The unit had six rooms filled with rows of flat warming beds, boxy Isolettes with latched portholes, and small metallic cribs. The nurse led us through the back door of Room 1, the admitting area with extra-bright lights and a hard, shiny floor. I scanned the room, wondering if I'd recognize our child. There—in the far right corner, I saw a scrap of a baby stretched out on a warming bed, with a face scrunched just like the one in the ultrasound photos. As Reed wheeled me near, my hand reached for the small, dark head. So little, so new. Thomas.

I studied him. At four pounds, three ounces, he was twice the size of many babies in the room, yet only about half the size of Sam at birth. Still, all the familiar features were his, in miniature—the mop of brown hair, the flat nose, the lashless eyes. I saw no evidence of the extra chromosome supposedly lurking in each of his cells.

The resident who'd delivered the diagnosis waited by the wall, watching me, probably expecting some emotional outburst. But all I felt was an eerie calm, as if my feelings had been left behind in the birthing room, absorbed by the cotton sheets along with my sweat and blood.

After a few minutes the resident leaned forward. "What questions do you have?" she asked with a Southern lilt.

"How can you tell?" I asked. She stepped closer and pointed to Thomas's eyes, noting they were spaced slightly farther apart than normal. There were pale flecks in the dark gray irises and tiny folds of skin in the inner corners. She showed me the extra roll of skin on the back of his neck, the barrel shape of his chest, the gap between his first and second toes.

It didn't seem like much proof to me. "How sure are you?"

"Ninety-nine percent."

Down syndrome. When I was a few months pregnant with Thomas, I'd quizzed my OB about prenatal testing. He said blood screening would be inconclusive without amniocentesis, and that my chance of miscarriage from amnio was the same as my chance of a positive diagnosis: about one in three hundred. But the former seemed far more likely to me than the latter. All my life I'd been painfully uneasy around people with mental disabilities— my childhood neighbor, my friend's little brother, random people on buses and in shopping malls. I kept my distance, avoiding conversation and even eye contact. I was the last woman on earth who should mother a baby with Down syndrome.

But there he was. My son.

"Do you have any other questions?" the resident asked. I shook my head. Actually, I had at least a thousand questions, but I couldn't articulate even one of them.

Reed's face was resigned, as if he were preparing himself for an unpleasant, unavoidable task. "What happens now?" he asked.

The resident explained the battery of tests Thomas would endure over the next few days: A chromosome karyotype to confirm his diagnosis. Regular blood draws to monitor his chemistry. An echocardiogram to look for heart problems, a CAT scan to look for brain bleeds. Her words sounded like dialogue from a TV drama, set in a NICU with lavender walls and flickering lights and a slack-bellied mother in a bloodstained gown.

Thomas stirred on his warming bed. It was surreal to see him, once a hazy possibility in my imagination, now blinking and breathing. Yet he was real. Solid. His skin hummed with new life, irresistible.

"Can I hold him?" I asked. The resident nodded. The nurse gathered up the bundle of blanket, wires, and baby and placed it in my arms. I believed in destiny and in God's benevolent management of the universe. Surely Thomas's arrival was part of the divine plan governing my life. I waited for a sign that he belonged with me—a bright spark of assurance, a firm sense of peace. But all I felt was the gentle warmth seeping from his skin into mine.

3 a.m. Reed wheeled me back into my hospital room twelve hours after the nurses had wheeled me out. During our hour with Thomas, shock had cushioned us in a protective bubble. We didn't talk much, didn't cry, didn't even feel tired. But as soon as

we crossed the threshold Reed sank onto the spare bed, fading fast.

When the night nurse appeared she gave Reed a withering look. "I'm sorry, but the beds are for patients only. We provide a fold-out chair for visitors who spend the night." She pointed to the armchair in the corner of the room.

"You've got to be kidding me," I protested. "We passed a bunch of empty rooms on our way down the hall. And it's the middle of the night. Why can't he just lie down for a few hours?"

The nurse pursed her lips. "We must keep the beds available for patients." She fetched a blanket and pillow from the closet and handed them to Reed. "May I help you set up the chair? It fits right here, between the beds."

"I think I can manage," Reed said, his voice carefully controlled.

He got to work while the nurse helped me change out of my crusty gown, climb into bed, and position an ice pack between my legs. Once we were both settled the nurse walked out of the room with prim little steps, clicking off the light on her way, as if we were two naughty children up past bedtime. We kept quiet until the door swung shut. Then we burst out laughing.

Gallows laughter. Once it was spent, we lay side by side like friends at a bizarre slumber party, whispering in the dark. We had a new baby. He had Down syndrome. In the cover of night none of it seemed real, not even as I felt the ice melting between my legs and the killer afterpains cramping my empty womb. But dawn was only a few hours away.

Solitaire

Reed crawled off the fold-out chair, stiff as a zombie. Neither of us had slept much. The prim nurse had appeared every hour to prod my womb with her blunt fingers, sending shooting stars of pain through my pelvis. Every time I jolted from sleep I remembered: *Thomas.*

The fuzzy numbness that had cocooned me the night before was gone, leaving me bare and blinking in the stark light of morning. Reed pulled on his sweatshirt, kissed me good-bye, and headed for the door. If he hurried, he could catch the next commuter train, then the bus that would take him home. Home, where our one car waited in the garage in case my mother needed it. When my preterm labor had started two weeks before, she'd flown to Utah from Maryland, coming to my rescue just as she always did.

My earliest memory: I was two years old. My mother was holding me over the kitchen sink, pressing my stomach against the edge of the countertop, her arm wrapped around me from behind, her free hand scrabbling frantically at my face. Her long fingernails dug into my mouth, scratching the back of my tongue and the top of my throat. The white, knobby top of a chicken leg was wedged in my airway, just beyond her reach. I tasted fright on her knuckles and palm. In the emergency room, doctors opted to wait until my stomach emptied to remove the piece, to avoid the high risk of aspiration and possible death. Mom sat at my bedside for hours as I slept, her hand on my chest to monitor my slow, labored breaths.

The sentinel. She'd been waiting half a day to hear the news about the baby's delivery, waiting ever since she brought the kids home from an outing at the park and found Reed's note on the kitchen counter: *Kathy's water broke.* She probably slept in my bed that night, so she could hear any calls from the little boys' bedroom. Or any calls from my hospital room.

The telephone waited on the bedside table. Next to it rested the plastic calling card Mom bought for me when my hospital stay began. Since then I'd clocked a dozen or more hours on that card, making the rounds through my circle of friends, telling everyone the story: Preterm labor. Four centimeters. Hospital bed rest. Each time I delivered the news I was rewarded with a little gasp coming from the phone receiver, a little piece of my crisis absorbed by proxy. Call by call, I parceled out the shock and fear as if I were dealing a pack of cards. And nobody was more willing to take a loaded hand than my mother.

I dialed my house. Mom answered right away.

"You have a new grandson," I said.

"Oh, Kathy! Congratulations!" Her crisis voice. I'd heard it too many times—worry wound tight, like dental floss around a fingertip, so tight it squeaked with fake cheer. "How is he?"

"He's doing okay." Pause. "He's breathing a lot better than we expected him to."

"Oh, thank goodness. That's wonderful, sweetie!" I could almost hear the *whoosh* of stress releasing from her neck and shoulders. "How big is he?"

"Four pounds, three ounces."

"Really? He gained a whole pound in the hospital? Oh, I'm so glad he's okay."

This would never work. I had to speak before her muscles unwound one more turn. I cleared my throat, dredging up words.

"Mom, he has Down syndrome."

Pause.

"He does?" The pitch of her voice fell an octave. Long seconds of silence, then she gave a resolute sigh. "Well, Kathy, he must have come to your family for a good reason."

I flinched. Like many Mormons, Mom and I believed God chooses certain children to be born with disabilities and sends those children to specific families. Which meant Thomas was handpicked to have Down syndrome, and I was handpicked to be his mother. The whole situation was considered a blessing, even an honor. But to my shame, it didn't feel like one. And I couldn't bring myself to say so, not even to my mother.

I ended the conversation as quickly as I could, then rolled onto my side, wishing I could stay in bed forever. Mom, by contrast, would've hit the floor running. Nothing stopped that woman. Throughout her divorce from my father, her remarriage, and her struggle to blend two troubled families, she clung fiercely to hope, smiling when others would cry, or scream. Her emotional endurance seemed superhuman. This strength I loved, and hated—loved because it made me feel safe, hated because it made me feel lonely.

So lonely.

I picked up the phone again and called Kate, my touchstone since high school and a licensed social worker to boot. As soon as I heard her firm, warm voice I began to relax, as if she were sitting right next to me, holding my hand.

"Thomas has Down syndrome," I said.

"Oh, babe," she sighed. She began emotional triage, gathering all the pieces of the crisis as quickly as I could unpack them. Thomas's well-being was the chief concern—his health, even his survival. But there were many other players: my husband, my children. Myself. We, too, had urgent needs. Kate laid these pieces out, arranged them, studied them one by one.

"This is big," she said.

"Yes." I closed my eyes. Kate would take care of me.

Then, from somewhere in the background over Kate's shoulder, I heard a clatter and happy shouts—her children were awake. I opened my eyes, surprised by the obvious: *Kate isn't here.* She stood in her kitchen, two thousand miles away. Her children were probably climbing on the table, spilling the milk and Cheerios, taking advantage of their distracted mother. And soon, very soon, she would hang up the phone, mop up the milk, and get on with her life, which was not mine.

Kate promised to call later that evening. After we hung up I felt so empty that I picked up the phone again and called Kylie, a longtime confidante who was newly pregnant with her fifth child.

"The baby has Down syndrome," I said with a nervous laugh. The week before, she and I had been talking about the roll of the dice every couple makes at conception, and she mentioned a television news segment she'd just seen about children with Down syndrome. "You see things like that," she said, "and you think, 'Please, no.'"

Please, no. I pictured her standing with one hand on the phone and the other shielding her abdomen. I could hear her crying in sympathy, and likely in fear and gratitude as well—fear that the same thing might happen to her, gratitude that it probably wouldn't. I knew well that shameful relief which can come when tragedy strikes a friend, that sense of escape: *Since it happened to her, it's less likely to happen to me.*

It had happened to me. I had a son with Down syndrome; Kylie did not. Kate did not. My mother did not. And it wouldn't matter how many phone calls I made, how many times I told the tale. I was holding cards I couldn't give away.

An hour later I stripped off my soiled gown and stepped gingerly into the shower. I turned the water on full blast, as hot as I could bear, and stood directly under the spray. The water around my feet ran rusty with washed-off blood.

Six times before I'd stood like that, ravaged and spent, letting the hot water run until it was gone, avoiding the moment when I'd have to step out of the shower and into a daunting new life. As much as I'd loved and wanted each of my newborns, the postpartum period was always hell. Raging hormones, bleeding nipples. Thick, black exhaustion. A certain despair that comes only when you feel dead, yet must keep others alive. With Sam those weeks had included an extra layer of stress from the NICU stay, with its beeping monitors and needle-wielding nurses and thick, heavy air. All of that was waiting for me on the other side of the shower curtain—and it was only the beginning.

Ellen, my close friend from high school, has a brother with Down syndrome. He was little—two or three years old—when I first met him. At the time his dirty blond hair was cut pageboy style; his thick glasses magnified his gray eyes, making him look constantly astonished. But he seemed foreign to me, distasteful, even less appealing than typical kids with their crusty noses and constant demands. Ellen loved to play with him. She even got scolded by her mother once for dressing him up in girl clothes and makeup, then posing him for photographs. I laughed when I saw the photos of David in drag, but I couldn't imagine loving such a brother. Not the way I loved my own brother, who was part of me, like a limb.

Could I love such a son?

I rubbed my arms and legs with a rough washcloth, determined to scrub away not only blood and sweat and oil, but also doubt. Of course I could love Thomas. I already did. I loved him as I'd loved each of my new babies, with a primal strength full and fierce. My friends and family members couldn't share the burden of his disability, but they couldn't share this intense bond, either. Not even my mother could.

Yet I knew the bond wouldn't be enough, not for long. It was instinctual. Even animal. Thomas deserved human love, the delight and appreciation and tenderness one unique person feels for another. I'd never felt this for a person with Down syndrome or any other disability. I didn't know if I could.

Goose bumps rose on my arms—the hot water was gone. And my time to indulge in weakness was gone. A child waited in a plastic box down the hall, and six more were waiting at home, waiting for security to surround them like a warm mantle, soft yet strong. Waiting for their mother.

Soon after I dressed, Reed arrived, freshly showered himself. I shook my head when he offered me a wheelchair ride to the NICU. My muscles were loose and soft after two weeks of bed rest, but walking suddenly felt important.

Reed held the door to my room open as I staggered forward. Every bone in my skeleton seemed to have tripled in weight; my joints felt clogged with dust. As we moved down the hallway I kept tugging Reed's shirtsleeve to make him slow down.

When we entered the unit I did a double take—the night before we'd entered through a different door, and I hadn't seen the huge whiteboard on the wall by the nurse's desk. It listed the names of all the patients, over thirty of them. The Room 1 patients were at the top. My eyes snagged on his name: *Soper, Thomas.*

I hobbled into the room and sank gratefully into the swivel chair in Thomas's corner. Several things had changed since the night before. The warming bed had been replaced by an Isolette, a Plexiglas box with two latched portholes in each side. New IV lines snaked from Thomas's feet; a line for blood draws protruded from his navel. An oxygen cannula lodged in his nostrils—he needed help breathing after all. A fresh blanket covered his bed in bright green. A blue sign with alphabet stickers spelling THOMAS hung on the side of his bed.

I opened one of the portholes. Warm air streamed out, scented with baby sweat and rubbing alcohol. Thomas lounged on his back, asleep, legs stretched in repose, arms limp at his sides. His fingers were unfurled from his palms like loosening rose petals, so different from the clenched bud of a typical baby's fist. *Hypotonia,* the doctor had called it—low muscle tone that accompanies Down syndrome. I pressed my index finger against one palm, but he didn't grab it, so I reached my thumb around the other side and held his hand instead.

We were the only parents in the room. Six babies, three nurses, no windows. The other babies were hiding in Isolettes with small quilts covering the tops, shielding them from light and prying eyes. The nurses stood at their stations between the beds, checking and rechecking the numbers flashing on the monitors. Every few seconds an alarm sounded from one monitor or another, a flat, repeating tone signaling a loose wire, or a dropped heartbeat, or a pause in breath. After Sam's NICU stay I'd heard those tones in my sleep for weeks.

Reed sat quietly, his short brown hair still damp, his dark eyes cast downward. He hated hospitals. The sight of infirm bodies attached to machinery caused a visceral reaction he couldn't hide.

"Are you okay?" I asked.

He shrugged. "I just can't believe we're here again. When Sam came home I figured we were all done with babies in the hospital, but apparently it was only a warm-up for this."

I shuddered. The aftermath of Sam's delivery still felt fresh. Soon after he was discharged I hit a bad patch of depression—I'd cycled between mild to moderate symptoms since childhood, but that episode was the worst I'd experienced in years. Reed struggled as well, suffering chronic muscle pain and exhaustion. For over a year we merely existed, side by side yet rarely connecting, wondering if we would ever feel alive again.

Eventually we did. By the time Sam turned two our marriage was soaring through a passionate renaissance. We wanted another baby. And so Thomas was conceived, symbolizing all the beauty of our renewed relationship. *Our love child,* we'd said to each other, only half joking.

Reed took off his glasses and rubbed his eyes. "I don't know how we're going to manage. Even after we get Thomas out of here, there's a whole other thing waiting for us, you know?"

"I know."

"I mean, right now he's just like any baby born too soon. His disability doesn't matter. But at some point it's going to matter."

I couldn't think that far ahead. All my points of reference were gone. I felt small and exposed, like I was trying to sleep outdoors under a wide-open sky, unable to relax without the four walls of my bedroom enclosing me. It made me wish for the security of a small Plexiglas box, one without portholes, so reality couldn't reach in.

A nurse delivered a breast pump to my room that evening. I gave it a wary eye as she pushed it close to my bedside: a hospital-grade double pump, perched atop a wheeled stand for my milking convenience. Just like the pump I'd used during Sam's hospital stay. Back then, before I tried it for the first time, I figured pumping had to be less painful than nursing. I was sorely mistaken.

But there was no question—I would provide milk for Thomas. It was the least, and the most, I could do. And my mother would be arriving any minute to meet her new grandson, so I needed to get moving. I assembled the tubing and the collection bottles, then set my jaw and flicked the switch. The pump groaned as it set in motion, pulling my flesh into its flanges. With gritted teeth I watched the second hand of the clock sweep its circle ten times. When I turned the pump off there were ten drops of yellow colostrum at the bottom of one of the collection bottles. Victorious, I captured them in a tiny syringe.

My friend Kate called as I was finishing up. "How are you doing?" she asked.

"Just sitting here wishing male mammals could lactate."

She laughed. "No, really."

"Really, I'm okay." I sealed the syringe in a plastic bag and set it on the bedside table, then lay back against the pillows. "I'm just feeling lost. I can't wrap my mind around everything. Part of me still doesn't believe this is happening."

"Well, that doesn't surprise me. You've just gotten the shock of your life. How's Thomas?"

"Okay. They're going to start feeding him through his tube tomorrow. His brain scan was normal, and his echocardiogram looked pretty good at first glance—we're still waiting for the full results, but the doctors seem hopeful." As I spoke Mom entered the room and sat in the armchair next to my bed, smiling.

"Thank God," Kate sighed. "Is this a good sign overall? I know there's a wide range of abilities for people with Down syndrome, but is there a connection between physical heath and higher cognitive function?"

I'd asked the geneticist the same question. "No, there's no way of predicting how severe his delays might be. We'll just have to wait and see."

"Well, okay. He's healthy—that's the most important thing." She paused. "I've been thinking a lot today. You remember when

I was in graduate school and I did that rotation with the adults with Down syndrome?"

Yes, I remembered, vaguely. Years ago, when my first two children were small, and Kate was pursuing her master's degree, she had told me she was working with a group of people with Down syndrome as part of her social work curriculum. At the time I wondered how she could stand it. I couldn't think of anything more uncomfortable than having to spend all day in the company of people who struggled to communicate and lacked social graces. People who might even want to touch me.

Kate continued, "I believe Thomas can have a good life, especially if he doesn't have any major health issues. It might be a different kind of life, given his diagnosis, but it can still be a good life."

Tears came, unwelcome. I blinked them back. I wanted to believe her, but I didn't know if I could. And to my shame, as much as I wanted Thomas to have a good life, right then I cared more about whether *I* could have a good life.

I glanced at Mom in the armchair, her arms folded, her face relaxed. "Right," I said to Kate, clamping off my emotions. "We'll figure this out. Down syndrome might be a challenge, but it's not a tragedy."

Mom nodded, slowly. They were words she might have spoken, grounded and hopeful and firm. Maybe if I repeated them often enough I would know—really know—that they were true.

We crept along the hallways toward the NICU. Mom's hand rested on my shoulder; she paced her steps to my own. Always anticipating my needs, always adjusting hers around mine.

Another early memory: I was three years old, or four. I sat on Mom's lap. She was hugging me, stroking my hair. "I love you, Kathy," she said. "I love you so much. If I had to choose between my life and yours, I would die for you." I sat very still, frightened by the tears in her voice, frightened by her words. I pictured her dead, and fear gripped me tighter. But my relief was immense: She loved me *that* much.

I felt that same love for Thomas as we approached his Isolette. And as soon as Mom saw him, she did too. "He's so beautiful," she said, beginning to weep.

He was. His skin shone that night, supersaturated with life. Mom and I sat close to each other, inches from the Plexiglas wall of the Isolette, arms stretched through the portholes. I began teaching her what I knew. I touched Thomas's eyes, ears, and hands, explaining. I named each tube and wire and the glowing screens that spoke for them. Mom listened closely, nodding and murmuring, wiping her eyes with her free hand. For the first time since my labor began, I felt strong.

Mom put her hand on my shoulder. "How was your delivery?" she asked.

My mind jumped back through a day and a night, into the birthing room, onto the delivery bed. Tears came without warning, dripping from my cheeks to my lap, draining away my newfound strength and refreshing my despair.

The baby is too small to use forceps safely, Kathryn. And I hadn't cared.

I couldn't find words for the terrible shame: At the very time my son needed me most, I'd wanted to abandon him and save myself. And part of me still did.

Thomas stirred in his sleep, barely able to move with the IV lines tethering him, the needles that were keeping him alive. I let go of his hand as I began to sob. My lungs heaved. My bones shook. I felt my mother's fingers moving across my shoulder blades, lightly stroking the knotted, straining muscles. I wished she could reach through a porthole in my side and dig, sharp-nailed, at the grief lodged in my gut like a stone. Gouge it out. But all she could do was sit next to me, touch my back, feel me breathe.

Clan

The door swung open at 10 a.m. to admit a parade of children—my children. Six of the seven, at least. Seeing them en masse never failed to amaze me—they couldn't possibly *all* be ours. But two of them had my full lips, and three had my round, gold-brown eyes (cow eyes, my friends called them). Two had Reed's extra-broad shoulders, and four had his fine, dark brown hair, complete with a cowlick on the left temple. People commented all the time about how much the children looked like us.

I wondered if they'd say the same about Thomas.

My mother led everyone into the room with a confident smile. The two preschoolers made a beeline for the spare bed and started pushing the control buttons on the guardrails. The three oldest kids found the TV remote and started arguing over what to watch. Reed, bringing up the rear, rolled his eyes at me—at times like this, having such a large family seemed like sheer lunacy.

"When does the snack cart come?" asked Christine, the ill-fated middle child, six years old. The infamous snack cart: When I was on bed rest the kids had been entranced by my tales of cookies and chips delivered right to my bedside.

"We'll have snacks after you see Thomas," I promised.

Only two siblings were allowed at Thomas's bedside at a time. Mom offered to stay in the hospital room with the others. After a bit of negotiating over turns, Reed and I herded the little boys down the hall. The nurse at the NICU desk had them scrub their hands, then took their temperatures and checked the vaccination cards Reed had brought. After a long and fidgety minute we got the green light. The boys each took a turn hitting the square metal button that opened the heavy doors to Room 1. Their eyes grew round at the sight of all the strange equipment.

"Where's Thomas?" Matt asked.

Reed pointed. As we neared Thomas's bed, I caught my breath. Yards of tubing covered his little body. A thin hose rammed up his nostrils delivered a stream of air from a CPAP machine—his blood-oxygen levels must've dropped dramatically during the night. A tube to facilitate feedings snaked up his nose and down his throat into his stomach. A bilirubin lamp captured him in a bright blue circle of light; he wore a blindfold to protect his eyes. A striped cap covered his head.

"Here's your baby brother," I managed. He'd looked so brilliant the night before, so alive. Not anymore.

"I can't see!" Matt complained.

I wondered if he'd be better off not seeing. But it was too late to switch gears. Reed and I plunked the boys into tall swivel chairs and pushed them close. As they leaned even closer, I put a firm hand on the seats to keep them from rolling backward.

"He looks a little scary," Matt said with preschooler approval.

"It's my brother," Sam said, staring. He'd never before seen a newborn. Thomas moved one leg and Sam jumped, as if he wasn't expecting the strange creature to move.

Reed and I brought the two girls next. Feeling bold, I turned off the bili light and peeled back Thomas's blindfold for a moment.

Christine took one peek and turned away. "I don't want to look," she said.

"That's okay," I said. She kept her back to the Isolette and tried to find a comfortable place to rest her eyes.

Elizabeth, the eldest, hovered over the Isolette as if Thomas was one of the cat-ravaged birds we sometimes found in our backyard. The big boys did the same during their turn, making adoring whimpers like they would for a puppy in a pet store. But after a minute or two their attention turned from their tiny, naked brother to the mess of paraphernalia anchoring him to life. They looked at me, then at Thomas, then at me again, sober-eyed. Due to the strict visiting rules during winter months, none of them had seen Sam during his NICU stay. And nothing else could have prepared them.

After a few minutes, Reed and I led them through the swinging doors, back to the hospital room with cable TV, and chips from the snack cart, and a window that proved the world was still standing. When we walked in, my mother looked up and raised her eyebrows. "How's the little bub doing?"

I started to explain, but my throat was too tight to finish.

Suddenly the overhead light flickered like a strobe—Sam had discovered the switch on the wall. "I think that's our cue," Mom said. "Okay, everyone, let's get ready to go." She lined the kids up for good-byes, then came over to give me a hug.

"It's going to be okay," she said in the same cheery voice I'd heard all my life. She herded the kids out the door. I watched them go, wishing I could be a child again, instead of a mother.

Reed left early that evening. Alone in the empty hospital room, my head crowded with images of Thomas in his Isolette, stretched out like an offering before a blinking, beeping wall of machinery. Wide open to pain. A terrible paradox—every cell in my body screamed at me to keep Thomas safe, to fling myself across his bed and shield him from the tubes and needles and poking, prodding fingers. But that kind of protection would end his life.

Panicked, I picked up the phone and dialed the number of a dear friend in another state who had been calling every few days to check on me. Level-headed and kind, she would give me a firm arm to hold on to.

"I had the baby," I said when she answered. "He's not doing well. He can't eat without a tube, and he's on a breathing machine." I swallowed hard. "And he has Down syndrome."

After a moment she spoke. "Oh, Kathy. I'm so sorry. You must feel completely overwhelmed."

Yes.

"I know you were worried about complications, but you didn't know the baby had Down syndrome, right?"

No.

"I understand it's normal for parents in your situation to grieve," she said. "To, you know, mourn the child they were expecting to have."

Wham.

Pain squeezed my heart like a vise. I stuttered a response, then made up an excuse to get off the phone. The tightness in my chest flared into anger. *Don't tell me how to feel,* I fumed. *You don't know. You don't know.*

I hated her for assuming. I hated her more for being right. Yes, my love for Thomas was polluted with disappointment, resentment, even embarrassment. In the most secret corner of my heart, I was ashamed I'd given birth to a flawed baby. But what kind of mother mourned her living child? And what kind of Mormon doubted God's will?

I turned on the breast pump. Although I still winced in time with the suction, I welcomed the stabs of pain. The sacrifice showed devotion, devotion that Thomas needed and deserved. Twenty minutes later, there was enough bright yellow colostrum at the bottom of the milk collection bottles to fill a small syringe—two ccs.

I carried the guilt offering to Room 1, arriving just in time for "cares," the every-three-hour routine of attending to patients' basic needs. Glad to be useful for a few minutes, I held the digital thermometer wand in Thomas's armpit and watched the reading slowly creep upward. I changed his diaper, as small as an index card. The nurse began to flush each of his four IVs with saline. Remembering that Sam's IVs usually stopped functioning after only one day, I bit my lip, hoping Thomas would be spared. But one line was blocked.

The nurse scuffed his arm with an alcohol pad, searching for a good candidate in the rose-colored web of delicate veins. I held Thomas's other hand, closing my eyes when his back arched away from the sting of the needle. It was the first time I heard him wail.

When the nurse reached for tape to hold the new line in place, I bent close to his ear. "We're done, sweetie," I whispered. But when the nurse tried to flush the line, she shook her head.

"We've had a tough time getting lines on this little guy," she said as she moved to the other side of the bed. Another alcohol pad, another needle. Another wail. Another shake of the head.

My brow broke out in beads of sweat. I swayed slightly with a wave of nausea, gripping the floor with my toes. When the nurse made her third approach with the needle, I steeled myself, hoping to block my emotions through sheer force of will, but Thomas's scream pierced through every defense that I had.

The line failed again. The nurse called for help. Another nurse came, the IV expert, I was told. She brought a small, thin light with a glowing blue tip. Held under Thomas's arm, the light illuminated the network of threadlike vessels. He squirmed and yelled. She studied, selected. The needle went in. This time, the saline flushed through.

Dizzy and sick, I folded onto the swivel chair. If Thomas was lucky, the line would last until tomorrow. If we were lucky, he'd be out of the NICU by his due date. Ten weeks away. And what then? What then?

The floors felt strange when Reed and I walked to the unit the next morning. I was wearing shoes for the first time since I'd been admitted. My forty-eight-hour postpartum stay was over, and within hours I'd be going home.

I shivered as I pushed up my sleeves and scrubbed my hands and forearms with foamy white soap. Next to the sink was a basket of crocheted baby caps, gifts from the night nurses to the parents in the unit. Picking through the colors, I found a navy blue cap with a small, white, star-shaped button on the brim. A traveling hat.

I pushed back tears as I sat down at Thomas's bedside. Did he know I was leaving? When he woke in the fluorescent-lit night, feeling my milk stream up the tube in his nose, would he know I was gone?

The nurse pointed to a large brown envelope in the wire basket near the bed. The label read DOWN SYNDROME PACKET—ENGLISH. "From the geneticist," she said.

I opened the clasp and pulled out a stack of Xeroxed pages.

Cradling Thomas's palm with one hand, I leafed through the pages on my lap with the other. There were fact sheets and growth charts, diagrams of cells splitting, and photographs of genetic karyotypes with X-shaped chromosomes lined up in rows. The typical karyotypes showed chromosomes in pairs, like twins. But in the photo depicting Trisomy 21, there was one set of triplets. Three stubby Xs, so small compared to the other chromosomes, yet large enough to transform a body, a life, a family.

Absorbed, I was startled when the geneticist himself appeared. "Mrs. Soper, Mr. Soper," he greeted us. "Good, you've got the packet."

We thanked him.

"I have the results from the echocardiogram," he said. Then he smiled. "Thomas doesn't have the classic heart defect associated with Down syndrome. The only abnormalities we see are some enlargement on the right side of the heart and a small opening between two of the chambers. We'll keep a close eye on him, but both of these issues should resolve over time without intervention."

Reed's shoulders slumped with relief. No open-heart surgery.

The doctor grinned at us. "In fact, I'm not convinced Thomas has Trisomy 21."

I looked at him in shock.

"His heart looks great," he continued. "His muscle tone is better than I'd expect. He does have some soft markers, but those occur randomly in the general population. I have an uncle with Brushfield spots," he said, referring to the white flecks that spotted Thomas's irises like bits of starlight.

He was trying to be careful, I could tell. He knew how cruel it would be to get our hopes up. But his voice was charged with quiet excitement. "We'll have the results of the karyotype by Sunday," he said.

As he walked away I gripped the packet of papers, my head spinning. That very morning technicians were splitting Thomas's genes apart. The tiny third X might not be found after all. A door was swinging open—an exit back to the world we'd come from, back to the life we'd been living. Every rational thought I had, every nameable feeling, pushed me toward that exit. Yet when I pictured myself walking through, I felt resistance, like the mysterious force created when you try to push same-sided magnets together.

Reed raised his eyebrows. "Well," he said, and paused. "I guess we'll just have to wait and see." But I could tell that he knew, like I did, what the technician would see after arranging Thomas's chromosomes: Twenty-two sets of twins. One set of triplets.

I didn't want to leave—ever. But it was time to return to our other home, our other children. We said good-bye to Thomas and stroked his soft little fingers in farewell. Reed latched the porthole covers, picked up our coats, and headed for the exit. I hesitated, then followed behind him, stumbling slightly, clutching the blue hat with the tiny star.

The kitchen door opened to a bright wash of gold: An enormous bouquet of roses studded with tiny purple lilies, baby's breath, and green ferns blossomed from a glass vase in the center of the table. I was surprised to see something so beautiful on such a dark day. I knew Mom had placed it there so I'd see it first thing.

The house was empty. Mom had arranged that, too, taking the kids to the park so that I'd have some time and space for orientation, a buffer zone I desperately needed. Reed hauled my bags to our bedroom while I opened the small card lodged in the rose bouquet:

Our thoughts are with you and your family, and sweet little Thomas.

Love, your Segullah sisters.

My friends from the staff of the literary journal I edited. I cried as I felt their love and encouragement. But when I wiped my nose and read the card again, my eyes stuck on the words printed in scroll lettering at the top: *With Deepest Sympathy.* Then I cried harder. My friends must've phoned their message to the florist, long-distance; the florist must've chosen a card to match. The pity, although unintended, still hurt. It didn't fit the occasion—a new baby! And yet it did.

I edged down the hall to the master bedroom and eased myself onto the bed, frightened by the tears that kept coming. I'd been gone sixteen days. The children would soon burst through the front door, expecting the return of normal family life, with their mother in her rightful place. But that was impossible. Their family had changed. Their mother had changed. I felt like a stranger in my own bedroom, in my own skin.

I stood and began to unpack, focusing on the heap of belongings to put away: toothbrush, maxi pads, maternity jeans. It took forced concentration to decide where to put things. My hands and feet could barely move.

"Mom!"

Footsteps thumped down the hall. Christine ran through the doorway and grabbed me around the middle. The little boys followed. "Mom's home!" they chorused. I stiffened, overwhelmed by the sight and sound of them, by the hunger I felt in their hugs.

The big kids found us within seconds. "Do you like your flowers?" Elizabeth asked eagerly. I managed a smile and nodded, hoping she hadn't read the card. Despite our strange sense of certainty regarding the karyotype, Reed and I had decided to wait for the results before telling the kids.

Everyone started talking at once, their words and smiles and touches gathering quickly into a heap of wants and needs, feelings and thoughts. I picked up the topmost pieces and began my work of listening, absorbing, responding. Every time I put away one piece, ten more were added to the pile. I wanted to hide from everyone. Even more, I wanted to hide from the truth: I'd left a baby behind, a baby I both welcomed and feared. And I didn't know which hurt more—my longing to bring him home, or my relief that he wasn't home yet.

Saturday evening the phone rang. When I saw UNIVERSITY HOSPITAL on the caller ID, my heart jerked to a halt. Such calls rarely brought good news.

"Mrs. Soper?"

The geneticist. That could mean only one thing.

"I have the results from the karyotype here, a bit earlier than I expected."

Pause.

"I hesitate to deliver a diagnosis by telephone—"

"Please," I interrupted.

"Trisomy 21," he said. With deepest sympathy.

The exit door in my mind slowly swung shut.

After hanging up I found Reed on our bed, legs stretched out, watching TV. Thankfully, no kids were in sight—they were downstairs playing with their grandma.

I shut the door. "The hospital just called."

Reed looked up at me, sharp-eyed. "And?"

"And the karyotype confirmed Trisomy 21."

Reed clicked the remote to turn off the TV. "Well, we pretty much knew that already." He sat up in bed. "Are you okay?"

I sat down next to him. "I don't know. It's got to be the right thing, but I'm still scared."

He leaned back on the pillows, looking drained. "Maybe it's not right or wrong. Maybe it just *is*."

No. I needed the diagnosis to mean something—that's the only way I could handle it. When Sam was born ill, I'd clung to the belief that God gave us that trial for a wise purpose. My friend Kate, who isn't religious, called it a random occurrence. But I couldn't bear that thought. I feared a world where anything could happen at any given time for no good reason. Believing in divine will protected me from chaos—I was angry at God for giving Thomas Down syndrome, but at least I knew someone was in charge.

Reed was quiet. "How do *you* feel?" I asked.

He shrugged. "It's not like I'm excited to have a kid with Down syndrome, but I'm not horrified or anything. And in any case, we don't have a choice. No matter what it means or doesn't mean, we need to figure out how to deal with it."

His cool pragmatism sank my stomach. Didn't he understand? Didn't he feel fear pushing hard against his sternum? Didn't he feel *something*?

Apparently not. I wanted to cry, but I couldn't afford more tears. Needing comfort, I curled up next to Reed with my head resting on his heart. Over the years, I'd fallen asleep in that position hundreds of times, cradled by his smooth arm around my shoulder, soothed by his warm hand on the small of my back. I closed my eyes and tried to escape into silence. But I couldn't relax into Reed's stiff arm, his tense chest, his carefully measured breaths.

He *did* understand. He just couldn't afford tears either.

Sunday afternoon. The house was hushed; everyone except me was at church. I sat on my bed and hooked myself up to the rented breast pump, which lived on my nightstand. I was supposed to do eight twenty-minute sessions each day, but I usually did five or six, seven if I was lucky. I noted the starting time—only an hour left until the house would be hopping again.

Reed and I planned to discuss Thomas's diagnosis with the children in a family meeting that evening. I'd been envisioning the scene all afternoon: We'd sit the kids in a circle and explain that there was something different about their new brother. Then we'd calmly present simple facts about his condition. As a united front we'd project love and acceptance. We'd absorb any tremors of anxiety or fear. We'd hold ourselves together; we'd hold all of us together.

But first we needed a script. With one arm I steadied the two milk collection bottles; with the other I emptied the packet of information from the geneticist and picked up the stapled articles one at a time:

Trisomy 21: The Story of Down Syndrome
Risk and Recurrence of Down Syndrome
Treating People with Down Syndrome: Some Tips for Physicians

I scanned the pages, hoping to find a few sentences that we could memorize and recite to our children. Something easy to swallow. But there wasn't much to help us among the graphs and charts, lists of complications, medical guidelines, and contact information for Down syndrome organizations.

In the middle of the stack I came across a glossy, full-color pamphlet: *A Baby First.* I flipped through pages of children with

Down syndrome: Children in dance recital costumes, children posed for school pictures. Children at the beach and the park. Children fishing, boating, playing, swimming. Each child looked different, and the same.

The kitchen door banged open; footsteps approached. Matt and Sam came running into the bedroom, no doubt hoping for some free entertainment: watching Mom get milked. I shooed them out. Then Ben walked in and sat next to me on the bed, averting his ten-year-old eyes from my half-bared breasts. I set the papers down blank side up, attempting nonchalance. But before I could stop him, Ben picked up the top article and read the heading.

He looked up in confusion. "Mom, why are you reading this?"

I balked, not ready to explain. "We're going to talk about this a little later on."

"Why? What's the matter?" His voice raised in alarm. "Is Thomas okay?"

I couldn't make him wait, and I couldn't lie. "Ben, Thomas has Down syndrome."

He stared straight ahead, blank-faced. Then he steeled his jaw and nodded.

I had to say more. A brief explanation of chromosomes, perhaps. How one of the cells that became his brother didn't divide properly. Something cut-and-dried, something far removed from the emotions I didn't understand and couldn't bear.

But it was too late.

"There's another name for that," Ben said, voice quivering. "For Down syndrome. It's that he's retarded."

Retarded. Grief squeezed my ribs, as hard as a labor contraction.

Ben's shoulders trembled. He gulped back a sob. "I love Thomas, but I would rather not have a retarded brother." He shuddered and sniffed. "I'm sorry, Mom."

My teeth clenched. I couldn't break down, not in front of Ben. But then he looked right at me. "Mom, do you wish Thomas didn't have Down syndrome?"

His dark brown eyes were pleading for relief, for understanding. I couldn't give it. Empathy was treacherous. The grief gripping me was so strong, so dark, it would pull both of us under if I released it.

I willed my voice to stay steady, my eyes to stay dry. I stroked Ben's shaking back and told him that everything would be okay—even better than okay. That God sent Thomas to us as a blessing. That one day we'd look back on this time and wonder why we worried, why we cried. But when my words ran out, his still hung in the air: *I'd rather not.* And I couldn't save either of us from that truth.

I punched the square metal button to open the NICU doors. A chattering, laughing crowd stood just inside the entrance, blocking my way. In the middle stood a smiling woman; on her hip sat a slight, dark-haired child wearing a miniature pair of eyeglasses. A bunch of nurses surrounded the mother and son, hugging and patting and exclaiming, apparently celebrating. I wondered what the special occasion was.

It had been three days since our family meeting. All of the children knew about Thomas's diagnosis. Matt and Sam were too young to have concerns, but Christine had been asking anxious questions. Ben was still brooding over the news. Andrew had been unusually quiet. Elizabeth, on the other hand, seemed unperturbed. Reed and I alternated between weighty silence and fervent discussion, recycling questions like a dog chasing its tail.

As I maneuvered around the edge of the crowd and made my way to the scrubbing sink, I noticed a large bulletin board on the wall, lined with orange construction paper and framed with a black border. Halloween was coming. Large oval-shaped photographs were stapled here and there to the orange surface—

baby patients, in costume. A name tag was stapled beneath each photo. Gary wore a miniature football uniform and clutched a pint-size pigskin. Gabriella and Isabella, twin sisters, were wrapped in matching feather boas (what were they supposed to be, Vegas dancers?). Zane wore a yellow polo shirt and a white hunting cap and held his catch—a small plush lion—under one arm. He looked surprised, as if one of the safari animals had grabbed the camera and turned it on him.

Oh, the indignities children suffer to please adults. I was all for it. I approached the nurse at the adjacent front desk. "Can my son Thomas have his picture taken?"

"Any baby that's not on a ventilator can be photographed, but you need to sign a release form," she explained.

"Who takes the photos?"

"Penny, one of the night nurses. She sews all the costumes, too."

I took the sheet of paper the desk nurse handed me, glad women like Penny existed, even more glad that Thomas was healthy enough to qualify for a photo session. The babies, grinning or grimacing in their colorful costumes, were convincing messengers: *Nothing wrong here. We're just hanging out, having a party.* Optical illusions. Like the posters in the unit hallways, which showed rosy-cheeked children posing on garden pathways. In a corner of each poster was a small image of the child as a NICU patient, barely visible under yards of tubes and wires. *Look what was hiding in this sorry scrap of a body,* the contrasting images seemed to say.

Dodging the group still gathered by the doorway, I carried the release form to Thomas's bedside. He'd been moved to Room 3, a softer, more hopeful environment than the harsh lights and hard floors of Room 1. Here there was carpeting, cheerful pastel wallpaper, even a small, bright window adjacent to Thomas's Isolette.

As I pulled up a chair, the geneticist came in. I liked this guy. All the doctors and nurses had been kind to us, but he'd been especially attentive. "Mrs. Soper," he hailed me. "Looks like Thomas is doing well."

"He's doing great," I said. "They're increasing his feeds. They say I can try nursing him soon." I couldn't wait to feel his new baby skin against mine.

The doctor leaned one elbow on the top of the Isolette. "You seem to be handling all of this so well," he said.

I smiled. *Mission accomplished.*

"In fact," he continued, "we're concerned that perhaps you're handling things a little *too* well." He leaned a bit closer, eyes deepening with pity. "Are you sure you understand the diagnosis?"

My cheeks flushed. I stared at the floor, my mind flashing back to all the attention shown me these past few weeks. Now I understood: The nurses and therapists, the residents and specialists, the social worker that called me at home every few days—they'd been watching me, keeping tabs on my emotional state. I envisioned them huddling together in the hallway. *Have you seen her cry yet?* they'd ask each other in hushed tones, wondering when I'd crack.

"We're fine," I said, staring at the floor until the doctor got the message and walked away. Bristling with humiliation, I turned my attention to the photo release form on my lap.

Reed joined me at the usual time late in the day. He'd been taking the train from his office to the hospital nearly every afternoon to see Thomas and have some time alone with me. We rarely had privacy at home.

"The geneticist came by," I said. "He thinks we're too happy about the diagnosis."

Reed's eyes narrowed. "How we feel is none of his business."

I sighed in agreement. What did the doctor want me to do, cry on his shoulder? Rage and scream, while the parents of "normal" babies looked on? Would that make everyone happy? Ever since Thomas came along it seemed like our family was on display, our feelings public property. I was sick of it.

"Did you tell anyone today?" I asked. We'd been trying to decide who to tell about Thomas's diagnosis, and when, and how, and why. Reed had been stewing over what to say to coworkers when they asked about the baby; close associates should probably be told, but what about acquaintances? Was it better to make a group announcement of some kind or let the grapevine take care of it?

"I told my secretary," he said. "Since we talk about our kids pretty often, it would be weird to not say anything to her. But I don't feel like talking to anybody else."

I knew what he meant. There were still dozens of friends and family members who didn't know about the Down syndrome yet, and I was in no hurry to enlighten them. Every time we told someone about Thomas, we had to deal with *their* feelings about Down syndrome on top of our own. And we already had more feelings than we could handle.

At least it's not snowing, I thought as we set out for tricks and treats a few nights later. Utah weather was so unpredictable in late October. The previous year we were coated with an inch of snowflakes by the time the kids' candy bags were sufficiently full. But tonight as I walked down the driveway, the air felt mild, almost balmy.

The kids scampered from doorstep to doorstep; my mom and I trailed them, keeping to the sidewalk. Reed had opted to stay behind as candy distributor. The past weeks had been tough on him, juggling work and hospital visits and a mother-in-law at home. An empty house would do him good. And I wanted to be outside: My leg muscles still felt weak and watery, but I was relieved to be under the night sky after spending the day in the corner of Room 3, breathing stale air, hearing the constant tones of monitor alarms.

Ben, wearing a pair of trick glasses with a mustache attached, led his pack of siblings around the corner, excited to gather more loot. His melancholy had suddenly lifted after our bedtime conversation the night before:

"Mom, since Thomas has Down syndrome, does that mean we can cut to the front of the line at Disneyland?"

Disneyland?

"When the Ereksons went to Disneyland, they got a special pass because of Jake," he explained.

Aha. The Ereksons were old friends from our former neighborhood; their family included Jake, a ten-year-old with autism. "I suppose so," I said.

"All *right!*" Ben's face lit up with anticipation. I didn't bother to remind him that to afford a trip to Disneyland, we'd have to eat Ramen noodles at every meal for a year. Let him fantasize about riding Space Mountain as a VIP.

The kids were already on the next doorstep. I could hear my neighbor fawning over Elizabeth and Christine's "fancy lady" costumes, complete with wigs and costume jewelry from the dollar store. "Thank you," I called once the treats were doled out.

"Kathy?" The light from the porch lamp didn't quite reach me. "Is that you?"

I flinched. For weeks I'd been steering clear of social conversation, letting my mother or the answering machine take care of the stream of concerned callers. I hid in my room when visitors came, incapable of engaging in small talk. I needed every drop of energy to hold my joints together and keep my skin from peeling off in layers, revealing the mess of feelings that I was determined to ignore.

My neighbor stepped off her porch, looking for me. I couldn't keep hiding behind her shrubbery, so I reluctantly met her in the middle of the driveway. She hugged me. "It's so good to see you!" she said. "Congratulations on that sweet baby of yours."

Sweet baby. I bit my lip to keep sudden tears at bay. "Thank you."

"We're praying for him, and for you," she smiled. "We miss you on Sundays."

I tried to smile back. "Thanks." I hadn't been to church in more than a month, and I had no desire to be part of a congregation again, not anytime soon. But I didn't want my church family wondering and whispering about me, speculating about my emotional state like the hospital staff.

Voices called to me from half a block ahead, where the kids were gathered for their next candy conquest. I said good-bye to my neighbor and caught up as quickly as I could. Decision made: I would go back to church the coming Sunday. I'd sit on the pew, smile, and show them all. *I'm fine.*

"Somebody's been waiting for you," the nurse said as I took off my coat and scooted my chair close to Thomas's Isolette. He was wide awake, looking around with his dark gray eyes.

"Hey, buddy," I said as I flipped open one of the portholes. The air inside was surprisingly cool. I looked at the nurse in surprise.

"We've been slowly decreasing his bed temperature," she explained. "So far he's doing really well maintaining his own temp. If he keeps this up, we'll be able to move him to a crib pretty soon."

I couldn't wait. There were two half-sized cribs in the room, each with a colorful mobile attached to its bars, pastel baby clothes stacked underneath, and a plump-cheeked, bright-eyed baby inside.

"In fact," the nurse continued, "during rounds this morning the doctors were talking about a discharge date."

I froze. *"What?"*

"I know it's a shock. But since Thomas is almost ready for a crib, they're considering sending him home sooner rather than later."

"But—but he doesn't know how to eat!"

She looked apologetic. "They think it'll be a long time before he's taking all his feedings orally. They can send him home with the NG tube, if you're willing."

The nasal-gastric tube. I'd seen the nurses insert them, and it wasn't pretty. I couldn't possibly. Reed couldn't possibly. He couldn't even bear to see an eyelid flipped inside out.

I shook my head. They'd been warning me since day one that Thomas would likely be hospitalized until his due date. Why the sudden change? "I don't get it," I said to the nurse.

"They figure you'd rather have him home than keep him here." She sounded doubtful. "Would you like to speak with the attending physician? He'll be in tomorrow morning."

Yes. I would.

By the time I reached Room 3 the next morning, my palms were sweating. The night before, Reed and I had agreed it was way too soon to bring Thomas home, but I dreaded confronting the doctor about it. For all my tough talk, I hated conflicts with authority figures.

Within minutes the doctor strode into the room, his shoulders squared. "I understand you have some concerns," he said.

I had my response ready: *Yes, I'm deeply concerned that you want to discharge a medically fragile patient.* But that was before I looked him in the eye. "The nurse mentioned something about Thomas going home earlier than expected," I stammered.

"Yes, if he's maintaining his own temp, there's no need to keep him here. We'd get you set up with a home health service to cover his oxygen needs."

I pictured metallic tanks lined up against my bedroom wall. Sam hadn't needed oxygen when he came home, and I had no clue how to manage it. But that wasn't my biggest concern. "What about feeding?" I asked.

The doctor nodded. "We would train you to maintain his NG tube until he's eating well from the breast or bottle." He paused for a moment. "Mrs. Soper, if we keep Thomas here until he's able to breastfeed on his own, he might not be home until Christmas, or even later."

That shut me up. I couldn't deal with eight weeks or more of being split in two, alternating between life at the hospital and life at home.

"If you opt to bottle feed, which doesn't require as much muscle tone for the baby, he'll likely be discharged sooner," he continued. "But even so, he probably won't make much progress unless the same person feeds him every time. You'd need to be available every three to four hours, around the clock."

My stomach sank. There was no way I could swing that kind of schedule. But I didn't want to give Thomas his first oral feedings at home. What if he choked? What if his oxygen saturation plummeted from the effort? And how would Reed and I ever manage to shove that damned tube up his nose?

It was a trap. No matter which way we chose, we'd lose.

I looked at the doctor, my mouth dry. I was scared to cross him, but even more scared to bring Thomas home. "I won't be comfortable having him discharged until he's having at least some of his feedings by mouth."

His face hardened ever so slightly, but he nodded. "I understand."

After he left I slumped in my seat, feeling uneasy. I wanted to believe he had our best interests in mind, but I couldn't shake the suspicion in my gut.

Minutes later I heard whispers coming from the doorway behind me. *The nurse,* I thought. She sounded upset. Mildly curious, I tuned in to the conversation.

"I can't believe what the attending is doing to this family," she hissed at someone, presumably another nurse.

My ears pricked up: Was she talking about us?

"Just because the baby has T21, they don't want to give him a chance. They're pushing for an early discharge. But a baby like this needs *more* support, not less!"

I was incredulous. Reed and I relied on these professionals to provide the expertise we lacked—but who should we believe? The doctor, allegedly biased against kids with Down syndrome? The nurse, with her righteous indignation about "babies like this"? Prejudice might be shadowing either of their opinions, or neither—or both. *He'll be slow, so he should go home. He'll be slow, so he should stay here.*

I curled forward in my seat, feeling the deep sting of judgment and the deeper sting of truth. Even if Thomas didn't face discrimination at the hospital, he would face it elsewhere. And even if the doctor and nurse weren't biased, one thing was true: *He'll be slow.*

I was still stewing when Reed joined me late in the day. When I told him what I'd heard from the doctor and the nurse, his brow furrowed in anger.

"They can't kick him out," he said. "He's not ready. We're not ready." He shook his head. "I'll bet this never would've come up if Thomas didn't have Down syndrome."

With our heads bent together we hashed and rehashed the situation, wondering if we needed to take action. But after a dozen rounds we gave up. There was no way of knowing if Thomas was being discriminated against, no way of knowing who truly had his best interests in mind. Our trust in the doctors and nurses, which had stood like scaffolding around our new life, was crumbling fast.

Did we understand the diagnosis? Actually, I was sure we didn't.

We slumped in our seats, holding hands, tired beyond words. At 5:30 we gathered our coats and said good-bye to Thomas so that we could catch the express train to the station near our home. On our way out of the unit we paused by the Halloween bulletin board, which was nearly full with photos. I was admiring the new additions when Reed grabbed my arm and pointed to a photo on the bottom row.

Thomas.

I wouldn't have recognized him without the name tag below the photo. He was decked out in a brown-and-white reindeer suit, with black antlers on the hood and a red bow under his chin. His eyes were looking off-camera; his lips were pursed in a tiny half smirk, as if he knew the answers to all of life's mysteries but would never tell.

I smiled with anticipation as I led my mother into the unit. "Check it out!" I said as we approached the bulletin board. She'd seen the Halloween shot of Thomas—nurse Penny had created prints for us to take home—but she hadn't seen the other babies. Today there was another set of twins on the board: Joseph and Emma. *Only in Utah,* I thought, catching the reference to Joseph Smith, founder of the Mormon church, and his wife Emma. I took a closer look at their costumes: Emma wore a white angel dress, Joseph a red devil suit, complete with horns.

Mom and I looked at each other and burst into laughter.

This is good, I thought. *Keep it light.* It was Mom's last visit to the NICU. Just that morning she'd finished making a blanket for Thomas, an oversize baby quilt with swatches of blue, red, and green. Her parting gift. The next day, she would board a flight bound for Baltimore, where my stepfather would be waiting, eager to see her after nearly a month apart. I wanted these final hours to be happy ones.

When Mom and I walked into Room 3, I was relieved to find that the whispering nurse wasn't on duty. Instead there was a nurse I had never seen before, standing next to something new, something momentous: a metallic crib, positioned a few feet from Thomas's Isolette.

"Are you Thomas's mom?" the nurse asked, smiling. "He's ready for a big boy bed!"

I caught sight of a tiny blue onesie and a white terrycloth sleeper waiting in the crib. "Clothes!" I cheered.

"Oh, this is perfect!" Mom said as we quickly crossed the room. I knew she was torn about leaving us. A parting view of Thomas in his crib would help her make it home in one piece.

Our hero was waiting patiently in his Isolette, wide awake. Mom's face fell when she saw the new IV line attached to his scalp. "Why is there an IV in his head?" she asked the nurse, in her I'm-upset-but-polite voice.

"Sorry. We had a terrible time getting a line started this morning."

I blanched, wondering if they had called in the nurse with the little blue flashlight.

"I was hoping to get some good pictures," Mom said, digging her digital camera out of her purse.

Aha. No wonder she was so disappointed—the gauze-padded needle was going to ruin the "all was well" photo op. But I couldn't blame her. I had photo hang-ups of my own: The envelope of Halloween prints I had taken home a few nights before included several cross-eyed images of Thomas that made me squirm. It didn't matter that I had similar shots of each of my other newborns—seeing Thomas look so goofy and clueless cut too close to the bone.

The nurse helped disconnect the line from its supply bag so that we could thread it through the neck hole of the onesie. Hands shaking with excitement, I wiggled Thomas into his first set of clothes, careful not to yank his tubes.

Mom rallied quickly from the setback, snapping shot after shot in spite of the dratted scalp needle: Thomas in his sleeper. Thomas and his mom. Thomas and his grandma, with me holding the camera. Thomas and his mom and his grandma, with the nurse holding the camera. Thomas and his NG tube, getting milk up the nose. His tiny eyes blinked as the camera flashed again and again.

All too soon, it was time for us to go. Mom's hands slowed with significance as she helped me wrap Thomas in receiving blankets and lay him gently in his new bed. She took a few last shots with her camera, then leaned close to the crib, fighting back tears. "Good-bye, Thomas," she said. "I'll miss you." She sniffed a few times, then put on her bravest, most capable face. "But just think—next time I see you, you'll be at home with your brothers and sisters!"

As we headed for the door she held her chin high, clutching her camera full of almost-perfect photographs. I feigned confidence, not wanting her to worry, but I was afraid to lose her. I'd been pushing myself so hard these past weeks, pushing back feelings, pushing through hospital trips and pumping sessions and chaotic bedtimes. I didn't think I could do it without my mother. I needed her sheer presence, her wordless assurance that everything was under control. Her magic mom power. I didn't seem to have enough of my own.

The train platform was nearly empty, and cold. I shivered as the autumn air seeped through my thin cotton oxford. Thomas was ready for his first breastfeeding lesson, and I was wearing a button-front shirt for the occasion, as the lactation nurse had requested. "We want him to feel as much of your skin as possible," she explained.

I zipped up my jacket to keep the goods warm and craned my neck to see if the train was coming. For weeks I'd been driving our van the twenty miles, but with gasoline prices ridiculously high and legs finally sturdy enough to walk several blocks, I'd figured it was time to go by rail.

Morning rush hour was over; most of the blue vinyl seats in the coach I boarded were vacant. I sat by a window, feeling empty. My in-laws had arrived a few days before, and their presence nearly filled the void left by my mother, but not quite. As lonely as it was to stand near her marvelous strength and know I didn't share it, having her gone was even worse.

As the train moved on, the store backs and industrial yards out my window turned to the glass and granite buildings of downtown Salt Lake City. Students en route to the University of Utah began to fill the coach, sporting the ID badges that secured them a free ride. We stopped every few blocks as the train climbed into the foothills above the city, drawing close to the university campus. At every stop several students clambered on and off. They all looked pretty much the same, with their backpacks and iPod earphones and knit caps.

Except for one.

Short and heavyset, with dark, close-cropped hair and thick glasses, a man wearing a red U of U windbreaker lumbered down the aisle. One glance at his face told me he had Down syndrome. Before I could help it, I scrunched deeper into my seat, crossed my arms over my chest, and looked out the window with feigned nonchalance.

My face burned with shame. Just the other day my friend Ellen had sent me a tender note brimming with hope, assuring me that I'd be a good mother to Thomas. I wondered what she'd say if she saw me now. *What a wonderful gift you have been given,* she had written. *I had the opportunity to have David at my house for most of the summer and fell in love with him all over again. (Crying now!) You are beginning a journey with countless rewards and blessings. Thomas will touch so many lives and educate so many around him. Our kids are different because of David. I have no doubts you will love and appreciate Thomas as he grows and develops on his own timetable.*

She had no doubts. But as I hunched down in my seat, I sure did. I might as well have been eight years old again, hiding from Eddie, the teenager with mental retardation that lived across the street. Rumors flew that his gruff, reclusive parents were brother and sister. On warm days he would stand on his front lawn with his portable tape player blaring the Oak Ridge Boys. I used to peek at him from behind the curtain covering my bedroom window. "*Elvira!*" he'd shout in his gravelly voice, showing his stained, crooked teeth. "*Elvira! My heart's on fi-ya, for Elvira!*"

The high-school kids walking home from the bus stop would cross to the other side of the street when they approached his yard. "Hey, babe, wanna date?" Eddie would call to the girls as they slinked past. I would shudder, glad I was too young to draw his eye. I did the same thing as a teenager when I saw half-witted homeless men on the street, or clusters of blank-eyed, drooling adults being shepherded around the zoo or park or library. I knew it was good to help them, but I certainly didn't want to do it myself.

The train lurched forward. The man in the red jacket made his way down the aisle and chose a seat near mine, next to a young woman with a student ID. "Where you goin'?" he asked, a little too loudly.

"To school." She was stuck and she knew it.

"I'm goin' to work!"

"Oh yeah? That's great . . ." She turned away, toward the window.

"I work at the stadium!" he announced with pride. Then he launched into all the details of his job at the university's football arena, oblivious to her disinterest.

I bristled at the student's rudeness. *Is it so hard to give this man a few minutes of your time? Is it so hard to sit next to him?*

But I couldn't deny the truth, as pathetic as it was: I didn't want him to sit next to me, either.

"We won't expect much from him today," said Valerie, the lactation nurse. "To start, just let him nuzzle you and smell you."

The curtain around our corner of the room was shut; my shirt was open. Thomas, wrapped in a striped blanket, rested his head on my breast. His skin felt delicious against mine. I savored the sensation, trying not to think about what would come next. I figured it would be a teeth-clenching time as he learned to nurse, just like those awful first weeks with each of my newborns, with their little mouths clamping like staple guns on my nipples. But his tiny body needed breast milk even more than my other babies did—and not just any breast milk, either. In its mysterious wisdom, my body was custom-designing the perfect blend of nutrients for a preemie.

"Do you want to see if he'll latch on?" Valerie asked. "Most babies this age don't have their sucking reflex yet, but he really goes to town on his pacifier, so let's see what he'll do with Mom."

I arranged Thomas lengthwise on my arm, parallel to my thighs, with my hand cupping the back of his head—the football hold, they call it. But as I stroked his cheek with one finger, coaxing him to open his mouth, I began to panic.

It's okay, I told myself, trying to calm my racing heart. *Your body remembers the pain. Push past it.* As soon as Thomas opened up, I pulled his head toward me. He quickly turned away.

"I know, buddy," I said. "Crazy idea, huh?"

Valerie patted my shoulder. "He'll get the hang of it. Try again."

So we tried again. And again. Each time Thomas's mouth opened, my body shrank back. I forced my spine to stay straight; I forced my hand to move his little head close. *He needs this,* I told myself firmly. *He needs you.* Ever since his birth, I'd felt like he belonged to the doctors and nurses: They set the rules, called the shots, kept him well. Now, finally, I had a chance to mother him—and every cell of me was resisting.

On the fourth attempt Thomas fell asleep, his mouth limply touching my breast.

Valerie patted me on the shoulder. "Good job. We'll give it another shot tomorrow," she said, standing to leave.

I put Thomas back in his crib, my eyes dark with failure. Why did he pull away from me? And why, why did I pull away from him?

The pipe organ hummed prelude music as we entered the chapel and filed into a pew. The ten of us took up the whole row: Reed, myself, the children, and Reed's parents, Don and Nancy. Heads turned our way, eyes blinked in friendly recognition. I kept my lips frozen in a half smile as I nodded my greetings. I didn't want to be there, but I didn't want my kids to wonder why I'd stopped attending church.

All around me the ward members sat in their Sunday best, their hair carefully styled, their faces serene. I felt like an imposter. I looked the part, with my dress and heels and lipstick, but my insides were ragged. Maybe I should've shown up at the hospital chapel, where I'd attended Sunday services the week before Thomas was born. I had worn ratty gray fleece pajamas, ChapStick, and an elastic band to hold my disheveled ponytail. My fellow churchgoers were tired-looking doctors and nurses in scrubs and pale patients in gowns or bathrobes, some with IV poles as sidekicks. It was the scrappiest gathering of Mormons I'd ever seen. That's where I belonged.

The young couple in the next pew leaned over to say hello.

"Congratulations on your new baby!" the husband said.

"Thank you." I tried to keep my voice mild, but it came out tight and forbidding.

Does this guy know about the diagnosis? I wondered. *If he did, would he still congratulate us?*

Yes, he probably would. According to Mormon doctrine people with significant mental disabilities are considered incapable of sin. Many Mormons believe it's an honor to be given a child like Thomas, whose spirit will remain unsullied by the world. That was one reason my e-mail inbox was full of cheery responses to the informal birth announcement I'd finally sent last week:

Congratulations on your perfect child!
Special children come to special parents.
What a blessing for your family!

Ellen's reply was the only one I could swallow—at least she spoke from experience. The others were just repeating feel-good platitudes. I couldn't blame them, really. I'd said such things myself in the past. I'd seen parents of children with disabilities and considered them chosen—but at the same time, I was glad *I* hadn't been chosen. I figured most, if not all, of our well-wishers felt the same way. Like this young husband, smiling at me with straight white teeth.

It wasn't fair, of course. It wasn't fair of me to accuse him of hypocrisy, when all he did was congratulate me. The birth of a baby—any baby—merits congratulations. What was the poor guy supposed to say?

I didn't know. There was no way to comment on Thomas's birth without causing my defenses to flare. Cheerful comments made me angry. Pitying comments made me furious. Why did people insist on calling Down syndrome a blessing, or a tragedy?

Half the world wanted me to be happy, and the other half wanted me to be sad—and I was both. Reed was the only one who came close to understanding. I felt like I was behind a Plexiglas wall, separated from everyone and everything, including God.

Especially God. Many people said God had blessed me with a special child, but it seemed more like he was sabotaging my quest to be a good mother. I'd heard it dozens of times from the pulpit: *Motherhood is near to divinity. It is the highest, holiest service to be assumed by mankind. It places her who honors its holy calling and service next to the angels.* I'd been aiming for that ideal my whole adult life, and I counted on God to help me bridge the gap between who I was and who I needed to be—especially with Thomas. But instead he was jabbing my sore spots without mercy, as if he was determined to expose me as a failure, a fraud.

The organist sounded the first notes of the opening hymn. I mouthed the words, just barely, so my children wouldn't wonder why I wasn't singing. The sweet, pleading tones of the music pulled at me, pushed on me, threatening to break the emotional barrier that was holding back a torrent of overdue tears. I bit the inside of my cheek and clenched the muscles in my legs, willing myself to stay seated during the invocation.

The bishop began the service. It was one of our ward's monthly testimony meetings, when members took turns standing at the pulpit to share spiritual conviction and experiences. Often, those in a time of crisis took the opportunity to update the ward, give thanks for help received, and affirm their continued faith. As I watched a few people make their way toward the front of the chapel, I wondered if I was expected to speak. Like an extended family, the ward members had been praying for us, bringing meals, offering rides to the hospital. They'd inquired regularly about Thomas's health and our family's well-being. They deserved a few words of acknowledgment, a few words about how we'd been faring. And no doubt they'd like to hear a nice inspirational story about the "special" new member of our family.

But what would I tell them—that I appreciated their kindness but knew they secretly pitied me? That I loved Thomas but secretly pitied myself?

My mind drifted to the woman with Down syndrome who was part of the ward in our former neighborhood. She was charming, with a quick smile and an easy laugh, but I would smile back only from a distance, worried about getting sucked into one of her long, pointless conversations. At testimony meetings she was a regular at the pulpit. "I love my mom," she'd say, tears dripping off her flat, ruddy face. "I love Kim," with a quick glance at her friend on the second row. She'd go on and on, naming the people she loved. I would sit in my pew, half wishing she would say my name. But she never did, because I never deserved it. I gave her nothing of myself. I gave nothing to that man on the train, either. And I feared—I feared—I wouldn't give myself fully to my own child.

What would my church family say to that?

I spent the rest of the meeting staring at the wall behind the pulpit. In all the years I'd been attending church, I'd never felt so bitter, so false, so dark. As soon as the benediction ended I walked quickly from the chapel, trying not to run.

Thin November sunlight filled my bedroom as I chose an easy-access shirt for the day, dreading the upcoming practice session with Thomas and Valerie. I'd never been so reluctant to breastfeed. Something wasn't right.

I still had a half hour before I needed to leave for the hospital. Sitting at the computer desk, I launched Google and punched in my terms:

> *Down syndrome*
> *Parenting*
> *Support*

Nearly two hundred thousand links. I wasn't sure where to start. I didn't even know what I was looking for—I just knew I needed to get square with Thomas's diagnosis. I'd wrestled my grief into a cage, but I could still feel it rattling the bars. And try as I might, I couldn't shake my guilt over feeling grief to begin with.

I started clicking links. From Amazon I ordered three books about Down syndrome—two parenting guides and a picture book for siblings. Then I clicked over to a few personal Web sites run by parents of kids with Down syndrome.

One particularly impressive site created by a mom named Rebecca included hundreds of links to national, state, and local resources. From her lists I checked out sites for the National Down Syndrome Society, then the Utah Down Syndrome Foundation, then the group for the Salt Lake City metro area. *Uptown Downs,* it was called. They had a Christmas party scheduled for December, and there were some photos posted from the recent Halloween party, which appeared to have been a live-action version of nurse Penny's bulletin board, except the kids were twenty times bigger. There were also photos from a "Buddy Walk" event that had been held earlier in the fall. The photos showed families in matching T-shirts gathered at a local park, smiling for the camera.

I wondered if I'd ever feel ready to walk into a party full of people with Down syndrome and their families. I couldn't imagine it. Actually, I could. I could imagine myself standing awkwardly in a corner, holding Thomas, unsure how to interact. The people with Down syndrome I'd met in the past seemed to be from a foreign country. They lacked the subtlety one finds in typical company. Thoughts, feelings, quirks, whims—everything was right up front, right on the surface. Their absence of self-consciousness made me squirm.

Almost time to go. I checked my e-mail and found a message from Kylie, my pregnant friend who'd wept on the phone. *Just wanted you to know I sat down and had a good cry for you the other day,* she wrote. *You seem to be handling this much better than I am.* She had no idea. Someday I would tell her, but not yet. If I let my guard down, my emotions might eat me alive.

Kylie included in her message the name and phone number of a family friend who had a daughter with Down syndrome. *She says her daughter is the highlight of the family,* the message went. *She'd love to talk with you, if you're up to it.*

I wasn't up to it. Not even close. I didn't doubt this woman had all kinds of encouraging words, but I didn't want to hear them. Down syndrome was a language I didn't want to speak, a club I didn't want to join. No book or Web site or gung-ho comrade could change that.

I unbuttoned my shirt and held out my arms as Valerie lifted Thomas from his crib. Cradling him on my lap, I watched his dark gray eyes slide from my hairline to my chin, then back again. "Hungry, Mr. T?" I asked him.

After a week of trying, he still showed no interest in nursing, and I still dreaded each practice session. But the more I read about breastfeeding babies with Down syndrome, the more guilty I felt about wanting to quit. Thomas was prone to infection and digestive problems, so breast milk was a must. He also needed the IQ boost that recent research had linked to breastfeeding. And suckling would reportedly develop his facial muscles, helping to minimize the speech delays so common in kids with Down syndrome. Reed didn't mind if Thomas was bottle-fed, but I felt duty-bound to nurse him.

We had a routine down pat. Valerie leaned over my right shoulder, helping me position Thomas comfortably on my forearm. I psyched myself up. *You can do this. You must.* I stroked his cheek, touched his lips. I crooned at him, beckoning him to open wide. When he did I lifted his head smoothly to my breast, commanding myself not to flinch.

No luck. Thomas turned away and shut his mouth. I coaxed it open again, pulling him close. Valerie hovered over us, giving directions. "Hold his head firmly," she said. I applied gentle counterpressure to Thomas's skull as he tried to pull away.

Valerie put her hand behind mine and leaned even closer, her breath hot on my neck. My head and back began to sweat from the tangle of bodies and the strain of the effort. I fought the urge to push everyone away and run. "C'mon, Thomas!" I said through gritted teeth, trying to sound chipper, trying to fool us all.

He stared blandly at my shoulder, his lips slack. Then without warning his eyes fluttered shut. *Dong dong dong.* I glanced at the numbers on the monitor screen—his oxygen saturation, which was supposed to be 90 percent or higher, had dropped to 79.

Valerie jiggled his shoulder. "What's up, Thomas?" His eyes opened again, and the alarm shut off.

"Are you a sleepy boy?" I said, relieved that naptime might cut our feeding session short. I held him against my chest and rocked him gently. Within seconds the alarm sounded again: 74 percent.

Valerie's eyes creased with concern. "Wake up, Thomas," she said, jiggling his foot. No response. Swiftly she dialed up the oxygen flow, then lifted Thomas from my arms, calling his name. "There you are!" Valerie said when his eyes finally opened. She turned to me. "Are apnea spells typical for him?"

I shook my head. "He hasn't had one since they moved him out of Room 1."

She frowned. "Let's call it a day. Looks like he's worn out." She laid him in his crib and tucked the blanket snugly under his bottom. I watched from the rocking chair, stung by guilt: If Thomas had repeated apnea spells, he'd have to stay in the hospital longer—and part of me would be glad.

When I got home the little kids were in the kitchen, clamoring for snacks. A package from Amazon waited on the kitchen counter. I let my mother-in-law take snack duty while I carried the package to my room.

I opened it to find the three Down syndrome books I'd ordered online. Just what I needed. On one of the covers, a little blond boy smiled out at me. He looked like David, my friend Ellen's little brother. One afternoon Ellen and I had sat side by side, watching David play as a preschooler. *He's so adorable now,* she said, her forehead wrinkling with worry, *but what will happen when he grows up?*

Still holding the books, I sat on my bed, suddenly faint. The man in the red jacket—that was Thomas. He would ride public transportation someday, having awkward conversations with unwilling seatmates as he headed to some menial job—if he was lucky. If *we* were lucky. I didn't want that kind of life for my family, for my child.

Did that mean I didn't want my child? Was that why I shrank from him? Was that why I refused to bring him home?

The little boys pushed open my bedroom door. "Mom, come swing me!" Matt pleaded.

"Me, too!" Sam said.

There was no escape. I put the books on my nightstand and followed the boys outside.

It was a beautiful afternoon, the light golden, the sky impossibly clear and blue. From our deck I could see patches of brilliant yellow on the Wasatch mountains—the aspen groves turning with the season. The green leaves on our peach tree had curling brown edges. Winter was on its way.

After swinging the boys for a few minutes, I retreated to the deck and dialed Kate's number on the cordless phone. As soon as she answered, I blurted out the truth: "I'm scared I won't love Thomas."

Kate was quiet for a minute. "What do you mean, you *won't* love him? Do you love him now?"

Tears stung my eyes. "Yes," I said, breathing deeply so I wouldn't sob. I loved him as much as I'd ever loved a child—but love wasn't all I felt. When I looked at Thomas I saw not just a baby, but a baby with Down syndrome. My intense mother-love was tainted by pity and by subtle yet unmistakable distaste.

"Babe, if you love him now, why do you think that will ever change?"

I shook my head in distress. "I try to nurse him, but whenever he opens his mouth I pull away. And if I'm pulling away from him now, what will happen when he's not even cute anymore? What will I do when he's a pimply sixteen-year-old? What if I don't want to hug him?"

"Kathy," Kate said firmly, "there will be times you won't want to hug *any* of your pimply sixteen-year-olds. That's just life with teenagers. Why should it be any different with Thomas?"

The question stopped me short. In the silence of my thoughts, I could hear Matt and Sam's happy shouts as they swung on their tummies, legs kicking behind them. "I don't know," I finally said. "I don't know."

"Have you considered the possibility that you don't want to breastfeed simply because you're exhausted?"

I wiped my nose on my sleeve. "Yes. No. I don't know." I knew I was tired from making so many babies, feeding so many babies. But something still wasn't right. I pressed my fingers to my temples, trying to push back the self-accusations swelling in my veins like too much blood.

"Kathy?"

I opened my eyes. My mother-in-law, Nancy, was standing in my bedroom doorway. I rolled onto my side and stretched my legs, annoyed to be summoned from my warm nest of blankets so early in the morning.

Nancy approached the bed and handed me the telephone. "It's the hospital," she said, her face tense.

I grabbed the phone. "Mrs. Soper?" It was the resident who'd delivered Thomas's diagnosis. My pulse quickened. Something was wrong. Something was wrong.

"I have some difficult news."

My stomach knotted. "Tell me."

"Last night Thomas got quite ill. His oxygen saturation dropped into the sixties, and his temp went way up." She paused. "We had to intubate him."

"*No.*" I closed my eyes against the words. Nancy's hand flew to her mouth.

The ventilator. A tube in his trachea, keeping him alive. He'd been so tired the day before, but I didn't know he was getting sick.

I should have. I should have known.

But before guilt could seize me, adrenaline kicked in and revved me into high gear, banishing all emotion. My eyes snapped open. "I'm on my way."

At my call Reed left work and met me at the unit doors. We rushed to Thomas's bed in Room 3 but then stopped short. He wasn't there.

I spun toward the nurse. "They moved him to Room 2," she said quickly.

Room 2 was actually eight cubicles with glass fronts, lined up like fish tanks in a pet store. We walked down the corridor connecting the tanks, peering into each one. Quilt-covered Isolettes in one, a sickly pale baby in another. We reached the end of the corridor—no Thomas.

I poked my head into the closest cubicle. "I'm looking for Thomas Soper," I said to the nurse. "He was moved here last night."

"Second section on your right," she said.

Perplexed, we turned back. *Second on the right?* I peeked in and shook my head. That was the pale baby on the warming bed.

And then I saw the name tag.

Thomas lay on his back, tethered to the bed by a tangle of tubes and wires, including one in his airway. His chest vibrated with the ventilator's pulse. His skin, ghost white, was spotted with a red rash. Reed and I exchanged glances, unable to speak.

The resident came in. "Sepsis," she said. Bloodstream infection. Only intensive antibiotic treatment could save his life.

Reed and I signed consent forms for the medication and took our places by Thomas's side. The sight of him, so chalky and limp, opened a void in my gut that I hadn't felt since Sam lay on the edge of death. Reed's head bowed to avoid the view. After a while I put my hand on his shoulder, knowing his urge to flee was as strong as my urge to stay. "It's okay," I said. "You can go."

His face flooded with relief. "Are you sure?"

I was. Truth be told, it would be easier if he left. I didn't want to worry about him, and I didn't want to share the room with another set of brooding thoughts. Reed kissed me good-bye, and I settled in for a long vigil.

Hours later, Thomas still hadn't moved or shown any other signs of life. "Is he sedated, or just too sick to move?" I asked the nurse.

She smiled in sympathy. "He's been sleepy, so we haven't had to give him anything."

I nodded. It was a relief, in a backwards sort of way: He was too zonked to be miserable. "He looks awful," I said.

"I'm glad you didn't see him before the transfusion." I looked up in surprise. "He needed a few units of blood last night," she explained.

A few units. Someone else's blood circulated through my child's body. Dazed, I put a hand against the side of the bed to steady myself. "He was doing so well," I said faintly. "They were even talking about sending him home."

She shook her head. "There's just no telling with these little guys. I've worked here for ten years, and I've seen it happen again and again. There are kids that seem to be sailing along, and then they hit the wall. And there are kids that arrive in really bad shape, kids that none of us think will make it. Sometimes they don't. But other times, they do."

I wondered which category Thomas was in.

"There was this one little boy," the nurse continued. "He was born at twenty-six weeks, just over a pound. Had stage 4 brain bleeds, the worst. One infection after another, on the vent for more than a month. Nobody thought he would survive, at least not without severe complications. But he's doing great. His mom brought him in to say hello a couple weeks ago. He's a year old now, and the only evidence of his neonatal problems is the glasses he has to wear."

Tiny glasses. That was him—the little kid in the middle of the happy crowd of nurses.

"We're not in charge here," the nurse finished. "We show up and do what we can, but we don't decide who lives and who dies."

There was nothing to say after that. For two days, Thomas lay like a corpse as potent drugs infused his blood. I perched at his bedside, my hand on his chest. Reed joined me as often as he could bear, but there was nothing we could do but sit, and wait, and listen to our hearts beating the same one-word prayer: *Please.*

On the third day, the nurse smiled as I entered the room. "Look who's up!"

I dropped my purse on the floor and came close. Thomas's eyes were wide open. That morning on the phone, the nurse had told me his fever was gone, but I didn't expect to see him so alert so soon. He'd responded well to the specialized antibiotics. We were safe.

I leaned over to stroke his forehead, feasting on the sight of his pinkening skin. "Hey, Thomas." He tried turning his head toward my voice, but the ventilator tube down his throat stopped him short. I watched in horror as he gagged in slow motion.

I turned to the nurse—a different one from the day before. "Has he had any sedatives?"

"No, I don't think he needs it. He's a real quiet kid."

I turned back to Thomas. His abdomen heaved as his muscles tried to dislodge the plastic tubing. Of course he was quiet—he couldn't cry with his larynx pried apart.

"He's miserable," I protested. "Look at him."

The nurse stepped over and peered at him. "I don't like to give narcotic medication unless it's urgently needed."

I fumed as Thomas gagged again. *Urgently needed? What do you call this?*

But she had a point. When Sam had been on a ventilator, the nurses sedated him every time he began to stir. Once he came off the vent he suffered intense narcotic withdrawal for two days, shaking and whimpering, howling. Demanding narcotics for Thomas would only cause him to suffer later.

I leaned close and whispered in his ear. "It's okay, Thomas. It's okay, sweetie. Mom's right here." I hoped my voice would soothe him into stillness. Instead he bent his knees and waved his arms, as if begging me to help.

By the time Reed arrived that afternoon, Thomas was so agitated that he pulled out the ventilator tube. I silently flogged myself for not demanding narcotics. When the resident came to reinsert the tube, she suggested we leave. "You don't want to see this," she said.

I wasn't so sure. Watching the procedure could be my penance for being so stupid. But when Reed headed for the door, I turned and followed, leaving Thomas to face his ordeal alone.

A dark evening. The kids bickered and whined, absorbing the stress I'd brought home from the hospital. After sending the older kids down to their rooms, Reed put the little boys to bed while I sorted through a pile of mail, started the dishwasher, locked the front door, then headed for our bedroom, ready to collapse. But as I passed Christine's room I heard muffled sobs.

I leaned into the doorway and tried to scrape together some motherly concern. "What's wrong, sweetie?"

She raised her face from the pillow, eyes red. Such a little girl. I could only imagine how scared and lonely she'd been over the past weeks. She needed me to comfort her, to promise her everything would be okay, but I couldn't do that. After my day at the hospital, I wasn't sure anything would ever be okay.

"Let's read a story," I said, remembering the picture book that had arrived with my Down syndrome parenting guides. "I even have a new book for you."

Her face relaxed slightly. "What is it?"

"I'll show you." I fetched the book from my bedroom and beckoned for Christine to follow me. We curled up on the couch in the living room and began to read about Emma, also six years old. She was so excited for her baby brother Isaac to come. But after the baby was born, Emma's dad came to her looking sad. He told her that Isaac had Down syndrome.

Christine slipped her hand around my arm and held on tight.

We read about Emma's worries: Would Isaac be able to do all the fun things she'd been planning? Would he be able to paint pictures, play ball, go on car trips? As I read the words aloud, another question, unspoken, filled the white spaces around the words. This was what Emma was really asking: *Will we love him?*

My voice cracked as I read the father's response. Yes, he assured her. Isaac would be able to take car trips, and play ball, and paint pictures. *Yes, Emma*, he said silently, *we will love him.*

I closed the book, picturing Thomas on the warming bed, pale and lifeless. I loved him. I loved him fully, completely. I would love him every day of our lives. And this love mattered more than anything else I felt about him, anything else I could ever feel.

Christine reached up and touched my cheek. I pulled her onto my lap and began to stroke her hair, rocking her gently in the warmth that filled and surrounded us. And suddenly I knew what she really needed, what all of us needed. We needed Thomas. As soon as he got better, we needed him to come home.

Valerie shook the slim plastic bottle filled with two ounces of warmed breast milk. "Are you ready?" she asked.

I nodded. It had been ten days since Thomas got sick, six since he got off the ventilator, five since he started getting milk through his NG tube again. Finally, he was ready to try eating by mouth. And finally, I was ready to feed him. After seeing him so close to death, I'd stopped caring about our failure at breastfeeding—I just wanted him out of the hospital as soon as possible, and using bottles meant an earlier discharge. But as Valerie lifted Thomas from his crib, my heart started pounding. What would he do when milk squirted into his mouth? What if he freaked out? What if he aspirated liquid into his delicate lungs?

I held out my arms and Valerie gently handed me the little guy, all cozy in a tiny blue sleeper and striped blanket. Then she helped me lay him on his side, supported by the pillow on my lap. "Okay, Thomas, it's time to eat!" I said, picking up the bottle and sliding the firm latex nipple into his mouth.

Slowly, his tiny pink tongue curled around the bottom of the nipple and began to pull. I heard a soft, smooth gulp. Then another. And another. A stream of little air bubbles flowed to the surface of the milk.

I beamed at Valerie. "He's drinking!"

"Look at him go!" she cheered.

Five weeks of tubes. Five weeks of dry hospital air. The warm milk washing down his throat must've felt glorious.

A wet patch began to spread across the pillow cradling Thomas—his grasp on the nipple was a bit slack. Valerie had me hold the bottle like a fat pencil between my thumb and forefinger. She showed me how to use my middle finger to stabilize his bottom jaw. The dribbling stopped; the gulps and bubbles continued.

"His numbers look great," Valerie said. I glanced at the monitor screen and smiled. Many preemies struggle to maintain their oxygen saturation when they're eating, but Thomas was managing beautifully.

Five minutes passed. Bit by bit, Thomas's sucking rhythm slowed. His eyes started to droop. His tongue released the bottle. I held it up to read the calibration: He'd drunk a full ounce. Feeding him hadn't been the blissful skin-to-skin symbiosis I idealized, but it was communion nonetheless. Cooperation. Nourishment for us both.

As I watched Thomas slip into sleep, hope lifted my heart with a hundred tiny wings.

Thanksgiving morning. I lay in bed alone. Reed had gotten up early, as usual, which was just as well—I didn't want any company.

Thomas was six weeks old. Our elation over his feeding success the week before had faded under the continuing strain of balancing home and hospital life. Reed and I were steadily retreating into long-term survival mode, which meant we didn't have much to say to each other.

When I appeared in the kitchen my mother-in-law, Nancy, was mixing the ingredients for stuffing and checking the progress of the turkey already roasting in the oven. She and Don had been staying with us for three weeks running, taking care of all the domestic work, keeping the kids as happy and occupied as possible. But they would be going home the next morning, using the last two days of Nancy's leave of absence from her teaching position to drive the eight hundred miles back to Portland.

I gathered milk from the freezer and packed it in my insulated bag. Reed was opting out of today's hospital trip. The kids were downstairs watching Macy's Thanksgiving parade on TV, waiting for Santa Claus to come to town. I headed out the door without saying good-bye.

When I entered the unit, I saw that the bulletin board was stripped bare of Halloween photos. There was no nurse at the front desk, only a row of Beanie Baby bears decked out in seasonal costumes—pilgrims, Native Americans, scarecrows. A sign was taped to the desk surface beside them: SUPPORT THE MARCH OF DIMES. $10 EACH.

There was no nurse in Thomas's room, either, but there was something unexpected waiting on the shelf next to his bed: a card. It was small, maybe four inches by three, made from heavy, dark green paper. On the front was a maple leaf cut from bronze-colored metallic foil. Inside I found a thumb-sized footprint, and a hand-written message: *Happy Thanksgiving! Love, Thomas.*

I looked at Thomas, snoozing on his tummy. There was no point in trying not to cry. I concentrated instead on moderating the flow, swallowing the sobs that bubbled in my throat. Tears dripped from the corners of my eyelids. I flicked them away with my forefinger, one after another.

"I'm back," the nurse said as she strolled in. "Potty break. Do you like your card?"

I nodded and sniffed.

"A former patient's mom made them. She came in early this morning to do all the footprints."

More tears. That mom must've gotten up at dawn to get all the cards ready before parents started arriving. I grabbed a Kleenex and wiped my nose, trying to pull myself together.

"It's just about feeding time for this little guy. Want to get his diaper changed while I warm the milk?"

"Okay." Carefully I turned Thomas over and stripped his bottom half. The cool air made a great alarm clock. "Hey, sweetie," I said as his eyes opened. He arched his back and pulled his knees close to his chest, then stretched his legs out like a waking cat. I wiggled him back into his pants. After we settled into the rocking chair, the nurse handed me a bottle, dripping wet from the hot water bath. Thomas latched on right away, pulling firmly and rhythmically on the nipple. The air bubbles flowed like crazy.

"Boy, he really knows what he's doing!" the nurse said. "He chugged two ounces earlier this morning."

"Really?" He'd been getting three bottles a day—one in the morning, one at night, and one when I came in to feed him. So far, having multiple people involved with feedings hadn't been an issue, contrary to the attending physician's prediction. "When will he move up to four?"

"Every forty-eight hours we can add another. We just need to be careful not to wear him out."

I did some quick addition in my head. "So that means he could be ready to come home within another week or so?"

"If he keeps this up, then I'd say it's pretty likely. And if you're willing to learn how to manage his NG tube, they'd discharge him even sooner."

I mulled this over while Thomas drank. I never thought I'd be willing to deal with that tube, and I still panicked at the thought of handling it. But I was even more panicked at the thought of juggling hospital visits after Don and Nancy left the following day. The kids' resilience was wearing thin, and the stress of reabsorbing all the housekeeping and child-tending might tip Reed and me over the edge.

Thomas pushed the nipple out of his mouth, and I handed the empty bottle to the nurse. "Would you like to give him his first tub bath today?" she asked.

My heart jumped—I'd been waiting for this for weeks. "I'd love to," I said.

She fetched a large plastic basin and filled it with warm water while I stripped Thomas down. Placing the basin on the countertop, she tested the water temperature and squirted in some baby bath liquid, then swished the water around. "Ready," she said.

I slid my hands under Thomas's neck and bottom and lifted him carefully. He waved his hands and kicked his feet as I stepped close to the basin and slowly lowered him into the water. His eyes widened, and the nurse and I laughed.

"Pretty wild, huh?" I asked him. "It's gotta feel good, though." I wondered if he could still remember floating in my womb, pummeling my bladder and kidneys with his hard little heels.

Thomas relaxed against my hand, which held him steady in the warm cradle of water. With a soft, wet cloth I wiped his cheeks and forehead, then the deep crease of his neck, then his whole body from shoulders to toes. I'd never seen anything more beautiful than his pale pink skin, strangely translucent, with faint webs of deeper pink just below the surface.

"He'll get cold quickly now, so let's dry him off," the nurse said. She unfolded a flannel blanket and draped it over her arms. As I lifted Thomas from the tub he let out a yell. A *loud* one. The nurse and I laughed again. I'd never heard such a noise from a baby—short and loud and forceful, as if he were yelling *Hey!* at a runaway thief.

Once I'd dressed him, it was already time for me to leave. We were putting up the Christmas tree that afternoon—I wanted to get it done while we still had help around—and the children wouldn't start without me. I hated that no matter where I went, I left part of my family behind. And I wanted Thomas home for Christmas.

All that stood in the way was that stupid NG tube.

"Okay," I told the nurse. "I want him to come home. I'll do whatever it takes."

She nodded. "I'll let the doctors know. And don't worry—the tube isn't that bad."

Somehow I doubted that. But my resolve was firm. Thomas didn't belong at the hospital, all alone under the fluorescent lights. He belonged with his family. He needed us—and we needed him, me especially. I needed to hold him, rock him, hear his breathing at night. I needed to finally be his mother.

I laid Thomas back in his crib, feeling sick at leaving him again. "It won't be much longer," I promised him. "Thanks for the card, buddy."

I picked up my coat and turned to the nurse. "Will you hold him whenever you can today? Please?"

She nodded. "Gladly."

On my way out I paused by the parade of stuffed bears. I picked up the one dressed like a boy pilgrim and peeked at the name tag: *Miles.* I shook my head, wondering if there was a whole staff of Beanie Baby people who came up with these names and designed the tiny outfits. *Patches*, with his straw hat and overalls. *Chief*, with his felt headdress. And the turkey bear, with a little red gobbler and bright, fuzzy tail feathers—*Tom.*

I didn't usually go for such cuteness, but this wasn't a usual day. I put a $10 bill in the envelope and grabbed Tom Turkey. I clutched the bear tightly as I moved past the bare bulletin board, through a dozen sets of doors, and across twenty gray miles.

Winter

The bulletin board was covered with red and green paper; the basket by the sink was full of knit caps to match. Christmas in the NICU—thankfully, not for us. Thomas would be coming home that afternoon.

I shifted from one foot to the other as the nurse went over the list of discharge requirements. Reed and I had completed the infant CPR class, and Thomas had completed the test to ensure he could breathe adequately in his car seat. He'd had his newborn hearing screening, which he failed; we'd have to get a more extensive hearing exam before too long. The only thing left to cover was an NG tube lesson.

"It's now or never," the nurse said as she unwrapped a new tube, a thin yellow catheter with tiny black centimeter markings on its surface. I stood at her elbow as she demonstrated how to measure Thomas's esophagus. "Okay, your turn," she said.

My hands shook as I measured. "Nineteen centimeters. That's what you got last time, right?"

"Right. Now, let's review what you'll do once the tube is in." She attached a syringe full of air to the end of the tube, then handed me a stethoscope. "You'll put the end of the stethoscope against his tummy, push some air from the syringe into the tube, then listen for a little puff as the air comes out the other end," she explained. "That tells you the tube is in his esophagus instead of his trachea. But actually, if it was in his trachea, you'd know right away."

"How?"

"Oh, he'd be coughing a lot. Maybe turning blue."

Perfect.

"Okay, I'll hold his little arms down and you push that tube in. Don't go too fast or you might push it in too far. Don't go too slow or you'll make him gag."

I set the end of the tube by Thomas's left nostril. The thought of shoving it up there was completely counterinstinctual—like sticking a finger in his eye. Red flags popped up all over my brain: *Warning. Security breach. Do not hurt the baby.* I gritted my teeth and made my hand push the tube upward. Thomas arched his back and squirmed, trying to get away from the miserable thing snaking up his nose. The nurse held him down tightly. I blocked out his cries and kept pushing the tube steadily until I got to nineteen centimeters.

"Great job!" the nurse said, patting me on the shoulder. "Now, let's check the placement and tape this sucker down."

Once that was done, I sank into a chair, trembling and damp. It was almost over. Reed would be arriving soon for his lesson; the oxygen delivery guy would be bringing us a travel tank any minute, and a large tank would be delivered once we were home. We had a new bassinette ready in the corner of our bedroom and a new dresser for Reed to assemble.

"Would you like to borrow some clothing for Thomas?" the nurse asked me. "You can choose four or five outfits from the stack, as long as you return them once he outgrows them."

Great idea. We had received a few preemie outfits as gifts, but we needed some more. I sorted through the folded clothing on the shelf under Thomas's crib and picked out some sleepers and play clothes, including my favorite outfit from the NICU cache: navy blue bottoms and a matching striped top with tiny tools embroidered on the front. I packed the clothing in my tote bag, which already held an insulated case to carry leftover breast milk from the hospital freezer, two blankets for the ride home, and the knit cap I'd chosen from the basket the day I was discharged. The traveling hat, inky blue like winter twilight, crowned with one tiny white star.

On my way to the pumping room for one last session, I walked through the "hall of fame," pausing in front of the posters of pink-cheeked children. My eyes moved from the small preemie shots in the corners to the full-color healthy-kid images, three feet tall. Once weak and fragile and sick, these kids had gotten better, much better. Just like Sam had. I'd been taking encouragement from that truth for the past six weeks.

But my heart sank as I realized another truth: Thomas would never get better. He would lose the NG tube and oxygen tube at some point, but he would have Down syndrome every day of his life. And I would have a son with Down syndrome every day of his life.

I couldn't do it. I couldn't deal with Thomas's disability *and* his medical issues *and* his adjustment to life at home, all at once. Down syndrome was the least pressing of the three issues. It would just have to wait.

The three youngest kids came running as soon as I pushed open the kitchen door.

"Mommy!"

"You're home!"

"Where's Thomas?"

Already weary, I managed a small smile. "In the car," I said. "Dad's bringing him in."

"Welcome home." My neighbor, who had been babysitting, gave me a wry grin.

Reed entered with the car seat in one hand, the travel-size oxygen tank in the other, and a pulse oximeter slung over his shoulder. We followed him to my bedroom, where Reed unloaded the bags. Matt and Sam clambered onto the bed and hovered over Thomas's car seat.

"Hi, Thomas," Matt crooned.

"He has a star!" Sam said, poking the button on Thomas's hat.

Dong dong dong. "What's that?" asked Christine.

"That's the machine that makes sure he's breathing well," I said, fiddling with the tank flow valve. The alarm sounded every time Thomas's oxygen saturation got too high or too low, and for some reason I couldn't get the oxygen flow just right to keep him in the safe zone. His reading had dipped and peaked all the way home.

Andrew came in. "Hi, Mom!" He eyed the stuff Reed was piling in the corner. "What's in the bags?"

"Things for Thomas. Nothing interesting," I said. He rifled through the syringes and tape and tubing spilling out of one bag, just to make sure.

Elizabeth and Ben showed up at the same time and gave me hugs, then joined the other kids, who were fawning over Thomas.

"Awwwwwww!"

"He's *so* cute!"

"*I* want to hold him first."

I held up my hands to cut the chatter. "Guys, now's not a good time to hold him, okay? Soon."

Dong dong dong. I pushed the alarm silence button, cursing under my breath.

"So, what's for dinner?" Ben asked.

Dinner?

My neighbor laid her hand on my shoulder. "I'll be back in thirty minutes with something hot."

I sighed. "Thank you."

"You're welcome. And congratulations—he's beautiful!"

"Thanks." I glanced at Thomas. Sam had pulled off the star hat and knocked the nasal cannula askew.

With the babysitter gone, Andrew sensed his opportunity. "When can we exchange my Transformer?" he asked. The night before we had given the kids gifts "from Thomas," a not-so-subtle distraction tactic. But apparently I'd picked the wrong one for Andrew.

"Not tonight, honey. There's no way."

His face crumpled. "By the time we go, the one I want will be gone!"

"I'll take him, if you think you'll be okay," Reed said, bringing in the last of the bags from the car.

I hesitated. I didn't want to be so indulgent, but everyone was wound dangerously tight, including Reed. The errand would give him some breathing room. And Thomas was still fast asleep. "Go ahead. I'll be fine."

Soon after Reed and Andrew left, my neighbor returned just long enough to hand me a covered casserole dish. "Good luck!" she said.

I peeked under the lid. Hamburger Helper. My mouth watered—after the day I'd had, anything would taste good. I put the dish on the table and called the kids in to eat. But when they saw the mysterious red stuff, they freaked.

"What's that?"

"Gross."

"I'm not hungry."

I nearly kicked myself for not being a clean-your-plate kind of mother. But it was too late to switch parenting strategies. And I was too tired to really care.

I heard a faint cry from the bedroom—Thomas waking up. I grabbed a cup of frozen milk from the freezer and threw it in the microwave, even though it was supposed to thaw in the fridge. Then I found the phone and ordered pizza, refusing to feel guilty. After hanging up I rushed to my room, fished a bottle out of one of the hospital bags, then ran back to grab the milk as the microwave dinged. When I got back to the bedroom, Thomas was fully awake, squirming against the straps of his car seat.

I was afraid to pick him up.

Don't be a wimp, I scolded myself. *You've been taking care of babies for a dozen years.* But my hands shook as I unbuckled the straps and lifted Thomas from his seat, mindful of the tube that tethered him to the tank on the bed. I grabbed a pillow, sat in the rocking chair, and tried to arrange Thomas on my lap.

Christine found me. "Is Thomas going to drink his bottle now?" she squealed, delighted.

"Yes, sweetie, can you hand it to me?" I had left it on the bed, out of reach.

She handed it over and ran out of the room. "Thomas is going to eat now!" she announced, and returned with Matt and Sam in tow. The kids surrounded my chair, twittering with excitement.

Dong dong dong. "Christine, will you push that big gray square?" I pointed to the alarm silence button.

I slid the bottle nipple into Thomas's mouth, but he wouldn't take it. *Crap.* I tried again, but he turned his head and started to cry. I lifted him against my shoulder and rocked, trying not to panic.

Ding-dong. "Pizza's here!" Ben shouted.

I set Thomas in his bassinette and paid the delivery man. Then I put the boxes on the table next to the casserole dish and headed back to the bedroom as the kids swarmed in for the kill.

I settled Thomas on my lap again and offered the bottle, but he was too restless to latch on. From the kitchen I could hear Elizabeth and Ben fighting over who got the bigger slice of pizza.

Dong dong dong.

Ding-dong.

I waited a minute, hoping one of the kids would get a clue and answer the door, but it only rang again, along with the alarm. *You've got to be kidding me.* I stood up, laid fussing Thomas in the bassinette, hit the silence button, and headed for the door.

It was the oxygen delivery guy, balancing a four-foot-tall tank. "Evening, ma'am. Where do you want this?"

When Reed and Andrew returned, an hour later than I expected, I was sitting on the bed with Thomas. And it seemed I'd be stuck on the bed for the foreseeable future, because the oxygen tubing was seven feet long, not the promised thirty—apparently the long tube wouldn't work for the low-flow oxygen Thomas was on.

"We had to go to three different stores," Reed apologized as he walked in, a slice of pizza in each hand. He saw the big tank set up behind the bassinette and the smaller tanks for car travel stacked against the wall. "Sheesh!" he said. Then he saw my face. "Are you okay?"

"No, I'm not." I felt my grip on control slipping away. "The tubing is so short, I can't leave the bedroom with Thomas. And the kids are bouncing off the walls, and we need to get them to bed, and Thomas doesn't want his bottle, and I'm starving but I haven't had a chance to eat." *Dong dong dong.* I hit the silence button. "And the alarm keeps sounding. When his levels are low I turn the flow up a tiny bit, but then his levels get too high. I had the oxygen guy swap our monitor for another one, and he even gave us a different flow regulator for the tank, but it hasn't helped! I don't know what I'm doing wrong!"

Reed picked Thomas up from my lap. "You need a break. I'll watch him while you get something to eat, okay?"

I escaped to the kitchen. I eyed the Hamburger Helper, thinking I'd better polish some off, since nobody else would. But I opted for pizza so I could eat with one hand and clean with the other. I searched for unscathed pieces in the remains of the feeding frenzy. No luck. By the time I'd shoved a few half-eaten pieces down my throat and cleaned up the worst of the mess, I heard Reed calling from the bedroom.

"This is crazy," he said when I appeared. "The thing alarms every two minutes."

I refrained from any smug remarks.

"How are we are ever going to sleep?"

I hadn't thought about that. We'd grown used to the alarm during our NICU visits, but we hadn't needed to fix meals or shower or sleep when we were there. And there'd been a nurse babysitting the alarm all day and night, nudging the flow up or down, hitting the silence button, adjusting the cannula or the monitor probe when necessary. I didn't know how we could manage.

Numbly I walked out of the room and begin corralling the little kids into their bedrooms. "What about stories?" Matt asked.

"Not tonight."

"But, Mom—"

"Not tonight!" I snapped, flipping off his light.

I went downstairs to say goodnight to the big kids. Usually I sat on the edge of their beds to chat for a few minutes, but at that point I was too wasted.

"Goodnight, Ben," I called through his open doorway.

"No, Mom, come talk to me."

I poked my head in. "Honey, I'm so sorry, but I just can't. I'm about to collapse."

His face pinched with anger. "I haven't talked to you in weeks. You're either at the hospital or you're home but you're too tired. Some mom!"

The words socked my solar plexus. A sucker punch when I was already down, already desperate. Fury exploded in my head, hard and fast, sending words flying like sparks. "Don't give me that crap," I spat, narrow-eyed, my finger jabbing the air. "I won't put up with that. I'm doing the best I can."

I wheeled around and stomped out of his room, half blinded by tears. At the bottom of the stairs I heard the *dong* of the monitor alarm drifting from my bedroom. I stopped, not sure I could make myself walk toward that sound. But there was nowhere else I could go.

The doorbell rang at 9 a.m. I made my way down the hall, hung over from Thomas's first night at home. When I opened the door, frigid air swirled into the entryway, smelling of frost. December was on the doorstep. And so was a short, round woman with pink cheeks, dark curls, and tortoiseshell glasses.

"Hi, I'm from Vista Heath Care," she said.

"Come in." I stepped aside to make room. As she bustled past, I shut the door against the cold. Matt and Sam came running to appraise the visitor. Sensing a willing audience, they began a running commentary of the last twenty-four hours, their voices rising steadily one above the other.

"Thomas came home!"

"He eats with a bottle!"

"He has a tank so he can breathe!"

The nurse smiled at me again, then turned toward the boys. "You must be the big brothers."

"Two of them," I said. Thankfully, it was a school day for the other kids.

"Is the baby sleeping?" she asked.

I nodded.

"Then let's get some paperwork done before I take a peek at him."

I shooed the boys down the hallway to my bedroom, where Reed was assembling the new dresser, and motioned for the nurse to follow me into the kitchen. The table was littered with remains from breakfast; I hastily cleared away bowls half full of milk and soggy Cheerios, then grabbed a dishcloth to wipe up puddles of spilled juice.

"Sorry," I said.

"That's perfectly fine." She set her bag on the table and unzipped it, then sat down. "How are things going?"

"We're surviving, kind of. We had a rough night last night." For eight hours I'd hung in a gray haze of consciousness, desperately wanting to drop into sleep. But every time I began to sink, I was yanked upward by the *dong dong dong* of the alarm. I used the silence button like a snooze feature, allowing myself three delays before I sat up, dizzy and stupid, to fiddle with the oxygen flow or reposition the infrared monitor probe, which would burn Thomas's perfect little foot if left in one place too long. Morning came like a curse.

The nurse gave me a sympathetic glance. "I'm sure this is a stressful time for you." She was the kind of woman you picture holding a hurting child to her ample bosom. I sat down next to her, tempted to crawl into her lap.

She pulled some papers out of a manila folder and clicked a ballpoint pen. "Let's get a health history for Thomas. Start when your labor first began."

And so I rewound my memory to October 4 and played the highlight reel while she recorded key details in a firm, curved hand: birth date and weight, T21 diagnosis, results of echocardiogram and CT scan, treatment for sepsis, hearing test results, progress of oral feedings. Every time the nurse asked a question, my mind strained to process her words and string together my reply. I heard the alarm's elevator tones from the bedroom down the hall, and muffled thumps as Reed scrambled to hit the silence button.

The nurse put down her pen. "Sounds like someone's waking up. Let's go take a peek."

I led her to the bedroom, where Matt and Sam were bouncing on the bed as Reed wrestled with the dresser.

"This is Thomas!" Matt announced.

"He's cute!" Sam added.

The nurse peered into the bassinette. "He sure is."

Matt and Sam bounced to the edge of the bed for a better view. The nurse pulled a stethoscope out of her bag, unsnapped Thomas's undershirt and listened to his heart and lungs. "He sounds good," she said. "Go ahead and get him undressed so I can weigh him. I'll set up the scale on the kitchen table."

"His tubing won't reach that far," I said.

"Unhook him from the tank," she said as she walked out. "It'll only take a minute."

I sat on the bed, weighed down by incredible fatigue. The paperwork session in the kitchen had only lasted an hour, but I felt like I'd put in a full day's work. With timid fingers I began to peel off the layers of Thomas's homecoming outfit (which had doubled as pajamas), trying and failing to get his undershirt off without dislodging his nasal cannula. Once he was naked, I wrapped him snugly in a blanket, then reached over to screw the oxygen tank shut, close the flow valve, and detach his tubing from the tank.

It was chilly in the kitchen. "We'll have to unwrap him," the nurse said while adjusting the electronic settings on the scale. "I'll be as quick as I can."

I gave Thomas a little squeeze. "Sorry, buddy." I removed his blanket and laid him on the cold, hard plastic scale, flinching at his indignant cry.

After recording the weight in kilograms, the nurse pushed the button to convert the measurement from metric to English: five pounds, five ounces. "He's gained two ounces already," I said, surprised and pleased.

Thomas yowled. "You can pick him up now," the nurse said.

Back in the bedroom I hustled to get Thomas dressed and hooked up to the tank. Cold and tired, he yelled while I fumbled with his undershirt and tubing. The nurse tried to give me instructions about increasing Thomas's feedings, but I couldn't hear a word. The alarm sounded. Matt and Sam jumped on the bed and chattered at full speed. Reed hammered the backing to the dresser.

The nurse cleared her throat. "You know, preemies can be very sensitive to noise," she said, glancing at Reed.

All at once, the stress of the past eight weeks came to a horrible, bulging head. I didn't want to sit on this woman's lap anymore—I wanted to slam her pink, pudgy face with the heel of my hand. "Sit down!" I snapped at the boys. They clambered off the bed and promptly grabbed the packages of screws, dumping them on the floor. Reed bellowed. Matt and Sam bawled. Thomas wailed. The alarm sounded. My tears spotted Thomas's blanket as I leaned over to adjust his cannula. I started to shake.

"Are you okay?" the nurse asked.

I nodded, just barely, willing her to pack up and go. Internal pressure would blow me open any second, and I didn't want her around to see. *Please leave. Please leave.*

Finally, she picked up her bag and walked out, her good-bye barely audible over the din. I clenched my fists to keep from exploding while Reed picked up the screws and the boys scampered off to play elsewhere.

Dong dong dong. Fingers trembling, I silenced the alarm. Saturation 79 percent. I increased the oxygen flow and watched expectantly for the percentage to increase. But instead, the numbers began to dip in a stomach-turning freefall: 74 . . . 71 . . .

Dong dong dong. I scooped Thomas out of his bassinette. His eyes were closed. "He's at 67!" I called to Reed.

He rushed over. "Turn up the flow." I pushed the valve open as wide as it could go.

Dong dong dong. 65. I watched in horror as pallor spread across Thomas's face.

"Make the call," Reed said, his voice mottled with fear.

Call. Call 911. The cordless phone was in the kitchen, but I couldn't make my legs move toward it. *He's dying. He's dying.*

Dong dong dong. Sixty percent. In desperation Reed grabbed for the dial on the top of the tank and wrenched it hard. A sudden rush of oxygen burst audibly through the tiny holes in Thomas's nasal cannula.

Reed turned to me, wild-eyed. "It was turned off," he said. "It was turned off."

Turned off. When I'd brought Thomas back from the kitchen, I'd opened the flow valve but never screwed open the tank itself.

I stood still, so still, watching the numbers on the monitor leap upward. *Dong dong dong.* One hundred percent. Reed turned the flow back down. Thomas still looked dangerously pale. I touched his cheek: cold.

"Get me a warm blanket!" I cried as I snatched Thomas from the bassinette. Reed grabbed a receiving blanket and ran downstairs to throw it in the dryer. I pulled off Thomas's clothes and held him against my chest, covering him with the flaps of my fleece cardigan until Reed returned. I wrapped Thomas in the blanket and sank into the rocking chair, holding him tight as we moved back and forth, back and forth. His body relaxed into sleep. His skin turned pink again, with a faint roadmap of veins showing just below the surface. When I touched his cheek, the skin felt thin and slightly dry, as fragile as vellum paper, as fragile as life itself.

I woke to sunlight streaming through my bedroom window, abnormally bright. I pushed the curtain aside: snow. Four or five inches coated the dead yellow grass and the withered tomato plants we'd never pulled out of the garden. The limbs of our peach tree bowed under the white weight.

"Have a good day," I told Reed as he headed out the front door. After two months of spotty appearances at work, he needed to resume his full-time schedule at the Utah Department of Transportation, where he managed environmental issues. The older kids were at school. I would be alone all day—alone with three kids under the age of five.

You've done this before, I told myself. *Make it work.* The first day flying solo with a new baby was always a panicky occasion, but for me it usually came a week or two after bringing the baby home. Thomas had only been home for three days, and even though he was more than six weeks old, he still felt brand new.

I wished Mom were still with me. She had stayed for at least a week after each of the other babies were born, typically showing up on Reed's first day back at the office. Even after I'd had several children and felt confident caring for a newborn, I still needed her help. A baby's arrival meant the reinvention of the family—a hard task to face when you're going on two hours of sleep at a time (at most) and leaking milk and hormones all over the house. And as our family grew bigger, the adjustment process got harder.

I had no clue how we'd make it work this time. The day before, I'd taken Thomas to the pediatrician, who told me Thomas would need weekly checkups for the next month or two. The NG tube could be out in a matter of weeks, but the oxygen would likely be needed for several months. Insurance might not cover the new RSV shot, essential for preventing respiratory infections in preemies—only a thousand bucks a stab. Thomas needed to be seen as soon as possible by the pediatric ophthalmologist and cardiologist, as well as the physician at the hospital genetics clinic. We had to call the hospital billing department and our health insurance company. And the Social Security office, so we could apply for disability aid. My temples throbbed at the prospect of all that talking, all that thinking. Plus the feeding and the holding and the dozen other facets of caring for a small child, times three. And later, the listening and helping and feeding required by a school-age child, times four.

It was a preschool day for Matt; he attended twice a week at a neighborhood home. I didn't want to take Thomas out in the cold, so the night before I'd asked my neighbor, Leslie, to take Matt to school. She readily agreed, which didn't surprise me—when Thomas was in the hospital, she'd brought us meals and gifts and even loaned us a set of keys to her spare car in case we needed it.

But as grateful as I was for Leslie's generosity, I hated asking for help. I hated needing help. I wanted to prove that we could handle this situation—that *I* could handle it. Plus, I felt unusually private about my home life these days. I didn't want any visitors, not even helpful ones.

I got breakfast and clean clothes for everyone, hurrying to finish before Thomas woke up, then hustled Matt into his coat. "Put your backpack by the door so you don't forget it."

He frowned. "Aren't you driving me?"

"No, Leslie is going to take you, so I can stay home with Thomas."

His face hardened. "I don't want to go in her car. I want *you* to take me." He started crying. "You never take me to school anymore!"

Crap. I reviewed my options: I could load Thomas and Sam into the van and drive Matt myself, but the very thought wore me out. I could keep Matt home, but he deserved the distraction and excitement of a school day. I could make him go with Leslie, but I couldn't stand the thought of forcing him out the door, tear-stained and wailing. I'd been neglecting him ever since this crisis began.

There had to be a way to make everyone happy.

Thomas was still fast asleep after his morning feeding. On impulse I called Leslie and asked if she would be willing to sit with Thomas while I drove Matt down the street to his preschool. Matt's face bloomed with relief when I told him the new plan. Proud that I had found an agreeable solution, I quickly wrote instructions for managing the pulse oximeter and the oxygen flow regulator. All Leslie would have to do was turn the flow up slightly if Thomas's numbers dropped. I taped down the NG tube and the monitor probe with fresh adhesive so they'd stay put.

When Leslie arrived, my tightly twisted stomach relaxed. She'd raised six children—she could probably care for Thomas even better than I could. In the bedroom, she listened carefully as I reviewed the written instructions and demonstrated how to turn up the flow if needed. "You don't even have to pick him up," I told her. "I'll be back in ten minutes, tops."

Outside, the frigid December air shocked my nostrils. I squinted against the clear blue brightness of the sky reflecting off the new snow. The weather had been gloomy all week, gray with winter smog, but the new morning was bursting with frozen glory.

After buckling Matt and Sam into their car seats, I guided the van through the neighborhood, tires pressing paths into the clean white streets. Virgin ground. The preschool teacher lived only a mile or so away; I dropped Matt off and glided home, giddy with fresh air and light and hope. *I'm alive,* I thought. *I'm alive.*

I listened carefully as I carried Sam back into the house—no baby crying, no alarm donging. Success.

But as I walked into my bedroom, I saw Leslie perched on the edge of my bed, clutching Thomas. She glanced up at me, then back down. I followed her gaze and my pulse froze: A length of stained yellow tubing hung from Thomas's nose. He'd pulled his NG tube most of the way out. The fresh tape I'd pressed to his cheek hung from one corner.

My arms shot forward to take Thomas. "He woke up as soon as you left," Leslie said. "He had his hands up by his face, and somehow he pulled that thing out. I didn't know what to do." There was a tremor in her voice. She was angry at me, although trying not to be. But she deserved to be angry. She deserved to be *furious* that I left her with Thomas after sixty seconds of instruction. What was I thinking? *What was I thinking?*

Hands shaking, I laid Thomas in his bassinette and pulled the rest of the tube out so he wouldn't choke on the tip. "I'm so sorry," I said. "I didn't think . . . I'd just taped it down . . ."

"It's okay," she said, her voice turning gentle. "At first I was scared something was wrong, but I kept watching the monitor like you told me, and the numbers stayed high, so I figured he was fine. It's okay."

But it wasn't okay. My stomach churned as I pictured what could have happened: Thomas could've gagged on the tube dangling partway down his throat; he could've vomited and aspirated. He could've died right there on Leslie's lap as she watched the numbers on the monitor plummet. It would be horrific enough if any of that happened on my watch. But how could I ever recover if it happened when I was gone? If my negligence had harmed or killed my child, and burdened my neighbor for the rest of her life? I had no right to pass off my responsibility. Thomas was *my* child, and no matter how hard I looked for an escape hatch, there wasn't one.

Leslie stood to leave. Desperate to erase what had happened, I apologized again and again, as if repetition could undo my reckless decision. She smiled to reassure me, then left. And I was alone again, alone with my incompetence and guilt. Alone with a baby who couldn't eat until that tube was put back in.

The nurse would arrive within two hours. Thomas was due for a feeding in one hour. I'd never inserted the tube alone before, and I was terrified to try. *He'd probably be fine if I made him wait*—but no, I couldn't do that. I wouldn't make him suffer because of my mistake. After being so careless, I needed to redeem myself.

I grabbed the TV remote and turned on Sesame Street for Sam, then gathered supplies: stethoscope, syringe, new tube, tape. Heart pounding, I laid Thomas on the bed, measured and marked the tube, then placed its tip just under his left nostril.

I can't do it.

You must. Right now.

Steeling myself, I pinned Thomas's arms down with one hand, grasped the tube with the other, and started to push. Two centimeters up, then four—Thomas twisted and cried. Numbly I kept pushing. *You must.* But the tube didn't move. I pushed again. Nothing.

I breathed in and out as Elmo on TV cackled in the background. Sweat coated my upper lip and dripped from my armpits. I tried again. Two centimeters, four—stuck again.

Stupid. *Stupid.* I flung the tube on the bed and picked up my screaming son.

Even after the nurse came and replaced the tube, even after I'd called my mom to confess my crime of negligence, I couldn't calm down. There was no getting around the fact that my judgment was failing, that *I* was failing. Instead of keeping Thomas safe, I'd endangered him—twice. And if something had gone terribly wrong, no nurse or mother could've made it right.

A gray afternoon. Instead of water vapor, the air was full of toxic gunk: Winter inversion was back, trapping smog like a heavy woolen blanket covering the Salt Lake valley, dulling the light.

Matt and Sam sat on my bed watching *Dragon Tales*. I hooked myself up to the pump flanges and began the latest round of the feeding repertoire: twenty minutes of pumping, then washing the equipment, then giving Thomas milk in a bottle. A logistical nightmare. I'd nursed Elizabeth sitting on the couch, reading a novel. By the time Sam was born, I nursed while flipping French toast, brushing kids' hair, checking homework. Sometimes I even vacuumed the carpets with him suctioned to my chest. But multitasking was impossible now.

The world had shrunk to the size of my bedroom.

I'd enjoyed such shrinkage in the past, under different circumstances. Motherhood was so saturating, so multifaceted and impossible to tame, that an excuse to narrow the focus usually felt like a vacation. In times past, when one of my kids got a fever or a bug, I'd happily abandon our usual routine to play nurse. We'd watch cartoons and drink juice and read books, just like I did with my mom when I was sick as a child, and for a few days life would be small and sweet and simple.

But life with Thomas was a different story. *This is big,* my friend Kate had said. And it wasn't just a matter of hunkering down and dealing with the medical equipment that had taken over a corner of my bedroom. I turned off the pump on my nightstand and eyed the Down syndrome parenting guides stacked on top of it—reminders of just how big this was.

I picked up *Babies with Down Syndrome* and skimmed a few pages, resisting the dense paragraphs that detailed a future I didn't want. But as I flipped through the chapters a subtitle jumped out at me: *Teach Your Baby Now.*

I started reading. "The importance of early intervention cannot be stressed enough . . . it should begin as soon as possible." By the time I'd finished the section, I'd learned that Thomas's fate depended on my taking every opportunity to stimulate his learning and development. And it kept getting better—a later section warned me that children with Down syndrome develop joint problems if they aren't held properly as infants. "Early patterns of movement can influence later development and are crucial to future social acceptance and self-esteem."

Uneasy, I picked up the other title, *A Parent's Guide to Down Syndrome,* opened to a random page, and found a chart. "Task Analysis: A Dressing Sequence." After a few startled seconds, I realized it was an outline of the different phases involved in learning to put on socks. Eight phases, to be exact. "Phase I: Child pulls on sock when just above heel. Phase II: Child pulls on sock when just below heel." I put the book down, feeling panicked. Twelve years of motherhood, and I didn't recall ever teaching a kid to put on socks. I just did it for them until the day they did it themselves—or until the day I decided I was done playing valet. What would it require of me for Thomas to learn basic self-care?

If putting on socks was such a complex cognitive activity, what would the task sequence look like for brushing teeth, or using the toilet?

Back in the springtime, when I found out I was pregnant, I'd thought it was the beginning of the end: a few more years of diapers and rice cereal and Fisher-Price before I graduated from baby raising and began the countdown to the well-earned empty nest. *This will be my easy baby,* I'd thought—my spoiled last-born, my final turn on the wild ride of motherhood. But the ride was supposed to last only a few years, not a few decades. My friend Ellen's parents finally retired to Hawaii with David as their sidekick. I might have a dependent child until the day I died.

After cleaning the pump equipment and stowing the milk in the fridge, I flipped through Thomas's discharge papers until I found the number for BabyWatch, our school district's early intervention program. The resident who discharged Thomas had said a representative would contact me, but since nobody had, I figured I'd better call. Not that I wanted to. All my conflicting feelings about Down syndrome still lurked within me, waiting to wreak havoc again. But my plan to ignore the whole issue for a few months wasn't going to fly. If I didn't take action immediately, where would that leave Thomas—sockless at fifteen? And where would that leave me?

While Thomas napped, I sat on the living room couch, ruler and pencil in hand, notepad on my lap. The pediatrician wanted me to chart Thomas's oral intake for a week, to see if he could manage without the NG tube.

On a fresh sheet of paper, I drew lines to make seven columns, then eight rows—seven days in a week, eight feedings in a day.

Fifty-six little boxes, fifty-six pieces of a decision. Still sobered by my gaffes with the closed oxygen tank and Leslie's babysitting stint, I resolved to be extra careful with this feeding chart. Precise. Every cc recorded. No shortcuts.

From my spot on the couch, I could hear Ben and Andrew's voices rising up the stairwell from the family room. From what I could hear, they were playing consecutive rounds of that create-an-insult game beloved by elementary-age boys. I considered hoisting myself off the couch and charging down there to break up the party. Or at least hollering a few choice words down the stairs.

"Your underpants are perma-brown," said Andrew.

"Well, *you* want a Barbie for Christmas," said Ben.

"Oh, yeah?" Andrew countered. "Well, *you have Down syndrome.*"

The words came like hard slaps to the face. Minutes later my cheeks were still stinging. Andrew, such a tenderhearted child. Where did such ugliness come from?

And then I remembered our patched-up attempt at a family meeting, when Reed and I had told the kids that it might take longer for Thomas to learn certain things, like walking, talking, and reading. After our spiel, the school-age kids looked concerned. All of them were stars in their respective classrooms; a couple were profoundly gifted. (*Keep reading those encyclopedias,* Ben's preschool teacher told him on his last day—and she wasn't kidding.) They'd seen themselves finishing work way ahead of the other kids. They'd heard themselves answering questions that stumped the rest of the class. Reed and I didn't pressure them to perform, at least not knowingly, but we did praise them for their talents. And voila! A simple logical inference, obvious to any eight-year-old: If learning quickly is good, learning slowly is bad. Thanks to me, Andrew equated *Down syndrome* with *loser.*

I hadn't seen this coming. But what was I supposed to do when my kids asked about Down syndrome—pretend it had no consequences? And what was I supposed to do when my kids excelled at school—pretend I didn't care?

Of course I cared. As a student I'd been in gifted programs; I'd taken honors and AP courses; I'd won academic awards. From kindergarten to my senior college seminars, teachers told me I could write my own ticket. Of course I was pleased that my firstborn child was precocious and creative and articulate. The psychologist who scored her IQ test in first grade called her remarkable. *There will be no doors closed to her,* she said. I wanted every one of my children to have that freedom.

Yet somehow I'd gotten my wires crossed, and theirs. I didn't mean to teach them that *smarter* meant *better*—I didn't believe that. Desperately, I wished I could live a thousand afternoons over again, when they came home with their tales of aced spelling tests and math triumphs and advanced reading groups. I pictured myself holding their report cards and opening my mouth to say the right thing. But I couldn't hear the words.

That evening, I headed downstairs to the older kids' bedrooms. Given Andrew's prize put-down, I knew the four of us needed to talk, although I worried that my attempt at damage control might just make things worse.

In the hallway the single lightbulb in the ceiling fixture burned yellow and dim. The bedrooms were dark. "Are you guys still up?" I called out.

All three of them were—Elizabeth, Ben, and Andrew. Separated by drywall, we couldn't see each other's faces. Maybe that would help.

"I heard you boys goofing around this afternoon," I began, as casually as I could. "I know you were just teasing each other, but I'm concerned about something that was said, and I was hoping we could talk about it."

Tense silence.

"When I heard Andrew use "Down syndrome" as an insult, I realized that I didn't do a very good job explaining it after Thomas was born. It's true that he'll need to work harder to learn, but everyone has gifts—things they're extra good at. Thomas might not be as talented as you are in reading or math, but he'll be good at other things."

After a pause, Ben spoke. "Like what?"

I hesitated. All I could think of were the warm fuzzies people kept telling me—*Down's kids are so happy, Down's kids are so loving.* I didn't want to perpetuate stereotypes, but I didn't know what else to say.

"Well, as Thomas grows up he'll show us," I answered. "Maybe his gifts won't have anything to do with schoolwork. But maybe he'll be good at accepting other people, or being cheerful. Maybe he'll have a talent for kindness, or gratitude." I wondered if my words sounded the way they felt—like cheap consolation.

More silence. Then a voice floated from Elizabeth's bedroom: "You mean he might be good at things that really matter?"

Things that really matter. There I was, trying to assure my kids that their brother was valuable, and I was the one who doubted.

"But Mom," Ben said, sounding bewildered, "what's wrong with being smart?"

"Nothing." I took a deep breath and cleared my throat. "Nothing's wrong with being smart. It's just that other things are more important."

Andrew's voice came from his bedroom, muffled with tears. "I love Thomas."

Winter

Love. I thought of Thomas's delicious little body, snuggling with his father upstairs. I imagined the silky feel of his dark hair, the warm smell of his neck, the soft heaviness of his head. And for one pure moment, my fear shrank to a flicker, as thin and weak as the yellow glow barely lighting the hallway.

Sunday. Reed took the kids to church, alone, just like he had for the past seven weeks. I'd never before missed so many weeks of church. But Thomas couldn't be around crowds yet, and neither could I. The skin of my new life was still too raw to be touched.

As soon as I got Thomas changed, fed, and tucked in for a nap, I sat at the computer and stared at the blank page on the monitor. With Christmas fast approaching I needed to get holiday cards into the mail, but I still hadn't written our annual family letter. Most of the people on our list didn't even know Thomas had been born, let alone that he had Down syndrome, and I had no idea how to phrase the news. We had a perfect photo to send—one of the reindeer images from nurse Penny's Halloween shoot—but that wouldn't be enough. People would be wondering how we felt about the diagnosis, and if we said nothing they might draw the wrong conclusions.

But what were the right conclusions?

Needing inspiration, I launched Google and typed in *Down syndrome birth announcement.* The top link opened a site called Diagnosis Down Syndrome. I scanned the page, which featured cute photos of kids with Down syndrome and encouraging words written by their parents. At the bottom was a message one set of parents had included in their son's birth announcement.

> *Sean is a very special baby, and the birth announcement can't possibly say it all. God has made Sean special and chosen us to be his parents—we feel blessed.*

I stared at the screen, bewildered. There was no way I could say such things in Thomas's birth announcement, even though I believed them to be true. At least, I thought I did.

> *We hope you will feel the same as we do, we're happy and proud. We would like you to see him as we do, a beautiful baby boy. We also want you to treat him just like any other baby. Congratulate us—Be happy we have a baby. We're a family now, this is not a sad moment. PLEASE do not apologize, we aren't sorry.*

More mixed feelings. I thought Thomas was beautiful, too. I wanted people to see him as a baby, not a diagnosis. I wanted to assure my friends and family that nothing was wrong. At the same time, I had a nurse visiting the house and a support group hoping I'd attend. I had a stack of literature on my nightstand and a team of specialists to consult. In short, I had ample evidence that something *was* wrong, and I couldn't honestly say that I wasn't sorry. Yet it would also feel false if I said I was.

I clicked and read and clicked some more, but I couldn't find any perspectives that matched mine. Which made sense, in a way. My thoughts and feelings were so conflicted, I was more like two women than one. I could write two completely different letters, and they'd both be true.

An hour later the printer hummed and buzzed with activity. When it stopped I picked up the sheet of paper, still damp with ink, and read the finished letter, focusing on the all-important paragraph that reported the diagnosis:

> *I finally made my appearance on October 18. There had been worries about my size and my health, but I surprised everyone by weighing in at a hefty 4 lbs. 3 oz, and being able to breathe without much help. I did bring along an extra chromosome, which landed me a subtitle of Trisomy 21 (otherwise known as Down syndrome). Some folks seemed a bit "down" when they heard the news, which confused me. Given the adoration I've gotten from my family (not to mention those poor, susceptible hospital nurses), I figure an extra measure of Thomas-ness can only be a good thing. Plus, it'll look great on Mom's license-plate frame:* MY KID HAS MORE CHROMOSOMES THAN YOUR KID.

The perfect solution. By writing from Thomas's point of view, I could avoid detailing my own. Satisfied, I picked up one of the photo cards that would accompany the letter: a blue-and-white winter scene with Thomas at the center, peering earnestly at the camera in his brown-and-white reindeer suit, his fuzzy black hooves resting on his chest.

I smiled. He was a Christmas baby after all.

I wrapped Thomas in a blanket and laid him on my bed, hardly recognizing him. The NG tube was finally gone. His face looked so bare and clean—no sniveling yellow snake winding across his face and no rubbery brown tape holding it down. His eyes, gray and brown all at once, peered up at me. *Here I am,* he seemed to say.

Hope warmed my chest. It was the first step forward since we had brought him home, the first sign that, under our care, he was healing from the trauma of coming to land ten weeks early. We needed a celebration.

"Ben, will you help me?" I called. I opened one of the small travel-size oxygen tanks and hooked up Thomas's tubing.

When Ben walked in and saw the travel tank, he turned to me with wide eyes. "Are you bringing Thomas out?"

"Yep! It's about time, huh?" I unplugged the monitor and hung it by its strap on Ben's shoulder, then hung the travel tank from his other shoulder. I scooped Thomas out of his bassinette and cradled him in the crook of my arm. Then we walked, slowly, down the hall toward the white glow of the Christmas tree.

Most of the family was gathered in the living room. Reed had gone grocery shopping, and Elizabeth was at her church youth group, but the other kids sprawled on the couches and the floor, reading books or playing quietly.

Christine jumped up when she saw us. "Thomas is here!"

"Can I hold him first?" Matt bounced in place.

Sam shook his head. "No, *me* first!"

My neck muscles tensed. "Everyone will get a turn," I said. "Line up on the couch." They scrambled into place. "Grab my camera," I told Ben. He scampered off to get it.

I laid Thomas on the kids' laps, one at a time: Sam, Matt, Christine, Andrew. While Ben snapped photos, they stroked Thomas's cheeks with gentle fingers, cooing softly. Never before had I seen such tenderness in the movement of their hands, the curves of their smiles.

Ben's turn. He set the camera down, sat in the wingback chair, and held out his arms. I placed Thomas in the crook of his elbow, keeping my hands in place until his brother's tiny, warm body curved gently into his lap. Ben tucked his finger into Thomas's palm and smiled at me. His soft brown eyes reflected the light from the tree, which shone as luminous as the truth:

We weren't sorry. And nothing was wrong.

The day's mail brought a handful of holiday cards, rich with red and green and gold. It'd been over a week since I sent ours. My friends and family members would have received them by now, opening the envelopes to find the holiday letter on bright red paper and the photo with Thomas's earnest, antlered face. But nobody had called. I wondered what they were thinking.

After dinner I shut the bedroom door, sat on the bed with the cordless phone in hand, and dialed my grandmother's number, feeling more than a little apprehensive. Although deeply affectionate, she was prone to worry. And she'd grown up during a time when people with Down syndrome were shut away in institutions. As the phone rang I psyched myself up to play cheerleader.

"Kathy?" she said when she heard my hello. "Oh, I'm so glad you called. I got your card!"

Definitely *not* concerned. I relaxed on the bed, surprised yet relieved.

"I've read your letter a dozen times," she continued. "It was so precious—I could hardly stand it!"

Her praise felt incredibly good. "Did you like the photo?" I asked, fishing for more.

"Oh, the *photo*—I've never seen anything so adorable. I'm completely smitten by my new great-grandson!"

I grinned as I pictured her opening the envelope and swooning in her armchair.

"Thomas is just *darling*," she gushed. "He doesn't *look* like there's anything wrong with him!"

My mouth opened, then shut again. *That's because there* is *nothing wrong with him,* I thought.

Say it! *Nothing's wrong with him. Nothing's wrong.*

The words wouldn't come.

"Do they know how severe it is?" my grandmother continued.

I closed my eyes. "No. There's no way to tell. We'll just have to see how things go as he grows."

"Don't worry," she said. "His brothers and sisters will help him. They'll teach him everything he needs to know."

Like the eight phases of putting on socks. I squeezed my eyes tighter.

My aunt came on the line, her voice soft and loving. "Your letter was delightful," she said. "I so admire your approach to this situation. You seem to have a true understanding of what really matters, and I find that very inspiring."

What really matters. "Well, it's easy to love Thomas," I said, my throat tightening. I forced emotion back down like bile. "Down syndrome is a challenge, not a tragedy."

The conversation ended. I put the phone on my nightstand, trembling. I wasn't upset with my grandmother—clearly her heart was sincere. But what about mine? All that talk about love, and I couldn't even defend my son. *Hypocrite,* hissed the voice in my mind. *Liar.*

But I wasn't a liar. I hadn't said anything untrue in the letter, or on the phone. I couldn't possibly call Thomas's life a tragedy, and his life was inextricably connected with his extra chromosome, so I couldn't call *that* a tragedy. And he *was* easy to love.

Oh, really? Images surfaced in my mind: the other Halloween photos, the ones that showed a cross-eyed disabled kid in a reindeer suit. The ones I kept hidden in a manila folder, shoved under a tall pile of papers on the top shelf of the computer desk.

I shook my head. I had cross-eyed photos of all my newborns, and I hadn't shown them off, either. This was no different.

Except it *was* different. I could laugh at my other babies' goofy-looking photos, but I couldn't laugh at Thomas's. They weren't harmless candid images catching him at an off moment. They were tokens of the future. And as much as I despised myself for dreading that future, I still did.

I lifted the breast pump off my nightstand, one hand gripping its handle and one supporting its weight beneath. The thing must've weighed twenty pounds. Carefully I lowered it into the blue plastic case waiting on my bed, taking care not to smash my fingers, then shut the lid and fastened its black leather strap. The home health guy would show up any time now. He'd lug a fresh four-foot oxygen tank from his truck to my bedroom. He'd take the almost-empty one away. And if I told him to, he'd take the pump away as well.

I'd been weaning myself off the beast for more than a week. A few containers of NICU breast milk remained in the freezer, but after those were gone, I'd have to crack open the extra-pricey high-calorie formula for preemies. The can had a list of ingredients hundreds of words long, man's best attempt at duplicating Mother Nature. I didn't want to feed Thomas a mix of corn syrup solids and whey protein and synthetic vitamins. I wanted to give him what only my body could make. Purity. Perfection. And I had plenty of milk to give. But I had no strength, no energy, no willpower. After twelve years and seven babies, those reserves had run dry.

I never thought I'd have such a big family. The only women I'd known with lots of children wore muumuus to church and never cut their hair. Really, I wasn't the type. I didn't even like kids before I had my own. As a teenager I had ordered my babysitting charges to bed as soon as their parents pulled out of the driveway, no matter how early the hour. I couldn't stand their mess, their whining, their wide-eyed neediness. When Reed and I were engaged, we talked about having a few children years down the road, after I earned the Ph.D. I dreamed about—maybe by then I'd actually *want* to be a mother.

But that was before I met a newborn baby for the first time.

After our wedding, Reed and I lived in a basement apartment near Brigham Young University, next door to our friends Luis and Eva. They brought their firstborn home one morning in the dry burn of August. When Eva opened the door to my knock, her eyes were shadowed, her hair limp, her curves sagging. But she smiled, quick and sure, as she glanced backward over her shoulder. Behind her I saw a pink blanket smoothed over the worn brown carpet, and on the blanket, an infant asleep. My legs moved forward as my eyes took in the sight: flesh and blood and bone, impossibly small, impossibly alive.

I sat at the edge of the blanket. Eva followed, gingerly, still sore from the birth. Time slowed as we watched the gentle rise and fall of the baby's chest, the short jerks of her limbs as she startled in her sleep. Dressed lightly for the summer heat, her pink skin glowed with a sheen that filled the room, washing the dullness from the worn furniture and yellowed linoleum and dark-paneled doors. The light touched me and sent me spinning.

I don't remember how long I sat on that brown carpet, transfixed, as Eva lifted her waking daughter, cradled her, brought her to breast. But as the afternoon sun slanted into evening, something gently opened within me. I wanted a child. More than that—I *needed* one, like I needed food and water. *Baby hungry*, friends teased me. I didn't know why I'd changed, or how. All I knew was that when I returned to my apartment that afternoon, I felt bereft. And when Eva's door opened the next day, and the next day, and the next, I felt like I was coming home.

Six months after my wedding, I told my senior advisor that I didn't need her letter of recommendation after all. I wasn't going to graduate school—I was going to have a baby. She shook her head, disappointed that I was succumbing to "cultural pressure," the Mormon expectation for young married couples to bear children as quickly as possible. She was wrong. My unexpected longing for a child didn't come from anything or anyone external. It was a deep, true desire that came from the deepest, truest part of myself, and I trusted it completely. So did Reed, once he got over the shock of my sudden one-eighty.

We still didn't think we wanted a big family. But baby hunger returned less than a year after Elizabeth was born, and again two years after that, and again and again. We welcomed six pregnancies in ten years. Then, as our thirteenth anniversary approached, a seventh. When the test came back positive, we'd never been so happy, we'd never been so confident. And we'd never been so clueless about what was to come: a baby born ten weeks early, a baby with Down syndrome.

A baby I couldn't feed anymore.

I never thought that would happen. All of my breastfeeding babies sucked life right out of me, yet I always manufactured more, and there was always enough for two, even if only just barely. But feeding Thomas was different. It had been different from the beginning. Within weeks of becoming pregnant I began to fall apart. I could hardly lift my arms to do simple tasks; climbing stairs required a rest every few steps; even my thoughts slowed to a near-stop. In the silence of inertia I heard my blood speak: *We can grow this baby, as long as we don't do anything else.*

That same sense of scarcity gripped me every time I pumped. Whatever power had sustained me through a dozen years of growing and feeding babies was gone. There were no refills on the life flowing out of my body—if I kept it up, I would shrink smaller and smaller until I dried up like a puddle in the sun.

Never again. Never again.

The doorbell rang. I held the door open for the home health guy and then led him to my bedroom, where he deposited the new tank. After he carried out the old tank and returned again, I pointed to the travel tanks in the corner.

"These all empty?" he asked.

I nodded. "You can take this, too." I motioned to the pump.

He looked a bit confused. "All done with that?"

I nodded again, frustrated by the delay. *Take it. Take it and go.*

He made some notes on his clipboard and handed it to me to sign. *Stay numb,* I warned myself as I signed my name.

I stayed numb as he picked up the heavy blue box by its handle and walked out the door. I stayed numb when I opened the last cup of frozen breast milk a few days later. And I stayed numb the day after that, when Thomas screamed with constipation from his high-iron preemie formula. He arched his back and twisted away from the cramps in his gut while I rocked him slowly, staring at the wall.

The doorbell rang at 9 a.m. I opened the door for the first time in days and shivered in the cold air. It was Suzanne, the early intervention therapist, a round woman with glasses, long brown hair, and the biggest smile I'd seen in a long time. Maybe she could help me resolve my crazy back-and-forth feelings about Down syndrome.

"I'll go get Thomas," I said. "He's just waking up."

"Great! While you do that, I'll wash my hands."

I hesitated—the kitchen and the bathroom were both disasters. I decided a crusty toilet was worse than a crusty sink. "There's hand soap in the kitchen," I said before heading down the hall. As I readied the travel tank and monitor, I could hear water running in the kitchen sink. Arms fully loaded, I made my way to the living room, where Suzanne was waiting.

"Here's Thomas." I slipped the tank and monitor straps off my shoulders so they rested on the floor, then tilted Thomas's face toward Suzanne.

"Oh my goodness, he's adorable! Did all your babies have lots of dark hair?"

I nodded. "Apparently that's the only recipe we have."

She laughed. "And he's two months old now?"

I nodded again.

"Wonderful." She pulled a clipboard out of her bag. "Let's start with a health history, okay?"

Not again. "Okay," I said, wishing the home health nurse could just send her a copy.

But as it turned out, I liked Suzanne more and more as she led me through the questions. When I told her I'd recently stopped pumping, and that Thomas was struggling to digest formula, she didn't skip a beat. "I think it's fantastic that you kept it up for two months," she said. "Those first weeks are what count the most. And don't worry—there are things we can do to help with the constipation."

I almost wished I'd called her sooner.

When the history was done, Suzanne put down her clipboard and scooted closer to Thomas, who was dozing in my arms. "Do you have a blanket we could lay on the floor? I'd like to take a good look at this little guy."

"Right over there." I pointed to the quilt neatly folded in the corner.

Suzanne spread out the soft folds of flannel. "This is beautiful," she said. "Did someone make it for Thomas?"

"My mom." The day before she left, she'd held it up with pride and said, *The bright colors will stimulate his eyes.*

"It's so big and warm—it'll be perfect for him to play on," she said. "And I love the bold colors." She opened her bag and took out a few toys. "Thomas, it's playtime!"

She took him with confident hands and arranged him gently on the blanket, explaining that her job was to assess his development and help me learn how to "maximize his potential." Roused from his nap, Thomas yawned and stretched. "Such big eyes!" said Suzanne. "He's so alert. See how he's studying my face?" I smiled, feeling better by the minute.

Suzanne picked up the toys—a rattle, a mirror—and used them to catch Thomas's attention, testing to see how far his eyes would track an object. Every time he followed her movements, my chest swelled with pride. The monitor alarm sounded a few times, but I barely heard it—I pushed the silence button and adjusted the oxygen flow without even thinking.

"Can he hold up his head yet?" Suzanne asked as she set the toys aside and grasped Thomas's hands.

"Sometimes, for a few seconds." I watched anxiously as she pulled his arms, lifting his shoulders slightly off the floor. At first his head lagged on the blanket, but then he rallied and lifted it upward.

"There you go, Thomas!" Suzanne turned to me. "His muscle tone is excellent."

I tried to play modest, but I couldn't stop a big proud-mama grin from spreading across my face.

She stayed for an hour, playing with Thomas, asking me questions about his hospital stay and our experience at home so far, and taking copious notes. After the evaluation, she made a list of ways our family could stimulate Thomas's senses. She gave me brochures from the school district's child development center and explained what programs they offered: home visits through age three, mother-toddler classes, special-needs preschool.

"Now tell me," she said, "have you contacted any of the local Down syndrome support groups yet?"

Uptown Downs. The Buddy Walk photos. The crowd of smiling faces I didn't want to join. "No," I said faintly. "No, I haven't."

"I can get you in touch with the leader of our local chapter. Would you like her phone number, or should I have her call you?"

"I—can't," I stammered.

Suzanne was quiet for a minute. "That's okay," she said. "Here's their most recent newsletter." She handed me a glossy leaflet. "They're a wonderful group, and they'd love to hear from you when you're ready."

I took the newsletter, said good-bye, and shut the door behind her, shivering again as winter air curled around my bones.

Standing at the kitchen counter, I opened the afternoon mail: hospital bills, credit card applications, more Christmas cards— and a large, flat envelope from our insurance company. Puzzled, I opened it to find a cover letter congratulating me on the birth of my new baby, and a calendar, pastel colored, with "Baby's First Year" on the front. I flipped through the pages. Each had a blank banner at the top and rows of blank squares beneath, so parents could fill in the dates beginning with their baby's birth month. The back page was a sheet of small, square stickers for marking developmental milestones: First Smile, First Tooth, First Step . . .

Ugh—cute stickers. I had an aversion to scrapbooking (to quote my husband, you can't spell *scrapbook* without *crap*). But I did value record keeping. I'd bought baby books for each of the kids and made myself fill them in, although Sam's book had a lot of blank pages. Maybe this calendar thingy would be a good idea for Thomas's baby record—I could just slap those little stickers on and call it good.

But I wondered what dates to use when recording Thomas's progress—should I go by his chronological age, starting on October 18? His corrected age for prematurity, starting on December 23? And given Thomas's diagnosis, how many of those little stickers would we actually use before twelve months had passed? My other babies sat up, crawled, and walked within the normal timeframe, or earlier. Elizabeth's book included a list of her vocabulary at fifteen months, with long columns of words covering the page: colors and animals, household objects, people. By that point she was walking, even running. But Thomas's first word and first step might be years away.

I set the calendar on the counter, next to the papers from Suzanne's visit. The top page in that pile was the list of interaction activities. Suzanne had been impressed with Thomas's muscle tone—maybe if I worked with him, he really would be high-functioning, like my mother predicted. I pictured Thomas's tiny, dark head lifting off the floor, Suzanne's praise, my big silly grin.

Without warning, awareness hit me hard: *This is how it all started.* My babies saw my relief (You're normal!) and delight (You're smart!) as they lifted their heads and swatted their rattles. They saw my satisfaction when they walked and talked, counted and spelled. That's how Andrew and all my kids learned to value success, quickness, competence. From day one I gave them my happiness in return for their achievement.

Guilt clenched my stomach. I didn't want to teach Thomas that his worth increased with his developmental success, and I didn't want to keep teaching that lie to my other kids. I wanted all of them to know, without question, that they were lovable and valuable no matter what they did or didn't accomplish.

And yet, according to the experts, Thomas needed my help to have a good life. *The importance of early intervention cannot be stressed enough.*

Early intervention. Its purpose was to intervene, to change the course of Thomas's development, accelerate his progress, and move him toward a more desirable end. But how could I feel and show unreserved love for Thomas if I was constantly trying to change him? On the other hand, how could I withhold my help and encouragement, even my praise, and call that love?

I put down the papers and picked up the calendar. *Maybe I should just chuck it,* I thought. I didn't want any reminders of what Thomas wasn't achieving. And I didn't want any incentive to pressure him. The last thing he needed was the burden of my self-serving expectations.

But if I threw the calendar away, wouldn't that be like giving up? I didn't know what Thomas might be capable of. I shouldn't sell him short.

I set the calendar down, picked it up, set it down again. More crazy thinking. Suzanne's visit had only made it worse.

"It's cookie week! It's cookie week!" Elizabeth sang as she walked into the kitchen, just home from school.

I groaned silently. Christmas was less than two weeks away, but it didn't feel like it. Every time I walked past the living room, I was surprised to see the tree twinkling. I'd hoped Elizabeth would forget cookie week, our pre-Christmas ritual of baking at least one different kind of treat each day: butter cookies with cherry centers, gingerbread men, sugar cutouts, peanut butter drops crowned with Hershey kisses. The crowning event was assembling small gingerbread houses for each member of the family, to be eaten on Christmas Eve.

Elizabeth hung up her coat and backpack. "What are we making today, Mom?"

I couldn't see myself baking. Not only was I exhausted, I could hardly walk around the house. I'd had my big toenail ripped off with steel pliers by a podiatrist a few days before—the timing was laughably bad, but the nail had become so badly ingrown I couldn't walk without bleeding. My foot was wrapped in layers of gauze. I couldn't get it into a shoe, and when I walked, I hobbled on my heel.

"Sweetie, it's not happening," I confessed.

She shot me a pained look. "But it's *tradition!*" she protested, dropping her backpack on the floor. Holiday routines meant a lot to Elizabeth, and most of our Christmas activities had already gone out the window. No handmade gifts from the kids for their grandparents and great-grandparents. No plates of treats for neighbors, friends, and teachers. If Nancy hadn't helped us put up the tree on Thanksgiving, it would have probably stayed in its box. And if it weren't for online shopping, the kids would have been scarred for life.

Elizabeth pouted.

I motioned to my bandaged toe. "I'm just not up to it. I can barely walk. And you know these past few weeks have been really hard." I hated myself for playing the pity card, but it did come in handy sometimes.

"How about if I make the cookies myself?" Elizabeth pressed.

I pictured the kitchen coated with butter, flour, and colored sugar, like it had been after her previous forays into baking.

"I'll clean up," she added.

I pictured the butter and flour and sugar smeared with a dishcloth.

Elizabeth put her hand on her hip. "Mom. It's *Christmas.*"

I sighed. "Okay, but only if you agree to make the gingerbread houses." Wicked me. The houses were a royal pain to assemble—before the frosting dried, they were highly unstable, prone to collapsing when you put the roofs on. More than once I'd vowed to never do them again. But *she* didn't know that. Yet.

"Yippee!" Elizabeth clapped her hands and spun around. I wondered where she got her energy and enthusiasm. She hadn't had a troubled reaction to Thomas's diagnosis, like Ben, Christine, and Andrew had. Maybe it just didn't bother her. Maybe it did, but she was over it now. I didn't know. But she seemed fine—and I'd gladly scrape cookie dough off the kitchen floor to keep it that way.

Once the little kids were in bed, Reed headed downstairs to his computer desk and I headed to our bedroom for my new evening ritual: soaking my raw toe. Doctor's orders were to soak in salt water for twenty minutes twice a day, to hasten healing.

I prepared a basin of warm water and Epsom salt, following the directions on the bag. Gritting my teeth, I lowered my foot inside, gasping as hellfire gathered on the tip of my toe, then spread through my foot and up my leg. For twenty minutes I sweated from the heat, wondering why healing had to hurt so much.

Not long after I finished the torture session, Elizabeth walked in, just returned from her weekly youth group activity. I felt a flash of annoyance—I wanted to be alone with my traumatized toe. But then I saw her face: pale, empty, shaken.

"Are you okay?" I asked, my heart picking up pace. What had happened—a conflict with one of the leaders? A tiff with one of the other teens?

She nodded, biting her lip and staring at the floor—definitely not okay. "We went to the care center."

The care center for the mentally disabled. I'd forgotten she was going. But I hadn't forgotten the sights, sounds, and smells of my own visit a few years back, when I was a church youth group leader. The slow, shuffling gait of the residents as they entered the room. The flat tones of their voices. The disinfectant fumes and body odor. How proud I'd been of our little program of songs and stories, the cookies we brought, the few minutes of our time we spent in service there. I even mingled with the residents after the program, making bizarre small talk, giving a few perfunctory pats on the back. But when one of them tried to hug me, I stiffened and pulled away. Right after that another resident, a short Latino man with terrible teeth, insisted on holding both my hands and guiding me through random dance moves.

I was afraid to ask. "How'd it go?"

"I don't know." She sniffled back tears. I shuddered to think of the connections she might be building between what she'd seen tonight and what she saw in her future. How would I have felt as a twelve-year-old if I knew my baby brother would grow up to be like Eddie across the street?

I pushed my panic down and snapped into wise-counselor mode, telling Elizabeth it was normal to feel uncomfortable around people who behave and communicate in ways we're not used to. She listened and nodded, dripping tears. But I saw the defeat in her slumped shoulders. Elizabeth, my firstborn—my child with such confidence, such drive, such optimism. For two months she'd been holding on, keeping her chin up. But tonight had been too much.

"Did it get easier once you were there for a while?" I asked, hoping for a feel-good ending.

She gave a half smile. "Yeah, I guess." But her eyes were like Ben's the night he found the Down syndrome packet—sad, imploring. *I'm sorry, Mom.*

I was about to stand up (painfully) and hug her, when her face brightened. "But Mom, the funniest thing happened. You know Jeff?"

One of the guys in the youth group. I nodded.

"It was hilarious, Mom. We were sitting there making these snowmen out of paper plates . . ."

An image flashed in my mind, not from the past, but from a possible future: two men, one young and one older, sitting next to each other at a long table holding scissors and glue, pipe cleaners and paper plates. The older man's hands were fumbling with the scissors. *Thomas.*

Elizabeth smiled and laughed as she told the rest of the story, but her voice sounded faint, as if it were coming from very far away.

Christmas Eve. Elizabeth was busy in the kitchen, putting together the dratted gingerbread houses. I was soaking my toe again. It hadn't hurt since I started following the doctor's instruction sheet, which had been lost in the pile of papers on my counter. *Soak in a solution of one tablespoon of Epsom salt per half gallon of warm water,* it said.

One tablespoon. I'd been using half a cup.

Typical. The past few weeks I'd been having a terrible time thinking straight. My brain felt cloudy. Forming sentences took a lot of effort; whole conversations were nearly impossible. And right then I was having real trouble mustering up strength for the evening festivities: Holiday ham for dinner. The candy-covered houses for dessert. The gift exchange—each year the kids drew one sibling's name and bought him or her a small gift for Christmas Eve. And the nativity play, when we dressed up in bathrobes and towel headdresses and reenacted the birth of Christ.

Christmas Eve. My mother's birthday. When I was a kid, the occasion meant cake and pizza and root beer. Shy and pleased, we'd give Mom the presents we made at Brownies or bought from the drugstore with our allowance. I didn't have a present for her this year, but I'd called her earlier to wish her a happy birthday.

"I talked to my mother," she said. "About Thomas." Spooked by the chat with my other grandmother, I'd asked Mom to make the call. But when I asked how it went, she hesitated. "Well, she was pretty upset. I asked her why she was crying and she said, 'I'm sad.' I told her, 'Ma, there's nothing to be sad about.'"

Nothing to be sad about. I hung up the phone two thousand miles away in more ways than one.

My twenty minutes of soaking were up. I dried my foot and stood to empty the basin, feeling lonely. I missed my mom. I wanted to join her in that hopeful place where there was nothing to be sad about. I knew it was real. I kept reaching for it within myself, as if reaching for a light switch in a dark room. But all I touched was doubt.

After dinner everyone's blood sugar soared. As we gathered for the nativity play, the energy in the living room was strong enough to lift the roof.

"I'll be the innkeeper," Ben said, swaggering around the room with an empty wine vinegar bottle. "I'm drunk."

"I'm baby Jesus!" Sam announced.

"No, Thomas is baby Jesus," Elizabeth corrected. "I'm Mary."

Christine frowned. "You always get to be Mary."

"That's because I'm the oldest. Christine, you can be a sheep. Mom, will you be the angel like you were last year? And the narrator?"

I nodded. Christine sat on the couch in a huff.

Elizabeth continued with the assignments. "Okay, Matt, you and Sam are shepherds and wise men. Andrew can be Joseph, and Dad will be the donkey . . ."

I interrupted. "Honey, Dad's with Thomas in the bedroom."

She rolled her eyes and sighed. "We need him to be the donkey!"

"You mean the ass?" Ben said with a sly grin.

Christine's eyes widened. "Mom, Ben said 'ass'!"

Ben gave me an innocent smile. "It's in the Bible."

"We'll just have to pretend we have a donkey," I said, ignoring them both.

"But won't he be bringing Thomas out to put in the manger?" Elizabeth pointed to the laundry basket in the corner, awaiting the arrival of the newborn king.

"Sorry. We'll have to travel to see baby Jesus, just like the real shepherds did."

"Can I give him my present?" Matt asked. He'd drawn Thomas's name for the gift exchange and had the present all wrapped: a board book with photos of babies in animal costumes. We'd found it at the dollar store, and I'd bought it before I realized what it reminded me of—the bulletin board in the NICU.

Elizabeth seized the idea. "Perfect! You're a wise man, so you can bring it to him when you make your visit."

I wondered if we'd be able to get through the play before midnight. Matt jumped off the couch and rolled on the ground. Sam climbed in and out of the basket. Christine still sat sullenly with her arms crossed. Ben "drank" out of the red-wine vinegar bottle and belched, much to Andrew's delight.

I stood at the front of the room and began the narration as loudly as I could. Elizabeth crouched down and pretended to ride a donkey; Andrew pulled an invisible rope. Ben pointed the way to the stable. An angel appeared to frisky shepherds and led them down the hall.

We burst into the room and gathered around the bed. Thomas rested on Reed's shoulder, unspeakably cute in his striped shirt with the tiny tools. Matt stepped forward to offer his gift, and we began to sing, in a variety of keys.

Silent night, holy night . . .

Thomas raised his head briefly.

All is calm, all is bright . . .

The words rang with light, the light that emerged from a dark corner of the world over two thousand years ago, the light shining from my children's faces. I could see it. I could hear it.

If only I could feel it.

January gloom settled in the house like a nasty winter cold. On school days the big kids trudged in and out, backpacks coated with white residue from salty snow. The little boys hunkered down with me and Thomas, except when Matt went to preschool. We had three more months until spring weather would make it safer for Thomas to be in public. Three more months of house arrest.

The days were all the same. Matt and Sam played in their room and watched TV on my bed. I held Thomas in the rocking chair, sometimes kissing the top of his head, sometimes stroking his little arms. He had the most beautiful skin—pale and soft, delicate, nearly transparent, as if he weren't fully grounded in time and space.

It was his skin that triggered the thought that came unbidden, every day: *Thomas will be leaving soon.* That was it. No explanation. No fear, no sorrow, no panic. Just words, lying calm and plain in my consciousness. And a deep, sweet longing, as if he had already gone but wasn't very far away.

As time moved forward, these impressions became stronger, more urgent. When I started envisioning a tiny tombstone, I called my friend Kate, hoping she'd tell me I wasn't going mad.

"I don't know how to explain this," I began, "but I think Thomas is going to die."

She didn't hesitate. "Of course you do."

I sighed with relief.

"Think about it," she continued. "Both you and Thomas have been through the wringer these past few months, and life feels really unstable right now. It's post-traumatic stress."

No, no. That wasn't it. "It's not just that I'm scared he *might* die. I actually have a feeling that he *will* die—not right away, but sometime kind of soon. While he's still a kid." I swallowed hard. The words felt even more true spoken aloud.

She exhaled. "Okay, tell me more. What brought this on?"

"Well, when I hold him, I have this overwhelming sense that he isn't going to stay with us for long. It's hard to describe." But it came even as I spoke, a strange sense of transience, as if Thomas could disappear like fading frost.

"Is he having any new medical problems, anything that would make you suspect his health might fail?"

"No," I said. "Nothing." His regular checkups with the pediatrician were normal; his visits to the cardiologist yielded no new concerns.

"Kath, I don't want to discount your feelings, but to me they make perfect sense. You have a new baby at home on oxygen—your *seventh* child—and he was in the hospital for weeks and weeks, and he has this diagnosis to deal with on top of everything else, right?"

I nodded dumbly, even though she couldn't see me.

She continued. "I would expect you to have troubled feelings, and I don't think they necessarily mean Thomas is going to die. You're under incredible stress right now. Quite frankly, it's a wonder you're still standing."

I didn't say anything for a minute. Kate lined things up so logically, and her conclusions made so much sense. There was no rational reason to suspect early death. But this impression wasn't based on anything rational.

"Okay, I'll try not to worry," I finally said, just to appease her.

It got worse before it got better. For several days my mind kept turning its morbid thoughts over and over, as though they were some benign curiosity. Changing Thomas's diaper, I wondered what size he'd be wearing when he passed away—or would he be potty-trained? Placing him in his bassinette, I wondered if he'd be in a crib or a big-boy bed when the time came. I figured it would be within a few years: When I tried, I could picture Thomas as a toddler, and as a preschooler. But when I projected past kindergarten age, there was nothing. Empty space.

Even when my fixation began to fade, that emptiness remained an indelible mark on the future. Thomas's expected life span was 30 percent shorter than mine—we were, statistically speaking, destined to depart right around the same time. But I considered myself warned that he might go long before I'd had my full share of tomorrows.

The garage door slid shut as Reed backed the van down the icy driveway. I sat on the front bench next to Thomas's car seat, his travel tank and monitor by my feet. We were leaving for an evening out. Our plan—eating takeout in the restaurant parking lot—was minimal, but at least we were getting out of the house. Elizabeth was old enough to keep an eye on Sam, Matt, and Christine, and the older boys could watch after themselves.

It was dark, January-dark, and we hadn't been out to dinner since late September. Reed drove toward our favorite restaurant a couple of miles away, over streets crusted with dirty slush. Out the window our neighborhood passed by, looking the same as it always did, yet different somehow. It reminded me of the car trip Reed and I made soon after we married, when we loaded up his Honda Civic and drove from California to Utah. We'd made the drive before, but after our wedding the once-familiar landscape seemed alien—the sagebrush desert, the curving mountain passes, the wide-open sky. We'd started a new life, and the world had changed.

Reed pulled into the parking lot of the Mexican place and maneuvered the van into a spot rows apart from the cars clustered around the entrance. "Do you want me to go in and order?" he asked.

Through the plate-glass windows I saw the Friday night dinner crowd already building up, though it was barely 6 p.m. I nodded. One of us needed to stay in the car with Thomas, and I didn't want to be around all those people.

I watched Thomas sleep, grateful his health was finally stabilizing. He was adjusting to formula—although he still got constipated, he didn't scream like he did the first few days. And he needed less and less oxygen each week. I couldn't wait to get rid of the tanks and tubes and wires for good. I wondered how long it would take to stop hearing the monitor alarm in my dreams.

When Reed returned, we sat in the van and ate, engine still running, windows steaming from the food in our take-out containers. I had the green chile enchiladas I'd eaten dozens of times before, but they tasted different. Everything was different— being there, being together, being alive.

I watched people walking in and out of the restaurant, unaware of us sitting in the van with our disabled baby and his oxygen tank. "Do you think we'll ever feel normal again?" I asked Reed.

He shrugged. "Were we ever normal?"

I smiled. We told our kids we married each other because we were the same kind of weird—same quirky taste in music, movies, and people; same obnoxious sense of humor. Our shared oddities were a strangely important part of our relationship, the bedrock of our sense of belonging together. And Thomas was our newest oddity—in the most endearing sense.

As I looked through the restaurant window at couples and families eating, I thought about the outbursts my friend Jen's son Jake sometimes had in public. "Do you think you'll be embarrassed to take Thomas places?" I asked Reed.

He finished chewing and swallowed. "I might be," he admitted. "But I don't want to be."

I nodded, grateful for his honesty.

"I'm trying not to think about stuff like that," he continued. "I'm more worried about logistics. The rest of the hospital bills are coming in, and it's a good thing our insurance has that out-of-pocket maximum or we'd be screwed. Even so, our savings are as good as gone. And it's not just a short-term issue, you know? We've got a kid we'll likely need to support financially his whole life."

I watched Reed's profile as he finished his grilled steak burrito. We didn't want thick, gray winter smog creeping into our relationship, yet it was coming anyway. We were tired. So tired. In fact, the stronger Thomas got, the worse we seemed to feel. The same thing happened during Sam's illness: Crisis adrenaline kept us numb for weeks, but as the emergency waned, our blocked-off feelings began to surface. And with Thomas our feelings were exponentially more complex, and more dangerous—so dangerous we didn't dare dig too deep. I didn't talk about my lingering thoughts of Thomas dying. I didn't talk about my dread of the future, either, or any other dark secrets. I sensed that Reed was hiding his, too, whatever they were. Maybe he feared, like I did, that air and light would bring them to life.

Dong dong dong. Thomas was stirring, and our food was gone. "Here, I'll do the dishes," Reed said, taking the Styrofoam containers and stuffing them into the plastic sack. "Ready to go?"

Home again. Back to our bedroom, back to the four walls that enclosed my life. "No," I said. "Not yet. Let's get a movie or something."

As we cut through the supermarket parking lot to get to Blockbuster, we saw an employee gathering shopping carts in the freezing night. Reed slowed the van to let him pass. I glanced up and froze—the man had Down syndrome.

Reed and I looked at him, then at each other. But we didn't say anything.

"They're here!" Andrew called from his perch on the couch, watching out the front window. My friend Jen had just pulled up, her kids in tow. Within moments they burst through the door: two boys who were Ben and Andrew's buddies, a girl Christine's age, and Jake, ten years old, tall and round and handsome with his olive complexion and big brown eyes.

The other boys clattered downstairs with shouts of laughter. Jake stood in the entryway, his head cocked to the side, his eyes darting back and forth. "The computer is downstairs, buddy," I said. He usually spent most of his time at our house playing computer games—the kid was a pro.

As Jake lumbered away Jen walked in, a chilled-out mom in a sweatshirt and jeans. Christine looked at her with anxious eyes. "Thomas has Down syndrome!" she blurted.

Jen grinned at me and tousled Christine's hair. "Yeah, I heard."

I put my arm around Jen's daughter. "Christine has new Christmas toys to show you. Want to see?" She nodded, and the two girls scampered off.

"Where's the boy?" Jen asked. "I've got something for him."

"Asleep in my room."

She pulled a blanket from her bag: Thomas the Tank Engine flannel on one side, red fleece on the other. I cracked up. Our sons had been Thomas fanatics when they were preschoolers.

Alone in the living room, Jen and I chose our spots to collapse in—she took the armchair, I took the couch. "How are things going?" she asked.

"Okay. We got rid of the tube, and we're almost done with the oxygen. I can't wait to get rid of those tanks." Then I stopped and looked at Jen. "It's been hard," I blurted.

She nodded. She knew.

Jake had been three years old when he was diagnosed with autism. Jen had thought his speech delays were due to chronic ear infections, but an evaluation proved otherwise. After the diagnosis Jen was a different person. She and I both had new baby girls, but her lethargy went beyond the usual postpartum funk. When we talked I felt an unbridgeable barrier between us—it remained to some degree even after her initial adjustment to the diagnosis. But I didn't feel that separation anymore.

"I can't stand people feeling sorry for me," I began. "The neighbors want to do everything for us, like there's been some big tragedy here. And then they tell me how special Thomas is. Well, would they want a special kid?"

Jen waited while I took a few breaths.

"But I love him. I love him so much I can barely stand it. I wouldn't give him up for anything." All my morbid thoughts came rushing back from their distant hiding place. "This might sound weird, but sometimes I get the feeling he's going to die young. And if he does, then I'll want to die, too. I couldn't bear to see him go." Tears started leaking. I needed to cry, really cry, but I didn't dare. If I started wailing, I might never stop.

Jen's eyes were red. Yes, she knew. She'd known for seven years. And all that time, I'd been glad Jake was her kid and not mine. With his supersize build and his dazed eyes, he stuck out in their family photographs—and not in a good way. Secretly, I'd thought he messed up what could have been an ideal family. I hadn't understood how much Jen loved him. I hadn't understood anything.

"I need to tell you something," I said, my pulse starting to pound. "All those times your kids came over for birthday parties, I wondered if I needed to get Jake a party favor." The heavy words rolled off my tongue and onto my lap. "I'm so sorry."

Jen was quiet for a while. "It's okay," she finally said. "Sometimes I've wondered the same thing."

Her honesty gave me courage. With increasing relief I told her about Suzanne and my grandmothers; about the sock chart, the calendar, and the paper-plate snowmen; about the man with the red jacket on the train and the man gathering carts in the parking lot. "I'm scared," I confessed. "I'm scared he won't grow up, but I'm also scared that he will."

Jen wiped her eyes. "That's because you know what the world does to kids like Thomas. I don't have a problem sending my other kids out the door in the morning, but every school day, after Jake gets on the bus, I watch it go down the street until I can't see it anymore."

My heart twisted. The short bus: My brother and I called it the "retard bus" when we were kids. It had stopped outside Eddie's house every school day. In a few years it would stop at my house. And after Thomas climbed the steps and sat in one of the high-backed seats, it would close its doors and drive away.

6 a.m. I drove the van along the dark, frozen freeway with Thomas in the back seat. Adrenaline pushed my eyelids wide open. We were on our way to the hospital for a sophisticated hearing exam. Any moment, Thomas would wake up wanting breakfast, and I couldn't feed him—he needed an empty stomach to prevent aspiration when he was under anesthesia. I let that worry push away any thoughts about test results.

The procedure was called an Auditory Brainstem Response. Tones of different volumes and frequencies would be sent into Thomas's ear canals, one at a time; electrodes would measure his brain's reaction. The ENT would also be checking for fluid behind the eardrums, a common cause of mild hearing loss in kids with Down syndrome.

When we reached the children's hospital I parked the van; loaded up the travel tank, monitor, diaper bag, and car seat; and slowly made my way to Same-Day Surgery. After we signed in I sat down in the waiting room with a sigh of relief—Thomas was still asleep. But within a few minutes a nurse appeared, calling his name. "We need to do a physical exam," she explained.

I wilted. Procedure time was still more than an hour away, Thomas hadn't had milk since midnight, and I knew he would wake up starving. With reluctance I followed the nurse to the exam room, where I lifted Thomas from his seat, removed his sleeper, and started working his little limbs into a pair of hospital pajamas. The yellow polyester was rough and pilled from washing. I rolled the waistband and wrapped the tunic-style shirt around him more than once, trying to reduce the slack. Thomas squirmed and cried as the combination of cold and hunger set in.

After the exam (heart, lungs, and blood pressure—all fine) the nurse pointed me to the presurgery area, bare white with linoleum tiles and a few hospital beds. Another nurse found us a glider rocker. I sank into it, weak from my own lack of breakfast. Thomas's skin was mottled from the cold; I cocooned him in a warm blanket and held him against my heart. We rocked, smooth and swift, into a numb place somewhere between sleeping and waking.

"Mrs. Soper?"

I opened my eyes. The ENT stood by the rocker along with another man, whom he introduced as the anesthesiologist. They took turns explaining the sedation, testing, and recovery protocols. I nodded dumbly, unable to focus.

"Would you like to carry him to the surgery entrance?" the ENT asked. I stood and walked, slow and heavy, clutching Thomas in the blanket. We stopped at double wooden doors. The anesthesiologist pushed the button on the wall to open the way, then held out his hands toward me.

I unwrapped the blanket and lifted Thomas from his warm little nest. The air was so cold. Everything felt frozen—my pulse, my feelings. I handed Thomas over, barely aware of the sharp tug in my chest as the doctors crossed the threshold and the doors swung shut.

The ABR was scheduled to take an hour. In the parents' waiting area I sat in one of the padded chairs and pulled out the book I'd brought, a collection of Annie Dillard's essays. The first was titled "Expedition to the Pole"—perfect for a January morning. I read about crews of nineteenth-century explorers traversing miles of pack ice in gray, hazy light. Their quest: the Pole of Relative Inaccessibility, "that imaginary point in the Arctic Ocean farthest from land in every direction."

They had poetic intentions. "Polar explorers—one gathers from their accounts—sought at the Poles something of the sublime," Dillard writes. "Simplicity and purity attracted them; they set out to perform clear tasks in uncontaminated lands." Problem was, they were naïve and foolish beyond belief. They brought ridiculous things on their journeys—crystal and china, monogrammed sterling silver flatware—and wouldn't surrender them at any cost. Explorers from one ship, which had become lodged in pack ice, walked to find help in their blue silk uniforms. They were later found, frozen to death, with their flatware beside them.

In the essay Dillard compares the explorers to the members of her Catholic church congregation, an odd bunch who gathered weekly in a tiny chapel near her rural home, seeking the divine, not understanding the quest required them to surrender everything. At the end of the essay, Dillard imagines joining the explorers and her congregation for Mass on a drifting ice floe. They dance and sing, exposed and ill-equipped, lost in delirious rejoicing as they approach the Absolute. "Wherever we go," she writes, "there seems to be only one business at hand—that of finding workable compromises between the sublimity of our ideas, and the absurdity of the fact of us."

"Mrs. Soper?"

The ENT sat in the seat next to mine, his surgery mask pulled below his chin. "Things went well. Thomas had fluid in his middle ears, so I inserted tubes, as we discussed."

My heart began to beat again. *Things went well. Things went well.*

"The ABR gave us some good information about Thomas's hearing," he continued. He pulled a small notepad from his back pocket and drew a graph with an angled line across the middle. "This is how normal hearing readings look." He drew another line, lower than the first. "This is how the hearing in Thomas's right ear looks. What a typical baby could hear at twenty decibels, Thomas hears at twenty-five or thirty, depending on the frequency. We call that mild hearing loss." Then he drew a third line, still lower. "The loss in his left ear is more pronounced. His brain showed responses at forty and forty-five decibels. We call that moderate hearing loss."

I nodded again, clueless as to what all this would mean for Thomas. "So is this because he has Down syndrome?"

He paused. "That's possible, but not likely."

I looked at him, confused. "Then what *is* likely?"

"I saw on his chart that he had a round of vancomycin and gentramycin in the NICU. You were warned these antibiotics can cause hearing loss?"

I blinked. Yes, Thomas had received those meds when he had sepsis. I'd signed release forms, but I didn't remember reading any warning about hearing loss. Not that it would have changed anything—he needed treatment no matter what the cost. But still. Why Thomas? He had enough to deal with already.

"The test showed something else," the doctor said, closing his notebook. "The numbers I graphed for you reflect the ability of Thomas's ears to process sound, but we took other readings that measure brain function. There's some abnormality with Thomas's brain waves in response to sound. We call that central auditory dysfunction, or CAD."

Abnormal brain waves. The doctor's face blurred as my eyes lost focus. "What does that mean?"

He shook his head. "We don't know for sure what's causing it, and we may never know. We also don't know for sure how it will affect Thomas's hearing. It's likely that sounds are distorted for him."

Great. "So how do you treat that?" I asked, not wanting to hear the answer.

The doctor fidgeted in his seat. "Unfortunately, there isn't any treatment for CAD."

I was quiet.

"You could start Thomas with some hearing aids to address his other hearing issues, or you could wait a year and see if things improve as his physiology matures."

I tried to picture hearing aids that could fit a six-pound baby. "What do you recommend?"

"Thomas's optimum language development hinges on him having full hearing capacity by the time he's six months old," he said. "If you opt out of the aids and his hearing doesn't improve spontaneously, you might miss that window. But CAD may interfere even if you use aids. It's possible that amplifying sound for Thomas will only increase the volume of the distortion he hears."

I was quiet again.

"Do you have any other questions?" the doctor asked.

Yeah, I had questions: How was I supposed to know what to do? Even the doctor wasn't sure what Thomas needed. How would the hearing issues affect my kid? The doctor didn't know that, either. I counted all the strikes against him: extra chromosome, prematurity, hearing loss, brain abnormality—how could I ever compensate for all these setbacks? Nobody could answer. I shook my head no.

The doctor led me through a printed sheet of postsurgery instructions. He scribbled two phone numbers at the bottom of the page and pointed to the first one. "The local school for the deaf has a parent-infant program that includes home visits from a therapist. Give them a call." Then the second one. "If you choose to start hearing aids, you'll need to make an appointment with an audiologist. Here's one I recommend." He shook my hand and stood to leave. "Thomas will be waking up soon. The nurse will take you to see him."

I followed the nurse to the recovery area. From across the room I saw Thomas curled up on a bed, a little lump of flesh in yellow polyester, the one bright spot amidst the white sheets and bare walls. Wires twisted away from his hands and feet and chest. A wall of monitors beeped and flashed.

I pulled a chair close to the bed and sat on the cold vinyl seat, weak-kneed, as if the pale tile floor were a sheet of ice shifting beneath my feet.

Suzanne beamed as I brought Thomas out from the bedroom, sans oxygen tube. "Hooray!" she cheered. "He looks fantastic!"

Melody, a therapist from the school for the deaf, gave Thomas a big grin. "What a *doll!*" It was true. With all the tape gone from his face, he was nothing but cute.

Both women sat on the living-room floor, ready for a joint early intervention planning meeting. I laid Thomas on the quilt in front of them, feeling lighthearted. It was heavenly to be rid of the oxygen. No more tripping over the tube. No more repositioning the prongs in his nose, or the probe on his foot. No more tank swapping. No more bedroom exile. And *no more monitor alarms.* The timing was perfect—Groundhog Day had come and gone with no evidence winter would ever end, and I needed a sign of growth, of change.

After admiring Thomas for a few minutes, the therapists got out their clipboards. "We're going to set some goals for Thomas for the year," Suzanne explained. "Melody will work with you on language and communication goals, and I'll work with you on the others."

"Okay." I wondered how that might work. My Down syndrome books had charts in the back listing age ranges for various milestones, but there were huge variations listed for each: Walking, for example, had a range of eighteen months to four years. How was I supposed to know what to expect?

"Let's start with large motor skills," Suzanne said, pen poised above her clipboard. "What would you like to see Thomas doing this year?"

"Well, I'm not sure what he'll be ready for," I said. "Rolling over, I guess. Sitting up."

Suzanne nodded as she took notes.

"I don't know what else. Crawling?"

"Sure," she said. "A year from now Thomas will be fifteen months old. Many babies with Down syndrome can crawl by then."

"But writing the goal down doesn't mean he's going to be ready," I said, still confused.

She smiled. "That's true. But it will help you be motivated to help him. If you work with him, he'll reach his milestones more quickly than he would otherwise. We'll teach you how."

Aha. So these were goals for *me*. I thought of the baby calendar that I'd given to Christine to play with. The purpose of the joint meeting was to create a custom sticker-sheet for Thomas. Much better than using a generic one, but I still hadn't settled my feelings about the whole milestone-measuring business. Frankly, I didn't even want to think about it. With every passing week I felt more hazy-headed and lethargic. My only agenda was survival.

But survival wasn't good enough if Thomas was to reach his "maximum potential." There were motor skills, social skills, and language skills to worry about. There were plans and protocols, appointments and assignments. By the time Suzanne finished with me, I wanted to crawl into bed and never get out again. But Melody was waiting for *her* turn.

"I understand Thomas recently had an ABR test," she began.

I nodded. Yes, we had hearing loss to deal with on top of everything else. I relayed the test results and told her about our upcoming audiology appointment: Reed and I had arranged to borrow a set of hearing aids from the school for the deaf, a trial run before deciding whether to purchase our own.

"Excellent," Melody said. "We assess language skills according to what we call *hearing age,* which is measured by the number of days a child has had full hearing capacity. As soon as Thomas wears aids for a full day, we'll consider his hearing one day old. Right now his hearing age is zero."

I felt a flash of panic. Thomas was already two-and-a-half months behind, and Down syndrome would set him back even farther.

I sat up straighter as we talked about language and communication goals. Melody's pen moved across her clipboard as she recorded milestones to work toward: *Thomas will respond to music. Thomas will recognize his name when spoken. Thomas will wave bye-bye.*

"We're just about done," she said. "Is there anything else you'd like to work on with Thomas this year?"

Thomas fidgeted on his eye-stimulating quilt. The night before, for the first time, I'd taken him on my bedtime rounds. Ben was curled up under his fuzzy blue blanket, waiting for me. I perched on the edge of his bed and laid Thomas across his chest.

"Hi, Thomas," he crooned, rubbing his brother's back. We sat in the near-dark, the three of us, silent. Thomas's little head bobbed as he studied Ben's hairline. His eyes shone in the faint light coming through the window.

After a few minutes, Ben let out a big sigh of sleepy pleasure. "I'm just *so* glad he's here." Another big sigh. "I mean, he has a *condition,* but who cares?"

Good question. Sitting on the floor with Suzanne and Melody, I was tempted to ask them the same thing. Why did we have to focus on changing Thomas? Why did it matter when he reached his milestones? I didn't want to care about when he rolled over, or drank from a cup, or waved his hand. I didn't want to use his blanket as a learning tool. I just wanted to love him—without hesitation, without condition. And I wanted him to love me back.

I wondered if he would. I wondered if he *could* love me the way I wanted to love him—as a distinct, unique, irreplaceable individual. But according to the stereotypes, kids with Down syndrome love *everyone.* That seemed to water down the significance of any given relationship. Would Thomas distinguish me as his mother, or would my face just be one of many in his warm little world?

"There is one thing," I said.

Suzanne and Melody smiled their encouragement.

"I want Thomas to know me. I want him to know I'm his mom."

Both women were quiet. I couldn't read their faces.

"Will he know me?" I asked after a moment, feeling like a fool.

Suzanne smiled, her eyes tender. "Oh, yes," she said. "Yes, he will definitely know you."

I nodded, worried that if I spoke I'd start crying.

"It's a wonderful goal. We'll put it under 'social skills,'" Suzanne said, writing it down. She quickly scanned over her list and then looked up at me. "Okay, we're all set!"

They stood to leave, handing me copies of the goal sheets—ten pages of them. "We'll see you next time," they chorused. "Good luck at audiology!" I tried to smile back as I saw them out the door, into the endless winter.

I'd been wondering what hearing aids for a baby would look like, and there they were: curved pieces of hard beige plastic, about two inches long, with tiny earpieces attached. The earpieces, called molds, were custom-made to fit into Thomas's ear canals—we'd need to get new ones every few weeks as Thomas grew. The larger pieces, called amplifiers, would be tucked behind his ear.

It figured. We had finally gotten rid of all Thomas's tubes and wires, and now this: four thousand dollars' worth of little plastic bits. We were borrowing the amplifiers for now, but eventually we'd need to buy some of our own. And if we broke the borrowed ones we'd need to pay for them. On one of the clinic walls, the audiologist had taped a ziplock bag full of aids that had been dropped on hard surfaces or chewed by dogs. A sign below the bag read PLEASE BE CAREFUL.

The audiologist was slim and soft-spoken, with wire-framed glasses and graying hair in short curls. We'd been working together for over an hour, holding a squirming, crying Thomas still for various tests and measurements. Every time one of our hands came near his face, he flinched and lifted his arm in protest, trying to swat it away.

"Why don't you lay Thomas on your lap, and I'll show you how to put the aids in," the audiologist said, pushing her chair close to mine. "Let's start with his right ear."

I held Thomas's arms down as she angled the tip of the mold into Thomas's ear canal, twisting it slightly to make a snug fit. He jerked his head away, and the mold fell out. I gripped his head with my knees while the audiologist leaned in closer, her wiry curls nearly touching my cheek, her hands fumbling by Thomas's face. The air got hot. My teeth clenched. It was breastfeeding practice all over again.

"Got it!" she said, taking a step back. The mold and aid were both in place.

I helped Thomas sit up. The aid fell forward, pulling the mold out of his ear and landing in my lap.

"Let's try some adhesive. Since his ears are so small, the cartilage isn't wide enough to hold the aid in place." She cut a small piece of double-sided tape and stuck one end to the back of the amplifier. I held Thomas still as she leaned over us again.

"There we go," she said after a long minute. The amplifier was taped to Thomas's scalp right behind his ear. This time it stayed put when I sat him up, but as soon as he turned his head, the mold popped out. The amplifier pulled away from his scalp and dropped to the carpeted floor with a soft thud.

An hour later I carried Thomas's car seat into the house, my head pounding. Both aids were in place; I'd even affixed one of them myself. But my neck and shoulders were pinched tight from the effort, and my shirt was stained with sweat.

Time to start dinner. Reed had come home early to watch the kids, and everyone would be hungry soon. Thomas was calm in his car seat—I had turned the aids off for the ride home so the engine noise wouldn't frighten him. With one finger I reached to the back of each amplifier and flipped its tiny switch. A squeal of feedback ripped the air.

Crap. The audiologist had warned me that the amplifiers would squeak if they touched anything, and one of Thomas's ears was resting against the side of the car seat. I pushed his head to the center, but as soon as I let go, it flopped to the other side. Another squeal.

This is nuts.

I grabbed a receiving blanket from the diaper bag, rolled it up, and stuffed it into the space between Thomas's head and the side of the car seat, careful to keep it away from his ear. There.

I got a large pot from the cabinet and filled it with water to boil for spaghetti.

Sam came into the kitchen. "Mommy's home!" he said. "And Thomas!" He knelt next to the car seat. "What's this?" He reached for one of the aids.

"Don't touch that!" I snapped.

Sam pulled his hand back and started bawling. Thomas jumped and began to wail. As I picked him up, the molds popped out and the amplifiers flopped backward, their weight pulling the tape partway off his head.

Don't cry. Don't. I pulled the amplifiers off the rest of the way. Thomas yelled louder as the tape yanked his scalp. Maybe his hearing age would stay at zero forever?

I held both aids in my hand—their sticky sides covered with strands of Thomas's hair—and restrained myself from flinging them across the room. We couldn't afford a four-thousand-dollar tantrum. And Thomas couldn't afford to lose one more day.

The February sky was deep gray, the sun dimmed by the smog that hung in the air like steam in a shower stall. Health officials encouraged people to stay indoors to avoid the toxic gunk, which was just as well. I couldn't leave anyway.

My nerves were shot from dealing with the hearing aids. Every morning, I pinned Thomas against my bed while I twisted the ear molds into place and taped down the amplifiers. But no matter where he was—the bouncy seat, the floor, or my shoulder—one amplifier or the other would touch something and squeal. And no matter how carefully I taped them in place, every time Thomas turned his head, the molds popped out. At one point I'd had Melody come check my technique, thinking I wasn't inserting the molds correctly. But she said I was. I had no choice but to replace the aids every time they fell off, which was several times an hour. All day long my body ached with tension. I could barely hold basic conversations with the kids because my temper was so short.

The telephone rang. I glanced at the caller ID and saw that a church sister from down the street was on the line. I debated whether to answer.

"I'm just calling to see how you're doing," she said when I finally picked up the phone. "I haven't seen you at church for a while."

The faith police. "Thomas can't go because of the germ exposure," I explained. "And it makes more sense for Reed to take the other kids since he has clerk stuff to do."

"Well, I'd love to come stay with that cute baby of yours so you can go," she said.

"I don't want to go." The words slipped right out.

The sister was quiet. For Mormons, purposefully skipping church is a big no-no, a sign that Something Is Wrong. And something was. I wasn't just unexcited about church, I was repulsed by the very thought of going. The scriptures, prayers, and hymns I'd loved seemed useless. The people I'd loved felt like strangers. I didn't say this to the sister on the phone, of course. I'd already said enough.

I hung up and stared at the calendar on the refrigerator door: rows and rows of numbered squares, some with notes scrawled inside. It took several long minutes for me to figure out which one to consult for the day. Thankfully it was blank, but *Melody 2 p.m.* was in the next day's square, and *molds 10 a.m.* two squares after that. *Call dentist* was scrawled across several squares on the row below. Oral hygiene didn't exactly top my current list of concerns. But I really needed to get the kids in for a cleaning, especially the little boys, whose teeth crumbled at the slightest provocation.

I picked up the cordless phone and dialed the dentist's office. "I need cleaning appointments for six kids," I told the receptionist. (Yes, sentences like that did make me wonder why I hadn't spent more time on birth control.)

"What day would you like to come in?"

I turned back to the calendar. "What day is today?" I'd forgotten already.

She told me. I found the right square and scanned the rows underneath for empties. The little numbers in the corners of the squares looked foreign, like marks in an unknown language. I tried to pin one down with my eyes, but it slipped to the side.

"What day works for you?" she asked again.

"I don't know." I could barely hear her above the buzz in my head. "I don't know."

"Would you like to call back another time?"

I nodded to myself and hung up the phone, eyes still on the calendar. The squares seemed to grow larger. I put my hand against the smooth, cool surface of the refrigerator door so I wouldn't fall into the spaces.

After a long minute I left the kitchen and walked down the hall toward the bedrooms. Thomas was still asleep; Matt and Sam were playing quietly. I turned around and headed for the living room, where the window showed sludgy air and slushy streets. I returned to the kitchen, opened the refrigerator, shut it, and stared at the calendar. There was nothing to do but keep moving, a rat in a maze, moving from room to room, from thought to thought. My head clogged with thoughts squirming together like piled worms. I started with one and followed its curves and twists to another, then another. I was like the woman in "The Yellow Wallpaper," a short story I read in college, who couldn't stop staring at the paper on her bedroom walls. She followed the garish pattern with her eyes, hour after hour, just as I followed the turns in my mind, unable to break away.

> *There's nothing to be sad about.*
> *Do they know how severe it is?*
> *Babies like this need more support, not less.*
> *Why should it be any different with Thomas?*
> *What a wonderful gift you've been given.*

Are you sure you understand the diagnosis?
There's nothing to be sad about.

Mom knew something was wrong. "Kathy, you've been through so much these past few months," she'd said on the phone the previous week in her hiding-the-worry voice. "Maybe your doctor can give you something to help."

Something to help. She meant antidepressants.

Out of the question. Prozac had helped me through a short-term crisis way back in college, but I swore off the pills once I got pregnant with Elizabeth. And after her birth, when my spiritual life blossomed, I was even more determined to steer clear. Mothers didn't take drugs to be happy; neither did Mormons. There was no church-issued restriction, but it seemed obvious that anyone who lived close to God shouldn't need a crutch. Especially mothers, who were supposed to be near-angels already.

As my babies arrived the depression surged again and again, sapping my strength and clouding my mind, but I refused to acquiesce. My desire for children still burned too intensely to ignore. Transcending the gloom became a holy quest. When I hit painful lows, I forced myself to keep moving toward my own Pole of Relative Inaccessibility, that sublime point of existence that was farthest from weaknesses in all directions. I didn't care how punishing the journey became. I didn't believe in workable compromises between the real and the ideal.

The clincher came when Elizabeth started kindergarten. At back-to-school night I met a woman, one of the other moms, who seemed to glow in some inexplicable way. I felt a strange thrill when she invited Elizabeth and me to her home for a playdate. On the appointed day she and I sat in her sun-filled living room while the children played. Within minutes of conversation I knew this woman had what I'd always wanted: Serenity. Joy. A brightness of spirit so different from my chronic, crippling melancholy. "I hope I live a hundred years," she said at one point. I stared at her in envy—even on good days, I looked forward to leaving this earth and moving on to someplace better.

Later that afternoon she told me she took Zoloft for depression.

Cheater.

I had no interest in fake enlightenment. Even as the years passed and my depression worsened, even after Sam's birth crisis ground me to powder, I refused medication. I would not succumb to the worst in me. I would not admit defeat.

Thomas stirred in his bassinette, his almond-shaped eyes fluttering open. He was four months old, although his age corrected for prematurity was only two months. The week before he'd smiled for the first time, one of those heart-melting little grins that pay mothers back for all their spilled blood, milk, and sweat. Taking antidepressants would be a shameful show of weakness. But even worse, it would be an unspeakable insult to Thomas. *My baby with Down syndrome drove me crazy.*

Crazy, like that woman in the story. At night she started seeing strange figures behind the yellow wallpaper, shadowy almost-women creeping along the perimeter from wall to wall to wall. They poked their heads through the garish patterns, eyes bulging and necks strangling, desperate to escape.

From my bedroom window I could see the peach tree, still covered with snow. One of its large limbs had cracked from the weight. As I rocked Thomas on my shoulder, I heard the kids bouncing in from school, probably tracking clumps of dirty snow onto the already-dirty carpet. After the thump of backpacks being piled on the kitchen table, I heard footsteps coming down the hall. "Hi, Mom! Hi, Thomas!" the kids chorused as they came in, filling the room with palpable energy that made me panic. I forced a smile. They'd been getting nothing from me but the bare minimum—food at regular intervals, clean underwear, a tired kiss goodnight.

Christine stepped close to the rocking chair where I sat with Thomas. "Why isn't he wearing his hearing aids?" she asked, brow furrowed.

"We're taking a break," I said. Thanks to yet another set of ear molds, his right aid was staying put a bit longer these days, but the left was impossible to keep in. Something about the shape of his ear canal, the audiology tech told me. Which figured, since that ear was the one with greater hearing loss. All morning and afternoon I'd tried my best with both aids, but after several sweaty rounds of wrestling with the damned things, I gave up.

"Can we have snacks?" Andrew asked. I roused myself from the rocker and followed them into the kitchen, depositing Thomas in his bouncy seat. The latest batch of mail was scattered on the kitchen table amongst sandwich crusts from lunch and dry cereal from breakfast. Bills. Credit card applications. More bills. And a flat brown envelope—strangely familiar.

I set a box of crackers on the table, carried the envelope to my bedroom, and ripped it open to find blue and yellow lettering in a cutesy font. "Baby's First Year." The exact same calendar as the one I'd received the previous month.

I flipped through it in disbelief, ending at the page of stickers at the back. We'd need at least three years to use them all. But now that we had "hearing age" to measure by as well as "adjusted age" and "birth age," it was anyone's guess where the stickers would go anyway. So what should I do—give the calendar to Christine again, so she could start a collection?

Or maybe I should start a collection of my own. I could include a can of formula and the hearing aids. The ten pages of early intervention goals I didn't care about. Maybe those cross-eyed disabled-reindeer photos, for good measure. I could make an artistic arrangement somewhere prominent—the living room, perhaps—and charge a fee for people to come view my failure shrine.

Furious, I walked straight to the garbage can and stuffed the calendar in. I could get my calendar off the fridge, full of appointments with therapists and specialists, and chuck that, too. Plus the Down syndrome books and the pamphlets on hearing loss. Just trash it all.

And then I'd be left alone to raise Thomas, with his extra chromosome and faulty brain waves and feeble ears. He might not walk until age four. He might not ever hear or speak clearly. He might not ever leave home.

He might not ever leave home.

I exhaled once, twice, three times. That was it. That was why I started early intervention in the first place: I feared Thomas would need me for the rest of my life, long after he stopped being a cute baby, long after my other kids had grown and gone. The doctors and nurses, the therapists, even the neighbors—I'd made them easy targets for my indignation, seeing ulterior motives in their every move. But all along, the hidden motives had been my own.

At the end of "The Yellow Wallpaper," the woman's husband finds her crouched on the floor, creeping along the perimeter from wall to wall to wall. There's a rut in the wallboard a foot or so off the floor—a deep groove worn by her shoulder. Madness split her in two. Those almost-women behind the wallpaper? They were herself.

I glared at the pastel calendar pages poking out of the garbage can. With my fist I punched them deeper, shoving them beneath the torn brown envelope. I knew what the world did to kids like Thomas. I needed to protect him from anything that didn't measure his true value, from anyone who couldn't love him the way he deserved.

But how could I protect him from his own mother?

Spring

Early March. I'd been holed up in the house for three months. My neighbor from down the street sat on my couch, looking worried. I could imagine how I appeared to her: pale face, tangled hair, shirt stained with formula. A caricature of the disheveled mom with a disabled baby.

"How have things been going?" she asked.

I avoided her eyes. "Oh, you know. It's been tough, but we're surviving."

She knew me too well to buy it. For five years she'd been my visiting teacher in our ward's Relief Society (the church's organization for women), which meant she was supposed to visit me regularly to deliver inspirational messages and offer me service during times of need. Most of the women in Relief Society served as visiting teachers, including myself, although I'd completely ignored my assigned sisters since Thomas was born. But my visiting teacher had always been diligent. When Sam was in the NICU and I panicked over Christine's upcoming birthday, she made the cake I was too exhausted to make—a cat-shaped white cake with pink frosting and sprinkles. Another time, when

Spring

I was struggling to paint my bedroom while several small children "helped," she came over with a roller in hand. She'd brought us at least a dozen dinners over the years, including the Hamburger Helper on Thomas's homecoming day. As she studied me from her perch on the couch, I knew she could see right through my calm facade. I wished she hadn't come.

"How's little Thomas doing?"

"He's got a cold, but otherwise he's fine."

Silence.

She tried again. "Has it been a hard adjustment for the other kids? I know it's always tough to bring a new baby home, and with Thomas's medical issues I imagine you've been extra preoccupied."

I shrugged. "Yeah, they've had to fend for themselves more than usual. But of course they all love Thomas."

What was my problem? She had raised seven kids. She understood what it was like to be overwhelmed. Now she was a grandmother several times over, with practical, washable clothes and short, gray, finger-styled hair. She wasn't some über-hip mom raising an eyebrow at my pathetic state. But I didn't want her sympathy, or her help. I didn't want her to play the hero—not again.

After twenty minutes of her caring questions and my stilted answers, I walked her to the door. "I'll come back for another visit next week," she said.

My resentment flared. "You know, things are so crazy right now. I think the thing that would be most helpful for me is if you'd just call me every now and then. That would be easiest."

She looked straight at me. "Kathy, I'd really like to stop by, even if it's only for a minute. I don't want you stuck in the house, getting depressed and not telling anybody." Then she turned and walked toward her car.

I shut the door, fuming. *How dare she?* How dare she refuse my request to be left alone? If I wanted to waste away in my house that was my choice. If I was depressed that was *my* problem. I didn't owe her anything.

That evening I was browning ground beef for dinner when the doorbell rang. My next-door neighbor handed me a sealed envelope. "This was in my mailbox, but it's addressed to you."

"Thanks." I smiled politely and turned away.

"How are you doing?" she asked quickly.

I bristled. I had no interest in discussing my feelings with anyone else that day. And the meat on the stovetop would soon be black instead of brown. But I didn't want to be rude. Okay, I *did* want to be rude, but I was determined to resist the temptation.

"We're okay. Things have been tough, but we're fine."

"I heard it's been hard for you," she said. "We have the same visiting teacher—she came to my house this morning after yours."

"Oh."

Oh.

As soon as she turned to go, I shut the door, restraining myself from slamming it. They talked about me. They sat on the couch and chatted about poor Kathy. I couldn't believe it.

But then again, I could. Countless times I'd sat on some couch and hashed over the latest neighborhood news. Not gossip, I always assured myself, but concerned dialogue about those in need.

Someone in need—that's how my church sisters saw me.

I walked back into the kitchen, where Reed was stirring the over-crisp meat. "I *can't stand* this."

"What, having me cook?"

I shot him a look. "Not funny. They're talking about what a hard time we're having. Why can't they just mind their own business?"

"Who's talking?"

"Our neighbors. Probably the whole ward."

Reed turned off the stove burner and dumped the meat into a bowl, wisely remaining silent. Slowly, my anger turned to shame. These women truly cared about me. They were being good neighbors, good friends, good Christians. Would I really want them to pretend I wasn't in the middle of an exhausting situation? Did I want them to make small talk with me, completely ignoring the elephant stinking in the corner?

The phone rang. I sighed and checked caller ID: the Relief Society president.

"Who is it?" Reed asked. When I told him, he raised his eyebrows. "If you don't answer, she's only going to be more worried."

That was the last thing I wanted. I pushed the talk button.

"I just thought I'd check in and see how you're doing," the president said.

"We're fine." My visiting teacher must have called her. *Thanks a lot.*

"How's Thomas?"

I told her with as few words as possible. Ditto for her other questions.

"What can we do to help?" she finally asked, getting nowhere.

"Nothing," I said. "We're fine."

"Liar," Reed whispered, grinning.

Yep. I hung up the phone with no regrets. I would *not* crumble into the arms of my charitable church sisters. I would *not* lose any more dignity, any more control. It had shattered when my labor started, and I only had a few shards left.

"Thomas Soper?" the nurse called.

I lifted the car seat with one hand and the diaper bag with the other, then told Matt and Sam to follow me. We'd brought Thomas to the pediatrician for another checkup and one last dose of RSV vaccine. The antibodies would last one month, and by that time warmer weather would bring sick season to a close, which meant Thomas would soon be free to venture into public places. I was desperate for spring, but its coming meant the end of my excuse to skip church. In a few weeks there would be a conference for multiple wards on "Strengthening the Family." It would probably be packed with reminders about the weighty responsibilities of parents, and at least one reference to angelic mothers. Just what I wanted to hear.

In the exam room Matt and Sam made a beeline for the Lego table in the corner. I hefted the car seat onto the paper-covered table, unbuckled Thomas and removed his hearing aids, then sat on the table with him on my lap.

The nurse approached with an ear thermometer. Thomas turned his head away. "He hates having his ears touched," I explained, pinning his head against my chest while he wriggled and cried. Next, the nurse took Thomas's blood pressure using an ultra-tiny cuff. Matt and Sam chattered as they built Lego towers on the corner table, then knocked them down, sending pieces clattering to the floor. "The doctor will be in shortly," the nurse said over the din.

I should've put Thomas's aids back in, but I didn't have the heart to do it. Four weeks of trying the aids, three sets of molds made, and nothing had improved. Feedback squeals had replaced monitor alarms in my daily soundtrack. Melody came once a week, each time bringing more information for me to absorb. Some of the handouts had suggestions for listening exercises, like *Expose your baby to a variety of sounds—loud and soft, high pitched and low pitched.* Others described various communication methods for the hearing impaired. I learned there were deaf tutors available to teach families American Sign Language in their homes, as well as group classes through the school district. When I told my mother about it she got all excited—there were two missionaries in her ward who'd been trained in ASL, and she was impressed with their skill and finesse. *What a great thing to learn as a family!* she said. I almost laughed out loud. If I was struggling to wash dishes and make sandwiches, how could I learn a new language?

After a knock at the door, the pediatrician entered the room, followed by a man I didn't recognize. "I have a medical student working with me this week," the doctor said. "Do you mind if he observes Thomas's exam?"

"That's fine." I hopped off the table and laid Thomas down, then stepped back a bit to make room. Immediately the men moved close to the table, standing shoulder to shoulder. I had to crane my neck to see Thomas.

The doctor lifted Thomas's limbs one by one. "Mild hypotonia," he said in a low voice. No wonder this guy wanted to watch. Thomas was a living textbook for med students.

The two men continued muttering to each other, their voices now inaudible over Matt and Sam's noise from the corner and Thomas's indignant cries. I stood stiffly behind them, crossing and uncrossing my arms, angry at them for examining Thomas as if he were a curiosity, angry at myself for not stopping them. I stepped closer to the table, ready to snatch Thomas away and hold him close.

"You can see the epicanthal folds," the doctor was saying. The little flaps of skin covering the inner corners of Thomas's eyes. As he gestured, Thomas's little arm shot up and batted the intruding hand away. The doctor turned to me. "Definitely a NICU baby."

I stepped back. A NICU baby? I felt sick as I realized what he meant: Thomas remembered. He remembered that hands hurt. The first hands that held him had whisked him away from his mother, the next had laid him on a metallic exam table, several others poked and prodded him—all within his first five minutes of life. And every day for the next six weeks, hands reached out to stick him with needles and tape tubes to his face. Hands held him down while he cried. No wonder he'd resisted when my hands pulled his head toward my breast. No wonder he balked when my hands tried to stick plastic bits into his ear canals. No wonder.

I couldn't keep forcing him to wear those aids. But how could I give up *again*? I'd already given up breastfeeding, and pumping. I couldn't keep making compromises. And one of Melody's handouts had warned what would happen if Thomas's hearing loss wasn't treated: *Communication is significantly affected, and socialization with peers with normal hearing becomes increasingly difficult. There is an increasing impact on self-esteem.*

The doctor turned on a penlight and moved it slowly in front of Thomas's eyes to see if he'd follow the glowing tip. "He's tracking well," he noted. "Can he roll from front to back?"

Spring

I bit my lip and shook my head as Matt and Sam banged Legos in rhythmic patterns against the play table.

The doctor looked at Thomas's chart. "His corrected age is only three months, so I wouldn't be concerned. And of course delays aren't unusual for Down's kids."

Down's kids. I blinked back hot tears. It wasn't fair. It wasn't Thomas's fault that he had an extra chromosome. He didn't ask to be born ten weeks early. He didn't ask for the infection that required toxic drugs, drugs that likely stole away some of his hearing. He didn't ask for the pain that taught him to fear hands, even his own mother's hands.

A cruel trap. Thomas's NICU stay had saved his life, only to complicate it with problems. And the damage he suffered there prevented him from accepting the solutions.

The pile of unopened mail leaned far to one side, threatening to collapse. Reluctantly I started ripping envelopes open and sorting through the contents. One from Elizabeth's junior high school held a report card.

My stomach sank as I scanned the grades—for the first time she had some Bs and B-minuses, even in classes she could easily earn top scores in. I had no idea she'd been struggling. Early in the school year I had checked her grades online at the end of each week, but once Thomas was born I put all the school-age kids on the back burner. For the past month or so, I hadn't even peeked in their school backpacks.

But Elizabeth had never needed monitoring before. She'd worked independently since kindergarten, bringing home highest marks without any visible effort. A few months back she'd signed up for the school musical, which held practices during her homeroom period—I never considered that she might need the time to finish assignments. I was just glad she wouldn't be missing the bus for after-school rehearsals.

I put the report card back in its envelope, stung by regret. Was Elizabeth simply overwhelmed by junior high, or was the stress of our home life hurting her grades? Either way, I'd failed to give her the support she needed. And that wasn't the only ball I'd dropped regarding the kids' schooling. I'd missed the window for my elementary-age kids to apply for the school's gifted program—the required testing had been scheduled for the Saturday after Thomas came home, and at the time, nothing mattered except survival. But thanks to my oversight, the kids would miss out on a full year of specialized instruction and enrichment activities. And speaking of enrichment activities, I'd been completely failing at early intervention. Suzanne came dutifully every month to show me how to stimulate Thomas's cute little brain, but I never followed through.

Survival wasn't good enough anymore. I couldn't let these kids' potential go to waste. I needed to get on the ball with early intervention, I needed to get the elementary kids prepared for gifted testing the following fall, and I needed to get Elizabeth's grades out of the hole. Starting that very minute.

I called Elizabeth into the kitchen. "This came today," I said, handing her the envelope.

She pulled the card out, avoiding my eyes.

"I was surprised to see some of those grades. What's going on?"

She shrugged. "I guess I forgot to turn some things in."

"Well, what might help you remember?"

She shrugged again. "I'll just have to try harder."

I geared up for a big toe-the-line speech. We'd check her grades online every week. We'd make a chart to keep track of her progress, and she'd keep her scores up or lose privileges. I opened my mouth, ready to set her straight. Then I stopped myself.

It was no use.

I could make the grandest of plans, but I wouldn't follow through. I wouldn't start checking Elizabeth's grades, or drilling the elementary kids with practice test questions, or practicing fine-motor skills with Thomas. Instead I'd keep watching the older children come and go without much thought, glad they could get themselves dressed and take themselves to the bathroom. Matt and Sam would keep playing in their own little world, separate from mine. Thomas would remain thoroughly unstimulated. Reed and I would keep living more like roommates than lovers. And the problems would keep piling up, higher than the stack of mail on the kitchen counter.

I lifted my face toward the sun, drinking in warm light and air. It was the first mild day of the year. As I felt the largeness and brightness of the sky, I realized just how dark and cramped my winter had been.

We'd arrived at the park an hour before—Matt, Sam, Thomas, and I; the other kids were at school. When I opened the van doors, the boys took off running toward the play equipment, laughing, sweatshirt hoods bouncing against their backs. In fluid motion they climbed the rope ladder to the big slide, turned the metallic steering wheel at the top of the ladder, slid to the bottom, and started over again.

I sat on one of the steps leading to a smaller slide. In his car seat next to me, Thomas was nestled in layers of cozy flannel. Technically, he wasn't supposed to leave home yet, but this open, empty park didn't really qualify as a public place, not for a baby who wouldn't be touching anything. I pulled back a corner of the blankets to take a peek. His eyes blinked at me, more brown than gray with the passing weeks. His cheeks had fattened up, pink and soft. His newborn hair was starting to rub off on the sides and back of his head, and I had trimmed the sideburns to keep him from having Elvis chops. He wore a sage green stocking cap—the inky blue hat with the star was too small for him now.

I closed my eyes as my cheeks blushed with warmth. I hadn't felt the sun's full strength since before Thomas came home. There'd been so many weeks of cold and gray. Dirty slush tracked on the carpets, walls closing in, no escape. So much fear and sorrow and guilt. Maybe the change in the weather would help me make a fresh start.

I inhaled the air of almost-spring, then let it go.

Let it go.

Tightness lifted from my shoulders in the breeze. Eyes still closed, I sat motionless in the sun, breathing in and out until I couldn't quite feel my body anymore. I was transparent, weightless. The next breath of wind might carry me away.

Voices. I opened my eyes and saw a woman approaching, holding hands with a preschooler. I recognized her as a young mom in the neighborhood. On Sundays her son was in the church nursery with Sam. She was pregnant with her second child. As she came closer I could see the pronounced curve of her belly.

She spotted me and waved. I waved back, suddenly nervous. She knew about Thomas, knew I'd been skipping church for months. Likely she'd heard about my struggles through the grapevine. I didn't want to talk to her. For a second I considered grabbing Thomas's seat and walking away.

Too late. Her son joined Matt and Sam on the play structure, and she sat on the bench a few feet away from me.

"Isn't this great?" she asked, motioning to the clear sky.

I forced a smile. "Yeah, I couldn't resist. It feels like we've been inside forever."

"I'll say. We've been climbing the walls all winter."

We watched the three boys slip to the bottom of the slide. Matt turned to face the soccer field adjacent to the park—a vast expanse of yellow-brown grass—then looked back at me.

"Go for it," I called. He started running. The smaller boys followed, their short legs struggling to keep up. Three heads bobbed across the field, little bodies nearly swallowed by the open space.

"So, how's your pregnancy going?" I asked, hoping to steer the conversation away from me.

It worked. She had lots to say about her pregnancy, and her toddler, and being a mom in general. By the time the boys returned from their expedition, flushed and panting, I'd almost forgotten my earlier anxiety. All that hiding all winter long, and there I was at the park with my three boys, shooting the breeze as if nothing had happened. Obviously this mom wasn't interested in grilling me about my problems. In fact, she hadn't asked me anything about Thomas.

That was odd, though. She and I weren't really friends, but here she was six months pregnant, a point at which I could spot a new baby a mile away. And the car seat was right by her sneakers.

"Would you like to see Thomas?" I asked, folding the blankets back so that his face was fully visible.

"Sure." She took a quick peek. "Come say hello to the baby," she called to her son.

He ran over and peered into the car seat. "Hi," he said, then ran off again.

Was she snubbing me? I couldn't be sure, so I played it cool. I didn't want to be the hypersensitive mom-of-a-disabled-kid who cried discrimination at every turn.

"On my way here I saw a couple of houses up for sale," I said. "Looks like we'll be getting some new neighbors."

"I hope they've got some little kids. There's hardly any in our neighborhood."

"I know. Matt's getting to the age where he wants to play with friends, but there's nobody around."

She sighed. "I really wish there were more women having babies around here. The way things stand, there won't be any little friends around for mine to play with."

I stared at her, incredulous. No little friends for her baby— didn't she see Thomas sitting two feet away? Apparently he didn't count. Apparently he fell short of her standards.

But what about my standards? There *was* someone around for Matt to play with, a little boy down the street just his age: Aaron. He had spina bifida and couldn't walk.

I'd never considered inviting him to our home. Never.

I counted the people in my bedroom: nine. Reed lay on the bed, I held Thomas in the rocking chair, and six kids bounced from wall to wall, chitchatting over the drone of the TV. It was bedtime, but nobody seemed to know, or care, except for me.

"Hey, guys," I whispered. Sometimes the odd sound of my quietness got their attention, but this time they just got noisier. "Enough!" I barked, making Thomas jump. Maybe I could count this little scenario as therapy. *Expose your baby to a variety of sounds, loud and soft, high-pitched and low-pitched*—check.

I left Thomas with Reed, sent the big kids downstairs, hustled Matt and Sam to bed, and headed to Christine's room. She was already lying down. Good girl. I sat on the edge of her bed and started rubbing her back, trying to ignore the tangle of clothes, toys, and books on the floor.

"I like how you have Thomas's picture up," I said, pointing to her bulletin board. I'd given her an 8 x 10 print of one of nurse

Penny's decent shots. The original Baby's First Year calendar was hanging beneath it.

Christine looked over. "Why didn't you want to use that calendar for Thomas?" she asked.

"Oh, I just didn't need it," I hedged. "I thought you'd have more fun with it than I would."

"Can I put the stickers on when Thomas does things?"

"Sure," I said, wishing I'd thrown it away.

She relaxed into her pillow as I stroked her hair. "You know, it's okay if somebody is different."

My hand paused on her warm head. "That's true. Did you talk about that at school today?"

"Yesterday. My teacher said people might have braces or glasses, or have red hair or curly hair, or speak a foreign language, but they're not really different from you."

I swallowed hard. "That's right."

Christine turned to face me. Tears gathered in her eyes, glistening in the light coming from the hallway. "Mommy, it's okay for Thomas to be different, right? He has Down syndrome, but he's still important."

"Yes," I almost-whispered, hoping she couldn't see my face clearly. Yes, Thomas was important, even if he was invisible to some people. Just like Aaron.

Pretending not to see the tears, I kissed Christine goodnight and escaped to the kitchen. As I loaded the dishwasher I tried to talk myself off the ledge. *It's logistics,* I reminded myself. Aaron wouldn't feel comfortable at our house. Matt's favorite pastime was tearing around the house in some crazy dress-up outfit—how would that fly with a buddy in a wheelchair? It just wouldn't work. It was nothing personal against Aaron.

Liar. I shut the dishwasher and pressed the start button,

wishing the hum and buzz of the wash cycle could drown out the voice that filled my head, jabbering and whining and accusing.

In the bedroom Thomas was asleep on Reed's chest. Reed's eyes were closed. I crawled into bed and turned onto my side, away from them. My body was stone. My mind was chaos. I couldn't get away from its constant pull, sucking me inward and downward.

I leaned over to turn off the lamp on my nightstand. Wedged between the lamp and the alarm clock was an envelope. White, business size.

To A Very Perfect Person, it said on the front.

I pulled out the note inside and unfolded it. Hearts and balloons lined the message in the middle:

> *Balloons are red, balloons are blue.*
> *Some balloons say I love you!*
> *A perfect spring is coming. I hope you like it.*
> *Love, Christine*

That was when the tears began.

They wouldn't stop. Even when I wasn't really crying, with shaking shoulders and dribbling nose, tears flowed nearly constantly in two salty streams. My limbs felt full of lead. For weeks I couldn't open mail or fold laundry. I couldn't pick up dirty socks or dishes. I couldn't hold conversations with the kids. All I could do was feed and clean Thomas, and I doubted that would last much longer.

The kids might've been scared, or oblivious—I couldn't tell and couldn't care. Reed knew something was wrong, but I didn't say much about it. There was no point. He would solve any problem he could, but this wasn't one of them. I was at the mercy of something stronger than myself, something determined to claim me, to own me. It had been after me for so long. And I was done resisting.

My mother saw the breakdown coming. She didn't tell me she was scared, but she didn't have to. I could hear it in her voice.

"How's the baby?" she asked on the phone.

"Fine."

"And the other kids?"

"Fine."

Silence.

"Are the hearing aids working any better for you?"

"No."

"That must be so frustrating, sweetie. I feel for you."

Silence.

"Are you looking forward to going back to church in a couple of weeks?"

"No. I don't want to go."

I was hurting her, and it only made me feel worse. But I didn't care. "I might not ever go back," I said. "They're having a conference this weekend on strengthening families. There's no way I'm going. I don't want to hear it."

Silence.

"I don't blame you," Mom said. "But—"

"I don't want to hear it. I don't want to hear it!" My voice got louder and louder until something broke loose in my throat. "I don't want to hear *one more word* about what I'm supposed to be doing. I don't want to hear *one more thing* about strengthening my family." Yelling now. Yelling at my mother as if she were God. "I *know* what the ideal is. I *know* I'm failing. I don't *need* to be told again. Can't we *give it a rest?*"

After a minute Mom spoke. "It's okay," she said, her voice gentle. "You don't need to go to church. You don't need to worry about any of that right now. Just take care of Thomas. That's all that matters."

But that was the whole problem: I was failing at the only thing that mattered.

I lifted Thomas from his bassinette and held him against my heart. Just a baby, a soft little baby with a sweet-smelling neck. And yet he *wasn't* just a baby.

Why should it be any different with Thomas? Kate had asked. I knew the answer: because *he* was different. And I could never be sure if my responses to him were colored by that difference. Praising, playing, teaching—would I be enjoying my son as he was, or trying to change him into someone I could more easily enjoy? How could I separate his needs from my wants? How could I tell the difference between love and pity?

I rocked Thomas deep into sleep, the curve of his skull against my shoulder. The delicate skin of his cheek pressed against my neck. *A special spirit*—I still hated the phrase, but maybe it was true after all. His presence was ethereal, as if only the most delicate bonds tethered him to earth. He was not of this world—that I knew. If he died I would have no right to protest. *You cannot demand that he stay,* God would say. *You know he's just a traveler.*

Thomas would be leaving us. The muscles of my heart turned inside out with grief and terror. And something else, something else:

Relief.

I wanted to vomit.

I put Thomas in his bassinette and stumbled into the living room. *I would die for you,* my mother had said. That's what mothers did. They protected their children at any cost. And me? I wanted my son to die.

No, I didn't. I swear I didn't.

But I did. I was flat on my back again, feet in the stirrups, begging for someone to get the baby out, take him away. I didn't care what happened to him. I just wanted the pain to stop.

I would give up my son to save myself.

My sobs came in great heaves. Raw. Rhythmic. For months I'd tamped down my feelings again and again until they were as numb and hard as pack ice, but spring had come, thawing the ice that held me steady, dropping me into the roiling sea. After one wave crashed another would build. I could spill and spill and spill and never be dry, like the sea tumbling over itself in salt and foam, spreading in sheets over the sand, then pulling back and up again, higher, higher, too high. I was collapsing, grinding my own face into the sandy seafloor.

But then something happened.

A window. It slid open in my mind, wide and welcoming. I stepped over the sill and turned around. There I was, pacing the worn beige carpet, wiping my eyes and nose on my sleeves, weeping aloud to nobody. It didn't add up—this woman I saw loved her son yet thought she was his enemy. *She's ill*, I realized. *She needs to get help.*

Get help. The words rang like a silver bell in clear morning air. I knew what I needed. I needed to call my doctor. I needed to ask for medication. I needed to do it right away.

"Okay," I whispered. "Okay." I walked toward the phone as quickly as I could, hoping to reach it before I slipped back into the sea.

It was cold in the doctor's office. I sat on a soft blue chair, arms folded, shivering. Tears still streamed of their own accord, steady and silent.

The nurse came in with my file and flipped it open. "What are we seeing you for today?" she asked.

"Depression." The word lay thick and heavy on my tongue.

The nurse made a note in my chart, set it down, and picked up the blood pressure cuff. She wrapped it around my arm and pumped it full of air, squeezing, squeezing. Blood thumped against my vein walls, reminding me I was alive.

Reed was glad I'd made this appointment. "It's your decision, and I'll support you either way," he'd said. "But I think it's smart to give some meds a try." Secretly, I thought he was just sick of my crying.

The doctor walked in and picked up my chart. "How are you?" he asked as he scanned the nurse's notes.

"Not so well." I stared at the speckled gray carpet.

"You had a baby a few months ago. Boy or girl?"

"Boy."

"How's he doing?"

"He's okay," I said, my voice hoarse. "He was born ten weeks early but he's doing okay now."

"But you're not doing okay."

I shook my head. Tears plopped to the floor.

"Tell me what's going on."

My throat squeezed tight, tighter, as if my collar were a blood pressure cuff. "I'm sad," I finally managed.

"Do you feel sad every day?"

I nodded.

"Has this been happening for more than two weeks?"

I nodded.

"Do you feel like life isn't worth living anymore?"

I nodded. A hundred years on earth sounded like the ultimate punishment. Forget eighty years. Forget ten, or five, or even one.

I could hear the naysayers clucking their tongues.

She had so many kids she lost her mind.
She couldn't love a baby with Down syndrome.
Another oppressed Mormon housewife.

And what would my fellow Mormon housewives think?

Maybe if she'd had more faith . . .
Maybe if she'd prayed harder . . .

Spring

Maybe if she'd let us help her . . .

As the doctor's questions continued I felt pressure mounting in my chest. Fresh waves. I crossed my arms and dug my fingernails into my elbows, trying to contain the swelling between my ribs. Finally, the doctor handed me a little white slip of paper.

Cheater.

But I didn't care anymore. I couldn't. I folded the prescription and put it in my purse, then walked quickly out of the exam room and through the waiting area, eyes on the red exit sign above the door.

I walked down the chapel aisle, lugging Thomas's car seat. Ahead of me, Reed directed the children into a pew toward the front. As I sat down I sensed the ward members looking at us; in the corners of my eyes I saw them smiling.

It had been three days since my doctor's appointment. Hidden in my medicine cabinet was a bottle with thirty half doses of Celexa, a serotonin-enhancing antidepressant. If my symptoms didn't improve after two weeks on the half dose, I would move up to a full dose. I'd cut the little white discs in half with a paring knife; their rough edges dropped bitter particles on my tongue every morning.

The doctor told me it would take at least a week for the medication to take effect. I didn't know if I could wait that long. Thomas's house arrest was officially over, and whenever I brought him to a public place I felt painfully exposed, like a bug squirming in the dirt after its rock cover is lifted away.

Friday night Reed and I had taken Thomas shopping for the first time. When we walked into Target I'd half expected an alarm to go off. I kept stealing glances at the other shoppers, wondering if they'd notice us, but the only ones who did were the neighbors who spotted us by the checkout line. Their hellos made me jump. I stammered a greeting and tried to look casual, but my pulse was pounding. Should I pretend nothing was out of the ordinary, even though I had a kid with Down syndrome in the basket? Should I make preemptive comments so that others wouldn't wonder what to say?

Sitting in the pew, the kids leaned over each other to hold Thomas's little hands and kiss his cheeks, then looked around to see who might be noticing ("Does everyone know Thomas has Down syndrome?" Christine had asked earlier). Tension stiffened my neck and shoulders, making it difficult to lift Thomas from his car seat. Surely the ward members were watching me. Nothing sinister, but naturally they'd be curious. I knew I would be.

It was the first Sunday in April. Testimony meeting again. Five months before, I'd bolted from the chapel in shame. Not much had changed since then. I was wearing the same stony face, hiding the same stony heart. I still had to force myself to sing. The sacramental bread was still tasteless in my mouth. But Thomas was with us now, resting on my shoulder, his hearing aids squealing when they pressed against my shirt.

After the sacrament a few ward members made their way to the pulpit to share their testimonies. Back in November, I'd refused to stand and speak, even though I knew some people were expecting it. But over the winter Thomas had become a celebrity in the ward, the baby everyone prayed for. Trying to blend into the woodwork now would only make me more conspicuous. I needed to get up and play my part as the grateful mother who was emerging from a crisis with strengthened faith.

I handed Thomas to Reed and made my feet move forward. I rarely get nervous speaking in front of a crowd, yet as I stood behind the polished wooden pulpit my mouth was bone dry.

There was my next-door neighbor, smiling. And my visiting teacher. And the mom from the park. And the sister who offered to babysit, and the young father with the straight white teeth. They looked up at me expectantly.

I didn't know what to say. When I spoke in testimony meetings past, I typically related a recent experience that had strengthened my faith. But I didn't recognize my faith anymore. Its landscape seemed alien, like the sagebrush desert after my wedding. If God's will really did govern my life, then he'd failed me miserably. If it didn't, I had no framework to live within, no paradigm to order the universe. Either way I was lost.

Everyone was waiting.

There were several unfamiliar faces in the congregation, so I figured I should introduce myself. "I'm Kathy Soper," I began, barely recognizing my own voice. It sounded flat, toneless, as if it had been compressed by great weight.

I cleared my throat and looked out at my friends and neighbors, all smiling and nodding their encouragement. "I haven't been around for a while. Last fall my son Thomas was born premature and we've had to keep him home to preserve his health." I looked down at him, snoozing on Reed's shoulder. Big mistake. A wave began forming in my chest, pushing steadily against my insides. *No,* I thought. *Not now. Not here.*

"I just wanted to thank you for your help and your prayers," I said quickly, hoping to finish before the wave crested in tears. "We're so thankful Thomas is with us, and we appreciate your loving support."

No luck. The rush of emotion swelled through my chest and up my neck and into my head, filling every cell, pushing firmly on the backs of my eyeballs. I was going to cry. Nothing could stop it.

Yet something did. The salt water heading for my tear ducts pressed hard against my sinuses, harder, harder—but the way was blocked, as if an invisible wall had sprung up within me, damming the furious flow.

I concluded with a few hasty words and returned to the pew, weak with relief. The meds were working. I breathed slowly, in and out, in and out. Waves of emotion roared and tumbled, knocking against their barriers, but they couldn't break through. It was like the Bible pictures I'd seen of Moses raising his staff above the Red Sea, parting the waves, revealing a strip of sand between two watery walls. Beyond the walls the sea churned and tossed and foamed. But within the walls, it was dry.

The calendar made sense again—that was one of the first signs. I could read my notes in the squares; I could even make doctor's appointments and shopping lists like a coherent human being.

"You sound so much better," my mom said every time she called. Her relief came through the phone receiver as distinctly as her voice.

I *felt* so much better. Clear. Grounded. Like a terrible fever had broken, returning me to wellness. "Is this how everyone else feels?" I'd asked Reed one night. "Like it's not a burden to be alive?"

"No, that's not how everyone feels," he said. "But it's how *healthy* people feel."

Wild. Apparently I hadn't been healthy since . . . who knew when. From where I stood, I could look back and see the slow buildup of depression over the years. It had gotten worse every time I had a baby—I'd been the proverbial frog being boiled to death without realizing it. If only I'd taken action sooner. But depression was the ultimate trap—it twisted the mind and sapped the body in ways that made taking action close to impossible. Like Thomas's hospital trauma, the problem precluded its own solution.

It'd been two weeks since my return to church. I hadn't cried once. Strong emotions brought pressure, but no pain—like I'd had an epidural for my heart. Nearly every day I peeled back another layer of the black funk I'd been stuck in. One afternoon I spent some time lurking at Downsyn.com, a networking forum for parents. Another day, I went to the educational-supply store and bought workbooks to prepare the elementary kids for the gifted testing the coming fall. Another, I researched hearing aid helps online and made a few purchases: a bottle of roll-on adhesive that came highly recommended, and a set of soft plastic rings that wrapped around the outer ear and held the amplifiers in place.

But despite the progress, I was still worried. Melody's next visit would mark the end of my tutorial about different communication methods, and within a couple of weeks I needed to decide which one to pursue with Thomas. Reed wanted the final choice to be mine, since I'd be doing most of the teaching, but I couldn't even keep the methodologies straight. And according to the Down syndrome guides, I pretty much held Thomas's quality of life in my hands. I feared I'd make the wrong choice. It certainly wouldn't be the first time.

"Can we do it tonight, Mom?" Ben asked. "Please?"

For weeks Ben had been asking me to spike Thomas's hair into a Mohawk—the hair on the sides and back of his head had rubbed off, leaving a tantalizing long lock on the top. I kept refusing, lacking the energy to find a fine-tooth comb and the willingness to deal with hairspray residue along with everything else. But when he asked again, all I could think about were the hilarious photos of Ellen's brother David in a dress and lipstick.

"Okay," I said. "Go get the hairspray. And the camera."

"Yes!" He scooted off while I propped Thomas against the pillows on my bed and dug through my bathroom drawer for a comb. When Ben returned he held Thomas steady while I sprayed and teased and sprayed some more. Once we had liftoff I took a dozen photos, including some from the side, which captured the fin in its full glory. Thomas looked uncannily like one of my high-school boyfriends, sans tattoos and steel-toed boots.

"This is his T-Bone look," Ben said.

"Yeah," I said. "And if we had some gold chains, it would be his Mr. T look."

Washing out the clumps of hairspray was no fun, but the photos were worth it. I e-mailed some to Ellen, who would be proud of me for carrying on the legacy. I had half a mind to send them to nurse Penny, too—might give her some good ideas for next Halloween's victims. Although it would be awfully hard to sew a preemie-size studded leather jacket.

Melody sat on my living room floor, clipboard in hand. "Let's do a quick review."

She ran through the list of methods, noting the core philosophy and chief characteristics of each. As I listened I was amazed. For the first time in months I could absorb information and process ideas. The different communication options formed a tidy line in my mind: At one end was the auditory approach, which stressed developing audible speech and maximizing hearing ability through aids or implants. At the other was complete nonverbal communication, accomplished by teaching ASL as the child's primary language. Ranging between them were options such as cued speech and signed English.

"So, which approach are you leaning toward?" Melody asked.

"I'm wondering which method will work best once Thomas starts school," I said. "If he's dependant on cueing or signing, won't that backfire in the classroom?"

"It depends on the classroom. Thomas qualifies for placement in programs for hearing-impaired children. If he learns one of the nonverbal communication methods, there'd likely be a classroom suited for him at the school for the deaf, or at one of the district's magnet schools for the hearing impaired."

The gears in my head turned smoothly. "But Thomas's hearing loss isn't the only variable here. He'll probably need special education."

"An in-class interpreter at your neighborhood school is another possibility."

So many options. But instead of muddling together in a hopeless tangle, they remained smooth and separate. More layers had gone. My mind was alive again.

"Okay," I said. "We'll be thinking, and I'll let you know what we decide."

Melody smiled. "I hope you don't mind me saying this, but you seem more upbeat today than usual."

I smiled back. And I wasn't even pretending.

I pulled a flannel blanket over Thomas's legs, then stood back and watched him sleep. Six months old. He lay on his back, head turned to the side, fist near his mouth. Since his NICU days he'd grown big enough to fill his bassinette, but in the wide expanse of his crib he looked tiny again.

I knew Thomas was ready for the change—no health issues remained, and there was no other reason to keep him an arm's length away from my bedside. Matt and Sam were ready to have another roommate. Reed was ready to have our bedroom to ourselves again. But I wasn't sure I was ready. How could I sleep without hearing the soft snurgle of Thomas's breathing?

At the same time, I was relieved we were taking a big step forward. Since October I'd felt so tense, so naked to a thousand possible disasters. Seeing Thomas snoozing peacefully near his brothers' bunk beds did my heart good. It felt *normal,* a rare experience during the past six months. When I got into bed I gave a little sigh of satisfaction. *Finally, finally, life is settling down again.*

At 2 a.m. I woke with a start. Someone was crying from the little boys' room, but it wasn't Thomas. When I walked in, I saw Matt sitting up on the top bunk, looking disoriented.

"I need a big towel," he moaned.

Great, I thought. *A wet bed.* Then I saw a darkish puddle. *Even better. He threw up.* I took another look and froze.

Blood. Streaming from his nose, dripping down his hands and arms, splattering on the bed. Matt whimpered. Numb with panic, I grabbed a towel and started wiping him off. *He's dying. He's going to die.*

I whisked Matt to the bedroom and woke Reed. "We need to get him to the hospital," I said. "This is bad."

Reed turned on the light and sat up, then watched me swab blood with the towel. "Kath, it's just a nosebleed."

It wasn't *just* anything. "Look at him. Go look at his bed. This can't be normal." I laid Matt on the bed next to Reed and turned toward the closet. "I'll get my shoes."

Reed rubbed his eyes. "My nose bled like this when I was a kid. It's not a big deal."

"In the middle of the night? Did you wake up bleeding in the middle of the night? Nothing hit him. He didn't fall out of bed. His nose just started pouring blood. And you think that's no big deal?"

Reed got out of bed, lifted Matt from my arms, and propped him against our pillows. "Get me some Kleenex," he said.

I pulled a wad from the box on the nightstand and handed them over. Then I grabbed my pediatrics reference manual from the bookshelf.

"Don't believe me, huh?" Reed said as he pressed the tissues against Matt's septum.

I didn't answer. I scanned the book's index, then flipped to the section on nosebleeds and read it quickly. I put the book back on the shelf and sat on the edge of the bed, still trembling. Apparently I was overreacting, but I couldn't help it.

"It's *okay*," Reed said. "I know it's scary looking, but it's okay."

He was right. After ten minutes of applied pressure, the flow of blood stopped. I changed Matt's pajamas, careful not to bump his nose. The three of us settled into the big bed. But I couldn't sleep. I felt shaken and dizzy, like I had just been knocked hard by the cosmos. Yet nothing had happened, nothing was wrong. Just a nosebleed.

The next morning I surveyed the damage. Matt's bed looked like a crime scene. I got to work soaking the bedding and pajamas. Matt was tired but otherwise perfectly fine. After more swabbing and swiping, only the barest trace of dried blood around the rim of his nostril remained. But I couldn't relax. Why did I keep thinking my kids were going to die?

Post-traumatic stress, Kate had said months before, when I confided my morbid daydreams about Thomas dying young.

I didn't believe her at the time. I thought it was premonition, maybe even a sign from God. But as I scrubbed Matt's sheets with peroxide, Kate's words began to make sense.

I *remembered.*

I remembered the NICU. The sounds of machinery and new-baby screams. The smells of body fluids and alcohol. The sight of tiny bodies, naked and pierced, born too soon or too weak. The memories themselves rarely emerged, but that didn't matter. They were embedded in my very cells—a raw, living layer I couldn't peel away.

I poked my head into the bedroom where Reed lay on the bed, watching TV.

"I'm going to tuck in the kids downstairs. Can I get you anything afterward?" Those days, the nearest we came to connecting was bumping hands in a bowl of popcorn.

He shook his head, eyes riveted on the screen. He looked more tired than usual. He'd had a rough few weeks at work, and at home he'd been quiet and withdrawn. If anything, my feeling better was giving him room to feel worse.

I knew I needed to respect the emotional space between us. It was one of our vital tools for managing a crisis—it kept us from clashing when we were overwhelmed and gave us room to sort through our personal issues. But the longer that buffer zone remained in place, the harder it was to cross. I wondered if we'd ever regain the intense intimacy we'd enjoyed the year before, when Thomas was just a tadpole swimming in dark water and the TV was rarely on after dark. Currently, it was a regular third party in our bedroom.

At the moment Reed had tuned me out completely. Curious, I glanced at the screen and saw a very large man in a swimming pool. He had Down syndrome. I turned and walked out of the room. Quickly. That bloated guy flopping around the pool was the very image of my long-standing fear. I didn't want to watch.

And yet I *did*. As I made my rounds downstairs I felt anxious to return to the bedroom. Some deep-seated, strong-willed part of me wanted to see.

Once I made my way back, I sat on the edge of the bed and looked at the screen: The man ate dinner in a restaurant with two elderly companions while an unseen Southern woman narrated.

I turned to Reed. "What is this?"

He shrugged. "PBS documentary." His eyes never left the screen, and from that point on, neither did mine.

The man was Jon. He had just turned forty—the restaurant meal was his birthday dinner and the companions were his parents. He couldn't speak. His walk was a slow waddle. His chief pastimes were folding sheets of paper into compact strips, ripping the buttons out of his father's TV remote, and playing with Furby toys.

I listened as Jon's mother, the Southern woman, spoke about Jon's childhood. He'd been born in the sixties, when parents of babies with Down syndrome were strongly encouraged to institutionalize their newborns. Jon's parents were told that raising him would ruin their family. Devastated, they placed him with a caretaker in another state. But when the caretaker died seven years later, they brought Jon home. He couldn't walk, talk, or chew solid food. He'd spent his entire life in a crib. A photograph showed him gripping the crib rail, looking out with a blank stare.

I listened to Jon's siblings, one brother and two sisters, describe what it was like to bring him home. They were scared of him at first—one sister even refused to sit next to him in the car. They didn't want this strange creature as a brother. But once they started to play with him, they changed their minds.

Spring

I watched Jon grow up in photographs: A round kid with a bowl haircut and thick glasses. A chubby-faced teen in a succession of school pictures, each one goofier than the last. A high-school graduate, aged twenty-one, short and stumpy in his shiny gown. He went on to earn $12 per year (yes, $12) pulling thread off industrial-size spools.

I watched Jon's family gather to celebrate the holidays. Every year his siblings and parents competed to see who could come up with the best gifts for him. Christmas, they agreed, was all about watching Jon open stuff. That year they gave him rolling pins, reams of paper to fold, cheerleader pompons, new Furby dolls. Jon twirled the pompons while his family hooted with delight. He dragged the rolling pin up and down his ample stomach, hamming it up for his audience. He cradled a new Furby with a gentle hand, lifting it to his face and caressing it with his cheek.

The credits rolled. I braced myself as the mother of all waves swelled inside me, pushing harder and harder against the protective walls until emotion broke through. Reed stroked my back as I cried. I cried for Jon stuck in his crib, a dim-witted, homely child nobody wanted for seven years. I cried for his siblings, who began to love him once they heard him laugh. I cried for his parents, for their ignorance and regret. And for their tenderness, which began as tentative acceptance and soon blossomed into mighty love.

"What's this movie again?" Andrew asked as I popped the videotape in the VCR and turned on the TV.

"It's called *The Teachings of Jon*. It's about a man who has Down syndrome," I said. "Jon's sister made the movie."

"Cool!" Elizabeth said.

"Is it animated?" Matt asked.

I smiled, picturing a cartoon version of Jon, and shook my head no.

Thomas was napping upstairs with Reed, but all the other kids were gathered in the family room, curious about the video I wanted them to watch. After seeing Jon on TV I'd checked the PBS Web site for the next time the documentary would air. Reed and I had watched it again together, and I'd recorded it so we could share it with the kids at some point.

At first we weren't sure whether to do so right away. Jon had severe cognitive limitations. He was grossly obese and, by typical standards, ugly (even his mother said so). He had minimal life skills and depended on his family to care for him. My kids didn't know any adults with Down syndrome, and it was risky to use Jon as an example. The man slept with Furbies, for Pete's sake. And how would they feel if they thought their cute baby brother would grow up to be like *him?*

But I decided I wanted to take that risk, and Reed had no objection. If nothing else, I could tell the kids what impressed me about Jon and his family. After months of faking acceptance of Thomas's diagnosis, I didn't want to miss this chance to show sincere enthusiasm about a person with Down syndrome.

The opening scene unfolded: Jon face down on a yoga mat, wearing nothing but Fruit of the Looms, trying to lift both legs straight behind him. After heaving and straining a few times, he grabs a stuffed Winnie the Pooh bear and shoves it under his torso for balance. One more try and . . . ta-dah! The legs lift. A fanfare sounds.

The kids burst out laughing. And for the next forty minutes, they were entranced. They giggled at Jon's obsession with Mickey Mouse T-shirts. They howled at his paper-folding antics. When they watched him cuddle his Furbies, they grew very still—even reverent. By the time we got to the Christmas scene, the four older kids were crying.

Once the screen grew dark, they turned to me. Ben was the first to speak. "Jon is awesome."

"Yeah, he's cool."

"I want Thomas to be just like Jon."

"Me, too. And watching Jon makes me love Thomas even more."

"I want to go hug him right now."

I wiped my eyes. "I know." We all smiled at each other, full of shared understanding: Jon was everything we'd feared. And he was beautiful.

Later, I found the phone and dialed Kate's number.

"Hey, how's my favorite punk baby doing?" she asked. I'd e-mailed her one of the Mohawk photos.

I looked at Thomas, sitting in his bouncy seat, chewing on his hand. "He's great." The tears started again. "Really great."

Kate paused. "Kath, are you okay?"

I sniffed a few times and nodded to myself. "Something happened."

She gasped.

"No no no," I said quickly. "Something good."

She exhaled. "Okay, you scared me. What happened?"

"I saw this show," I began. "On PBS. About this man with Down syndrome." I sniffed a few more times and swallowed. "And he was really limited. He was at the bottom of the barrel, ability-wise. And I loved him. I just wanted to hug him. And—" I turned away from Thomas, not sure if I could say it. "And now I know I don't want Thomas to die."

Fresh tears. "I mean, *of course* I don't want him to die, but part of me did." I wiped my nose. "I'd think about him dying, and I couldn't imagine anything worse. But then I could imagine something worse: having him grow up."

Kate sighed. "Oh, babe. Don't you know that's normal? It must've hurt like hell to feel it, but it's so normal. It's human, hon."

Normal. Human. I shook my head. A mother doesn't have the luxury of being human. Especially if being human means wishing her child gone.

"And what about now?" Kate asked. "How do you feel now?"

"Well, obviously I'm a mess at the moment. I can't stop crying, and in a way it hurts really bad, like I'm turning inside out, and in another way it feels good." I took a deep breath to calm myself. "Even when I'm crying I feel happy. And I thought antidepressants would only make me fake-happy, but I don't think this is fake."

"Of course it's not. This is who you are, Kath. Those meds don't change who you are. They just clear away the crap so you can *live* again."

Yes. I only wish I'd known it sooner. *Believed* it sooner.

"And babe," she continued, "I can't tell you how happy I am you're feeling so much better. But you know this isn't the end, right? You've made a big step, but there will be others."

"I know, I know," I said, only half listening. There were more layers to peel away, and some of them would hurt. But I didn't care right then. I wasn't thinking about endings—only beginnings.

"The Easter stuff!" Christine cheered as I dragged two big Rubbermaid containers into the living room. She loved holiday decorating almost as much as Elizabeth did.

I pulled off the lids. Christine dug out the personalized bunny baskets my mom had bought for each of the kids. "Mommy, will Thomas get a basket this year?"

"Yep, Grandma already ordered him one." She'd even sent him a bag of candy in the kids' Easter box, which Reed and I were happy to help him eat (Reed had dibs on the jelly beans, but the chocolate was mine).

Christine rifled her hands through the dozens of plastic eggs at the bottom of one container. "When will we do the egg hunt?"

Elizabeth walked in. "At Easter time, silly." She pulled a door decoration from one of the boxes. "It's the big bunny! Mom, can we put this up?"

"Be my guest." I stood back and let the girls take over. After unpacking some of the decorations, they put on some rabbit ear headbands from the boxes and hopped around the room, laughing.

I smiled. Ever since they'd "met" Jon, the kids had been laughing more than usual. They couldn't stop talking about how funny he was, how loveable. And they couldn't keep their hands off Thomas. He'd always been a big draw for their hugs and kisses, but these days he was irresistible, especially with all his new tricks: laughing, cooing, grabbing toys. He had the funniest hands, with stubby little fingers and plump, pink palms, and he spent long stretches of time studying them with rapt attention. And he loved to stand up, with one of us supporting his weight. The kids often bickered over who got to play with him next.

"Can we hang these in the kitchen?" Elizabeth asked, holding a large bag full of papier-mâché eggs in pastel colors.

"You can hang them wherever you want," I said. "Knock yourselves out." The girls scampered off with the bag, excited to have free rein. I had always been particular about holiday decorating—everything had to be done the right way, *my* way. But such rigidity seemed pointless now. So did decorating. Spring was bursting in our backyard—the peach tree was covered with pale pink blossoms, and the dead lawn was starting to green. Nothing we did with bunnies or eggs could even begin to compare.

I flipped Thomas over so I could reach the tiny snaps on the back of his outfit. Dressing my daughters for their baby blessings had been easy—tiny white gowns weren't hard to find, and my mother-in-law had sewn a beautiful one for Christine. But high-quality white outfits for newborn boys were in short supply, unless I wanted a miniature tuxedo, complete with bow tie. Which I most emphatically did not. So Thomas was wearing a soft cotton jumpsuit with satin piping.

Spring

Mormons don't christen babies—baptism takes place at age eight, which is considered the age of moral accountability. But we do have a blessing ceremony in which several elders encircle the infant while one of them, typically the father, announces the child's name and proclaims a blessing. This usually takes place in the chapel, but Reed and I had arranged for Thomas to be blessed at home. Even though I was growing more comfortable among my church family, I still wasn't ready to share this intimate occasion with a couple hundred people.

On our mantel we had photographs of each of our newborns on their blessing day, and I was excited to add Thomas to the lineup. I stacked up my bed pillows, covered them with a white crocheted blanket, and propped Thomas against them. He could hold his head up with no problem, but he couldn't sit unsupported, not even for a few seconds.

I knelt on the bed in front of him, camera ready. "Tho-mas!" I called. He looked up. *Click.* I checked the viewing window—cute, but not good enough for the mantel.

I kept shooting. Thomas lifted his hands in front of his face, put them in his mouth, waved them around. I couldn't get a decent shot. He was bored after hearing his name called a dozen times, so I decided to switch tactics. "Boo!" I said. He looked right at me and smiled. *Click.*

"Boo!" He laughed. *Click.*

A hundred clicks later—literally—I had a bunch of great photos. I used the camera's view feature to flip through them. Lots of funny faces, lots of big grins. In some of the images, it was obvious Thomas had Down syndrome; in others, the likeness was subtle. The one I picked for the mantel collection showed him looking straight ahead, with a barely-there smile. A stranger probably wouldn't guess his diagnosis just from that photo.

Wait a minute. Is that why I liked it so much?

I thought about it and decided no. I liked it because it was a perfect formal pose. Thomas looked so wise, so charming. There were plenty of other images I liked that highlighted his extra chromosome, and I would share them with relatives and include them in our photo albums. And there were some photos I would delete—ones where Thomas was blocking his face, or staring off into space, or closing his eyes. Speaking of which, those cross-eyed reindeer shots from Penny were still in their envelope, and I still had no plans to frame them. My original question had reversed: Instead of wondering why I felt compelled to hide those pictures (there must be something wrong with me!), I wondered why I ever felt obligated to display them in the first place.

I kept flipping through the digital images on the camera. Before Thomas in his blessing outfit, there were shots of the kids wearing Easter bunny headbands. Christine in fuzzy pink ears. Andrew in tall white ears and dark sunglasses, striking a cool-guy pose. I stopped on the next one: Ben holding Thomas. Thomas was wearing lavender rabbit ears and screaming; Ben was cracking up. I flinched for a split second—*don't tease the disabled kid!* Then I looked again at Thomas, so furious in fuzzy purple. And I laughed and laughed.

The doorbell rang. I wrapped Thomas in the white blanket and brought him to the living room. The bishop and his two counselors had arrived, along with a few of our close neighbors. Our living room was already filled with our kids, plus Reed's brother and his family, who were in town for the weekend and were (thankfully) keeping Matt and Sam occupied.

Spring

Reed greeted the elders and shook their hands, looking a bit nervous. Baby blessings are sacred occasions, intimate interactions between a father, his child, and God. Yet because others witnessed the ceremony, there's a touch of performance pressure.

I was nervous, too, not knowing what to expect. Every baby blessing is specific to the individual, but most mention basic things like physical health and spiritual strength, and there are often references to the infant's adult life, such as future missionary work, education, marriage, and parenthood. What kind of blessing would Thomas receive? He would never have children (with rare exceptions, men with Down syndrome are sterile). He might be able to marry—the wedding of a couple with Down syndrome had been in the news recently, and I figured such marriages would become more common in coming years—yet that capacity wasn't a given. He probably wouldn't be able to serve a traditional mission, which meant two years living away from home and full days of proselytizing.

I wondered, too, what might be said regarding Thomas's disability. The term "special spirit" still rankled me, but I couldn't deny that there was something special about Thomas. I didn't know what that was, though, or what it meant. Did he have Down syndrome *because* he was special, or did having Down syndrome *make* him special? Or did his diagnosis have nothing to do with his specialness? And how did God and/or fate fit into this whole scenario?

"Ready, Kath?" Reed held his arms out. I handed Thomas to him and stood back as the elders formed a circle around them. All of us bowed heads and closed eyes. The room stilled. In the silence Reed addressed God the Father and presented Thomas Reed Soper before him. Then he began to pronounce the blessing.

"We bless Thomas that he may fulfill his unique mission on earth.

"We bless him that any burdens presented by his health will not be too great for his family to bear.

"We bless him to be a teacher in his family, to show them how to love each other."

I started crying.

Reed continued for several minutes, using words that filled the air with near-palpable charge. Then he paused.

"And Thomas, we say unto you—"

Reed began to weep.

"We say that any good thing denied you in this life will be given in the life to come."

The blessing ended. I didn't want to open my eyes, didn't want to lose the sensation of light filling my skin. But all around me, sound and motion were breaking the stillness. I shared hugs with my family, my neighbors, my friends. I saw light in their faces, felt it in the touch of their hands. And when Thomas was back in my arms, I knew he was the reason.

That night, Reed and I lay together in bed, my head on his chest. There was so much we could talk about—the day, the blessing, the future. My unanswered questions, and his. But instead we stayed quiet, savoring the golden glow that lingered between the slow, steady beats of our hearts.

Reed and I zipped up our duffle bags and stowed them in the trunk of his car. Christine threw her arms around my waist. I kissed the top of her head. "We'll be back tomorrow," I promised her. My mother was visiting that week, and she'd agreed to hold down the fort so Reed and I could celebrate our fourteenth anniversary—alone.

I was reluctant to leave Thomas. Since he came home from the hospital, we'd never been apart for more than an hour or two. And Reed and I had never left the kids overnight, except in emergencies. But for the first time in over a dozen years, all the planets were aligned: We had a willing babysitter and money for a hotel. We had no other obligations, no sick kids, no nursing baby. No pregnancy-induced vomiting. No toddler who couldn't sleep alone. If we didn't leave now, we might be stuck for another twelve years.

We backed down the driveway, waving to all the kids. Mom held Thomas on her hip and waved his hand at us. "Is there anything special I need to do for him?" she had asked before we left—I thought I heard a hint of anxiety in her voice, but I wasn't sure. I told her he was just like any other baby, except for his hearing aids, which would be put away until we got back. As we paused at the bottom of the driveway for one last good-bye, she flashed me her cheery, I-can-do-this smile. If anyone could do it, she could.

Once we reached the end of the street and rounded the corner, I turned to Reed and grinned. "Free at last!"

"Yeah. Think we'll ever come back?" He smiled, but I knew he was worried about Thomas. On evenings out he always had a harder time leaving the kids than I did.

"Dunno. Think we'll still like each other tomorrow?" A joke, of course, yet it held a bit of truth. Our marriage had barely begun recovering from the stress of months past. Thomas's blessing had drawn us closer, but not as close as we used to be.

We headed up I-15 and then took I-80 toward Park City, the resort town that hosts the Sundance film festival. Reed turned on the iPod, and we relaxed as the freeway narrowed into a winding canyon road, carrying us far from the sprawling suburbs of Salt Lake valley. When we pulled into the loading zone of the hotel, I fidgeted in the car while Reed got our room key.

We opened the door and saw freedom. One bed. One TV. One window. One bathroom. No children. For the next twenty-four hours we wouldn't be interrupted or spit up on. We wouldn't have to make a sandwich or wipe a bottom. We stood for a minute, taking in the quiet, empty space.

Reed shut the door and set the duffel bags on the bed. Then he reached for me with both arms. And the space between us disappeared.

The next morning I lay in bed, awake, for a full hour. Because I could.

Spring

Amazing what one night could do. I didn't sleep especially well in the strange bed, but I woke feeling different, as if I'd been wiped clean by the neutral air of the hotel room. Reed found an old John Cusack movie on cable, and we drank Coke (Mormon coffee) and lounged around until we decided we were hungry. Before we kicked ourselves out of bed, we planned our remaining time: Breakfast—lots of it. A few stops at the outlet stores (I had my eye on babyGap). Then a long drive through Provo Canyon. A nice, lazy day.

By the time we hit the canyon road, I was more relaxed than I'd been in months. Years. Maybe a decade. We kept the iPod off and drove in gentle silence, taking serpentine curves, dips and hills. Spring was just beginning to touch the canyon. The mountains were waking up, shedding their blankets of snow. Green boughs poked through some of the drifts.

I leaned back in my seat, drowsy from so much food and rest. "Why did it take us fourteen years to do this?"

"I can think of seven reasons."

Seven *good* reasons. But still. "Think Thomas misses us?" I asked.

"Maybe, but I'm sure your mom's keeping him busy. I miss him, though."

"Me, too. I get this pang every time I think about him." And it was hard not to. The kid was a total ham. When he was hungry, he didn't cry. He yelled. Short and loud and forceful, like his debut yell in the chilly air of the NICU. *Hey!* he ordered. *Get me some food, stat.* And when he caught sight of the full bottle, he chuckled like a good-natured grandpa: *heh heh heh.*

"I can't believe he's seven months old already," I said. "It's been crazy, but it's getting better. At least, it is for me."

Reed's hand covered mine. "I'm glad."

"Have you felt any better since Thomas's blessing? I mean,

we both felt really good afterward, but did it change anything for you?"

He thought for a minute. "Yeah, in a way. I used to feel sad because he might miss out on a lot of things. And he'll definitely miss out on some. Like being a father."

He'd been thinking about it, too. I wondered what other thoughts we'd both had but hadn't shared.

"But now I feel like he won't really miss out. I don't know exactly what that means. But it makes me feel better. Some of the time, at least."

I waited for him to go on.

"When I think about how things might be down the road, I still get stressed out. We don't know how independent Thomas might be, or what he'll be able to do. It probably won't matter, as far as the big picture goes. But we'll still have to deal with the day-to-day stuff." He paused. "Watching that show about Jon really made me think about what our future could look like. That could be us, you know?"

"I know."

He paused again. "I don't worry about it all the time, though, like I used to. And whenever I'm with Thomas, I don't worry about anything. I just like being with him."

I smiled, thinking of Thomas sitting in his bouncy seat, studying his pudgy paws as if they were rare ancient texts. "I know exactly what you mean."

Reed squeezed my fingers. We were quiet for the rest of the ride, drinking in the rich views of the canyon, which was lined by a rushing, foaming creek swollen by the recent thaw. Winter was over—in more ways than one.

Spring

When we drove up our street late that afternoon, we could see our kids playing in the front yard. They ran to greet us as we pulled into the driveway. My mom waved from her seat on the porch. Thomas was on her lap, chewing on a rattle. I couldn't wait to hold him.

I hugged all the kids. "What'd you bring us?" Ben asked.

"A knuckle sandwich," Reed joked.

I showed Ben the shopping bags. "We did stop at babyGap, but they didn't have anything in your size."

"Hardy har har."

I headed for the porch. "He did just fine," Mom said as I approached. "I don't think he missed you at all!"

"Tho-mas," I called. He looked up from his rattle and looked down again. Had he forgotten me already?

I lifted him from Mom's lap. His limbs stiffened, as if I were a stranger. "T-Bone, we're home!" He looked at me, eyes sparkling in recognition. Then he started wriggling with glee. I kissed him again and again.

Reed got the bags while I carried Thomas into the house. "Did you miss me, buddy? I missed you." He patted his hands against my chest and my face, grinning nonstop.

Mom found us in the kitchen. "All the kids were terrific. They had lots of fun playing with Thomas, and they were a big help when we needed to clean up toys."

"Good. Thank you so much for doing this."

"You're very welcome, sweetie. I just wish I could do it more often. It was really nice to have this time with the kids, and Thomas is just a delight."

"Did you have fun with Grandma?" I said to Thomas, bouncing him on my hip.

"Really, Kathy, he is the sweetest baby." Her voice caught on the words.

I looked at her in surprise. Along with love, there was something else in her eyes, something unexpected: hope. She had hope for her relationship with Thomas, hope that she didn't have before I left. That *was* anxiety I'd heard in her voice—some part of her, however small, had worried she and her grandson might not connect.

Maybe, just maybe, she and I weren't so different after all.

I picked up Thomas for the third time in an hour and laid him on his back, then picked up the hearing aid that had fallen out. He turned his head, pressing his ear against the carpet, and the remaining aid squeaked. His hand flew up and batted at it, knocking the mold loose.

Swearing silently, I left him on the floor and carried both aids to my room. With my thumbnail I scraped the old tape off the backs of the aids and cut two more crescent-shaped pieces. I attached the fresh tape and headed back to Thomas for our latest round of the battle. Thomas fought the aids every time I laid him down, and gravity fought them every time I sat him up. At this point they were little more than torture devices.

We'd had the aids for ten weeks. None of the different molds we'd tried would stay in his left ear, and it didn't take much for them to fall out of his right ear as well. The plastic rings we'd ordered were useless on Thomas's tiny, floppy outer ears. The roll-on adhesive didn't work as well as the double-sided tape, and the tape didn't work well at all, especially since Thomas had gotten strong enough and coordinated enough to yank the aids off himself.

It would have been easier if Thomas weren't so self-protective. He loved to be held and cuddled, but vigorously resisted any invasion or manipulation of his body. During early intervention sessions with Suzanne, he yelled every time she tried to position him for exercises, and if she persisted he became hysterical. The same thing happened whenever I tried to wipe his nose, button his shirt, or comb his hair—as soon as he saw my hands approach, he went on high alert, pushing me away and protesting loudly.

With great reluctance I turned Thomas on his side, pinned his free arm down with my forearm, then used both hands to twist the mold into his ear canal and press the sticky amplifier in place. I felt torn. The sanity-saving move would be to give up the hearing aids, as well as anything else that drove him berserk, but I worried we'd pay the price later on. It was like deciding whether to sedate Thomas when he was on the ventilator—a no-win choice. Gag on the tube, or suffer narcotic withdrawal? Hourly wrestling matches, or loss of language skills? Forced exercises, or weak muscles?

To make matters trickier, we didn't know what would truly help Thomas. Given his central auditory dysfunction, the aids might have just been cranking up the distortion in his brain, like TV static at full blast. And while research suggested that early intervention helped kids with Down syndrome reach milestones more quickly on average, Thomas wasn't average. Given his unusual resistance to certain kinds of touch, it was possible, even likely, that physical therapy would have a strong *adverse* effect on his development.

After both hearing aids were in place, I lifted Thomas to my shoulder, taking care not to bump his ears, and walked around the room to help him calm down. But he wouldn't stop crying. He kept drawing up his knees and pushing against my chest with his feet, as if he were trying to get away. Suddenly his stomach heaved and a jet of milk spewed out of his mouth, landing on the carpet in a wet stripe several feet long.

Spring

He'd never thrown up from crying before. For the first time in weeks, tears of frustration pricked my eyes.

I slid into the row of movie theater seats, with Reed following right behind me. We settled into the middle of the row and wedged Thomas's car seat into an empty space next to us. His first movie: *Mission: Impossible III*. Not a bad metaphor for the past six and a half months.

"No aids?" Reed pointed to Thomas's bare ears.

"I left them at home. The volume's going to be earsplitting already."

"True."

"Besides, I'm totally sick of those things. I'm not sure I can keep dealing with them long-term."

"Well, maybe you won't have to. I've been getting the feeling that hearing aids aren't the solution for Thomas."

"Really? Why?"

"I don't know. It's just that when I think about it, I get the feeling that the problem will take care of itself. But I don't know what that means. Maybe his hearing is going to improve so much he won't need aids, or maybe his ears will get so bad that they wouldn't do him any good."

That stopped me short. "I hadn't thought about that."

He shrugged. "There's no use in worrying about it now. We'll just keep doing what we're doing until he gets another test. When's that going to be?"

"A few weeks." His second sedated ABR was on the calendar for the first week in May.

The previews started, a welcome distraction from thinking about Thomas going deaf. I thought the dark room and flashing light might freak him out and send us both to the lobby, but he ended up falling asleep. Halfway through the movie, though, he woke up crying. Reed got him out of the car seat while I fished for the bottle in the diaper bag. He chugged half the bottle while reclining on my lap, then started whimpering. I held him against my shoulder and bounced as best as I could, then passed him to Reed.

We were watching Tom Cruise jump out of some explosion when Thomas heaved and spewed milk all over the theater seats. I grabbed him from Reed and rushed to the lobby. That was the third time Thomas had forcibly vomited that week, and the first time I couldn't blame it on his crying. I used Reed's cell phone to call the pediatrician at home. *Probably a virus,* he said. But Thomas didn't have a fever, or diarrhea. I'd seen scores of tummy bugs in my mothering career, and this didn't seem like one.

Something was wrong—very wrong. My muscles tensed, ready for sudden action. Yet given my overreaction to Matt's nosebleed, could I trust my intuition? Reed was concerned about Thomas, but not scared. And I didn't want to waste a trip to the ER. So I told myself to calm down and see how things went.

By the following afternoon Thomas had vomited three more times—even clear liquids didn't stay down. After another phone consult I headed for the ER, fearing an obstruction in his stomach or bowels. The doctor who examined him suspected the same, but the x-rays came back normal. *Probably constipation,* he said. I rolled my eyes. Five hours and a $100 co-pay to diagnose constipation. Home we went to give Thomas an enema.

The next day the presumably cleaned-out Thomas woke up in obvious pain. I packed him in his car seat and sped to the children's hospital while he screamed. Adrenaline buzzed my brain as I carried him into the unit. The triage nurse got us a room right away. But once we got inside, Thomas calmed down. All the way down. He leaned back in my arms and peered around the strange room, quiet and content. I almost wished he would cry again, just so I wouldn't look like a fool for rushing him in.

The resident was a very tall man with a gorgeous Jamaican accent. He peppered me with questions, then ordered preliminary stool and urine tests. When the results came back normal, he recommended opting out of the next level of tests: a barium enema and exploratory scope. "Probably a virus," he said.

At that point I *did* look like a fool. Or at least, I felt like one. "Should I have brought him in or not?" I asked the resident.

He shrugged his massive shoulders. "If we find a problem, you think it's a good idea. If not, you think it's a bad idea. You cannot know," he said. "You cannot know."

He was right. As I drove home, I felt like I'd wasted lots of time and money indulging my motherly panic. Yet had there been a true emergency, I would be congratulating myself for taking action. How was I supposed to know?

Thomas seemed okay the next day—tired and cranky, but he didn't throw up again. We waited for the hospital to call with results from his urine culture. I wanted an explanation for Thomas's symptoms and my resulting feelings over the previous few days. I couldn't dismiss projectile vomiting with a shrug. At the same time, I feared my ability to sense true danger had been permanently skewed.

By dinnertime I was pretty testy, snapping at the kids and nursing a stress headache. "Mom, you should watch TV with us tonight," Ben said. "*Deal or No Deal* is coming on. It'll cheer you up."

"Which part will cheer me up—the scantily clad women?" I asked. But I let Ben talk me into it. I needed something to pass the time before I could escape to bed.

I slumped on the couch as Howie Mandel came on screen with his troupe of barely dressed Barbies, who seemed to be wearing a collection of sequined handkerchiefs. At first the contestant, a middle-aged blond, kept the odds of high winnings in her favor. But after the third round of play, her chances evened out. If she walked away, she'd have a hundred grand safely in hand; if she kept playing, she could win five times that amount—or lose it all.

Howie stepped close to the contestant and flashed his oily smile, then made his trademark ultimatum: "Deal, or no deal?"

"No deal!" Ben shouted. "Go for more cash!"

The other kids chimed in. "No deal! No deal!"

Nerves shot, the contestant turned to her husband and sister on the sidelines, then to the studio audience. "No deal!" the audience chanted. But she looked torn.

"Is she crazy?" Ben complained. "She could win half a million! She can't stop now!"

"Easy for you to say. You're not the one up there." I couldn't exactly pity someone being offered free money, but I knew how it felt to face a decision that might turn sour either way. My choices for Thomas could make or break his opportunities in life. But I couldn't see the outcomes of different options any more than the contestant could. I didn't know what would benefit Thomas most in the long run. Neither did Reed. Neither did the doctors or the therapists or anyone else we could look to in our studio audience.

The contestant agonized on-screen, biting her knuckle and squirming as if she needed a toilet. "We need an answer," Howie prodded.

Finally, she pushed the big red button that signaled the end of the game. "*Deal!*" she called out, with obvious relief.

"Nooo!" the kids shouted. The audience clapped politely.

Howie shook the contestant's hand and congratulated her. "Now, let's see if you made a good deal," he said. "What would've been your next move?"

Sadist. It'd been hard enough for the woman to make a choice—now she had to risk humiliation on top of it all. Sure enough, as she revealed her would-be strategy, the audience groaned—if she'd played even one more round, she would've won a quarter million. "Sorry," Howie said as he patted her on the shoulder. "Looks like you didn't make a good deal."

Suddenly I sat up straight.

"That's not true," I said, pointing at Howie's shiny bald head.

The kids looked at me like I was nuts.

"She *did* make a good deal." My voice got louder. "She didn't know what was going to happen. If she did, she would've chosen differently. But she didn't. She couldn't. She made a good choice based on what she knew."

Ben rolled his eyes. "Chill, Mom."

But I couldn't chill. Everything was suddenly making sense. *Let's see if you made a good deal*—I'd been pressuring myself the same way. After those ER visits I'd judged the wisdom of my decision based on the *outcome,* not the *odds.* I thought I'd made a poor decision. But given what I knew and felt beforehand, Thomas might have had a serious illness. I risked money and time against health. That was a good decision. A good deal.

The next morning the hospital called. Thomas's culture had grown E. coli, which indicated a urinary tract infection. I picked up antibiotics from the pharmacy, glad to have an explanation for Thomas's illness. But I knew the hospital visits were justified in any case. They were warranted by the risks we'd faced, not the reality that came to light after the fact.

It felt weird to take such a calm, rational approach. Weird in a good way. I was out of that hellish room where my mind followed the same pattern of thoughts over and over, trapping itself at every turn, unable to break out of the deep groove in the walls. The door to that room was still open a crack; I could still feel the pull of its heavy air. But I didn't have to go in. I could shut the door and walk away.

I set Thomas's car seat on the floor and then settled Matt and Sam onto two folding chairs, hoping some modern miracle would enable them to stay quiet for the next hour. Christine's first-grade musical would be starting in a few minutes. I pulled my camera from the diaper bag. We had a good view of the stage; with a bit of luck, I'd be able to get a few decent shots.

The auditorium was packed with families, seated in two sections of chairs with an aisle down the middle. Looking around, I caught sight of a family sitting across the aisle, a half dozen rows back. Mother and father, with a young son sitting on the chair between them. On the father's lap was a little girl, three or four years old, with a pink dress and light blond hair. I glanced at her face, then glanced again. Flat features, almond-shaped eyes—did she have Down syndrome?

She fiddled with her fingers, oblivious to my trying-not-to-stare stares. When she reached up and patted her father's cheek, I knew. Something about the curve of her jawline when she tilted her head back.

I studied the parents with careful nonchalance. The mother looked older than me—maybe forty?—and had a friendly smile.

With her faded jeans and polo shirt, she looked like a typical stay-at-home mom. The father had gray streaks in his hair and wore a dress shirt and trousers. He had both arms wrapped around his daughter, and he was smiling, too.

The mother caught me looking at their family a few times. I wanted to talk to her, but what would I say? *I noticed your daughter has Down syndrome. So does my baby!* I doubted she'd mind, but still, I felt too shy. And the program was about to start.

I turned on my camera as the first graders gathered on stage. One of the kids stood at the microphone and welcomed us to "Wish Upon a Star," a medley of Disney songs and fairy-tale vignettes. I spotted Christine, wearing a dress and apron for her role as Mama in "The Three Bears." She had two huge circles of rouge on her cheeks. I waved, along with every other parent in the audience—as if that would get her attention.

Between listening to songs, snapping photos, and wrestling Matt and Sam back onto their chairs, I kept peeking at the little blond girl's mother. I was a stranger to her, but I didn't feel like one. Wasn't that silly, though? We had one thing in common, but that didn't mean we were meant to be best friends. Even so, I sensed we would understand something essential about each other. And there was something about that little girl, something hard to capture in words.

I couldn't stop thinking about her all that night.

"Let's get a car-cart!" Matt said, pointing to a grocery shopping cart with a molded plastic car attached to the front. He and Sam climbed inside the car and started turning its steering wheels. I hooked Thomas's seat to the cart's produce basket, proud of myself for braving the supermarket with three little boys.

Spring

Reed did our grocery shopping, save the little in-between trips I made on occasion. The task used to overwhelm me. Too many things to look at, too many decisions. Regular produce (laden with pesticides) or organic (three times the price)? Froot Loops (which the kids would eat) or Wheaties (which they wouldn't)? Regular-size or bulk? National brand on sale or store brand? Which cut of meat, and how many pounds—or should we not be eating meat anyway? There wasn't one item I could pick up that didn't come with emotional baggage. But this time I felt sure I could choose some apples and milk and bread, and somehow escape cosmic judgment.

I pushed the cart closer to the checkout aisles, debating. The two open lanes both had baggers. One was a teenage girl with a ponytail. The other was the bag boy—bag *man*—whom Reed and I had seen in the parking lot back in January. Stocky and slow, he was filling the sacks two at a time, deep in concentration. On past shopping trips I usually refused his offer to load my van, but one day, feeling amiable, I'd agreed—then regretted my decision once I arrived home and unpacked squashed loaves of bread.

I took a deep breath and pushed the cart into his aisle.

My pulse thumped as the cashier scanned our groceries. Matt and Sam made honking and driving noises from the car-cart. Thomas surveyed the scene from his perch. As the cashier pulled the cart through the lane, she smiled at me. "Cute baby," she said.

"Thanks." I glanced at the bagger. His name was Eric. He had a ruddy face and close-cropped brown hair. He was quite trim and energetic, his eyes bright, his expression determined as he sorted our groceries into bags. I wondered if the cashier was thinking what I was thinking—my baby might be in Eric's shoes some day.

Feeling self-conscious, I mustered my courage and cleared my throat.

"Hi, Eric."

He looked up. "Hi," he said in a gruff voice.

Not sure what to say next, I leaned over so I could see the boys inside their plastic car. "Matt and Sam, this is Eric."

"Hi," they said.

"Hi," he said.

We were all quiet while Eric finished filling the bags. "Help you out with this today?"

I hesitated for a short second. "Sure."

Eric grabbed the cart handles. "Hi-ii!" he said to Thomas, smiling. Thomas smiled back.

"Hi-ii!" said Matt and Sam from the front of the cart.

"Hi-ii!" Eric repeated. The boys cracked up, and Eric looked very pleased with himself.

I walked next to him, not wanting Thomas to think I'd disappeared. It was the closest I'd ever been to an adult with Down syndrome since the Latino man at the care center had insisted on dancing with me. I didn't necessarily want Eric to grab me in a bear hug, but I didn't want to bolt, either.

As we walked, the boys continued their "hi" game. Every time Eric responded they dissolved into laughter. He seemed to enjoy it as much as they did.

When we got to the van I unhooked Thomas's car seat from the basket and latched it into place. Matt and Sam climbed into their booster seats while Eric loaded the groceries. I arranged the bags as he put them in so the bread stayed safe. "Thank you," I said, and I really meant it.

"Welcome," he replied. "By-eye!" he said to the boys.

"By-yye!" the boys said. And they giggled all the way home.

Spring

We pulled our vans into the parking lot, side by side—one twelve-seater, and one custom van with a wheelchair lift. The custom van was driven by Aaron's mother. Aaron, the little boy Matt's age with spina bifida. The boy I used to see right through.

I'd suggested the park because I wanted to make sure Matt had a good time on this play date. It would backfire if he decided he didn't like spending time with Aaron. The mom opened the back of her van and released the wheelchair ramp. Her adult daughter stood guard as Aaron wheeled himself down the ramp. As we crossed the grass toward the playground, I wondered how Aaron would be able to play. Wouldn't it be hard on him to watch Matt climb around, while he was stuck in his wheelchair?

I shook my head. No excuses. After our encounter with Eric the other day, I'd realized my info bank regarding people with disabilities was outmoded. I needed new data, new interactions. A playdate with Aaron and his mom was a good way to start, and it would be a good experience for Matt, too. But I felt sheepish about my self-interest. I wondered what Aaron's mom would think if she knew why I'd called out of the blue.

Matt took off for the slides. Aaron's sister unbuckled his straps and lifted him out, then carried him to the play structure. I watched, surprised, as she helped him place one of his feet on the lowest rung of the ladder, and his other foot on the one above. Once Aaron had reached the top his sister climbed up as well, long brown hair swinging, then sat next to Aaron and surveyed the view.

"Boy, I'll bet you're glad you don't have to do the climbing today," I said to the mom.

She laughed and nodded. "My daughter has been invaluable. She feels helping Aaron and Heather is part of her life's work." Heather, the family's other child with spina bifida. She and Aaron had been adopted a few years apart.

The first time I'd seen Aaron he was only a couple of days old. I was changing Matt's diaper in the restroom at church when the mom came in, carrying a tiny baby.

"Hey, I didn't even know you were pregnant!" I teased her.

"They called yesterday and asked if we would take him," she said, sounding as if she still couldn't believe it. "We said yes. I didn't have diapers or anything, but I knew he needed us."

Amazing, I'd thought. She'd brought disabled kids into her family *on purpose*. She was in a completely different class of human beings than people like me. As she changed Aaron's diaper, I'd looked at his squished-up new-baby face and thought about how lucky he was.

I thought the same thing as I watched Aaron on the slide, his sister waiting at the bottom with outstretched arms. Thomas lounged in his car seat next to us. As much as I'd adjusted to his diagnosis, I could barely imagine raising someone else's baby with Down syndrome.

"Has it been really hard?" I asked her. "I mean, one kid in a wheelchair would be a big challenge, but two?"

"It's difficult sometimes." She smiled a little. "But my other kids weren't always easy, either. It's just a different set of challenges, that's all."

"That makes sense." Thomas's diagnosis caused some problems, but it precluded others. *At least he'll never get his girlfriend pregnant*, Reed once joked.

From the top of the play structure, Aaron started crying. "It's okay, he just wants to come down," his sister called. She lifted him and began carrying him down the coated-wire steps.

"Wow, taxi service!" I said.

The mom laughed and nodded. "Aaron tends to get clingy, and his sister spoils him sometimes. But they're good together."

"I can tell. I think it's wonderful." I felt stupid for worrying about how Aaron would handle playing at the park. Obviously his family knew what would or wouldn't work for him. They didn't need me to protect him.

Aaron's sister set him down on the grass a few feet from us. "Ready for a snack, Matt?" I called. He came running over from the swings and sat next to Aaron.

"I want to take a picture," I said, digging the camera out of the diaper bag and pointing it at the two of them. Sitting down, Aaron and Matt looked the same. Nobody passing by could've guessed which child had been born with an open spine.

The boys seemed happy enough, but they didn't have much to say to each other. At first I was disappointed—I'd secretly hoped they would hit it off. Then I sat back and let the moment be what it was: two boys eating cookies, sitting together in the sunshine. It was more than enough.

Melody slipped off her shoes, set down her bag, and sat on the floor next to Thomas. "Hey, little guy!" He smiled. "Oh, you are just the cutest thing ever." She pulled a musical toy out of her bag and pressed one of its buttons, watching for Thomas's reaction. "How's he doing with the aids?" she asked.

"Well, we're still trying, but it's not getting any easier."

"Would you say he wears them all day, most of the day, or only occasionally?"

I hedged a bit. "Maybe not most of the day. But I keep putting them back in until neither of us can stand it anymore."

She smiled in sympathy. "I know it's not easy. It'll be a big help to him, though." She turned the page on her clipboard. "Okay, let's talk about which communication method you'd like to pursue. What did you and your husband decide?"

Even with my newfound clarity, the choice had been a challenge. Picking a method of managing hearing loss meant picking a philosophy and a goal as well. I felt caught between conflicting agendas—the same ones I'd wrestled with since

Suzanne's first visit. Should we help Thomas be as "normal" as possible, or should we accept and enjoy him as he was?

I took a deep breath. "Well, we want to use some sign language," I said. "But we want English to be his primary language."

She nodded. "Do you want me to put you on the waiting list for an ASL tutor, or get you some information about signing up for a class?"

I shook my head. "We're not ready for that. Right now we just want to focus on a few basic signs." The kids' favorite was *T-bone:* thumbs tucked between first and second fingers, arms crossed at the wrists. We'd learned the sign for *Mr. T* as well, but it wasn't as fun.

Meredith made some notes on her clipboard, looking a bit disappointed. She was fluent in ASL, and while she'd been careful to present all the options without bias, I could guess what she'd hoped for Thomas. "Do you have any interest in learning cued speech?" she asked. "The training for that is much simpler. There are daylong workshops that could teach you the basics."

"Maybe down the road we'll consider that. But I'm worried that if Thomas needs sign or cued speech to communicate, he won't be able to socialize. I want him to go to school with his siblings, even if he needs to be in a resource classroom."

"I understand," she said. "Of course your preferences will be considered, but ultimately the district decides where Thomas will be placed."

What? "So it's not up to us whether Thomas is in a special-education classroom, or a hearing-impaired classroom, or a regular classroom?"

She shook her head. "A team of professionals will consider his needs and the resources available at the time. Your input will be given close consideration, but parents don't have the final say."

I couldn't believe it. Thomas would be at the mercy of people who barely knew him. And I was supposed to sit back and let others decide his fate? That would be like watching Howie Mandel make my most important deals.

"I can see you're disappointed," the therapist said. "But there are some really good people in the district. They'll only want what's best for Thomas."

"It's not the same."

"I know. I'm sorry."

So was I. Just when I was ready to take charge, I found out I wasn't in charge after all. How could I create a good life for Thomas if I couldn't make the decisions?

I ripped open the envelope from Elizabeth's school and pulled out a progress report. Among the scattered As were several Bs and B-minuses, and one big fat C-minus.

"Elizabeth!" I called, walking down the hallway. I found her in the bedroom, e-mailing from my computer. "Look at this." I handed her the progress report.

Her face fell.

"Pull up the school Web site," I said. As we looked at her scores, it was clear she'd been acing her tests but failing to turn in projects and homework assignments. Elizabeth stared at the ground, as if bracing herself for the inevitable rant. She deserved one.

"You have so much ability, and you're not getting credit for it because of sloppiness," I told her. "Before long your grades will start showing up on your permanent transcript. If you keep this up, you won't be able to get the scholarships you want." Didn't she see that she was wasting her potential? This was the kid who scored in the highest category—very superior—on her IQ tests.

There will be no doors closed to her, we were told. But if she didn't get her act together, there certainly would be—in fact, she'd be closing and locking them herself. I couldn't let that happen.

"Elizabeth." She looked up. "If you can't keep your grades up, you're going to have to drop out of the play so you can get your assignments done in homeroom."

She burst into tears. She loved theater—I was hitting where it hurt. *Good,* I thought. She needed to learn her lesson.

But as I listened to her cry, my self-righteous anger faded and shame crept in. I wanted to punish Elizabeth. I wanted to punish her because I felt threatened. When she failed, I failed—and I couldn't bear another failure.

Elizabeth leaned forward, hiding her face in her hands. Her long hair curtained her shoulders in rich brown. Her hair was the first part of her I ever saw: a dark, slick scalp appearing in the birthing mirror. Once she emerged her newborn body squirmed in the open air, vibrant pink, full of light and life. The most precious thing I'd ever seen.

At what point had I forgotten? Was it when she started school, and I started anticipating glowing report cards? Or was it earlier, maybe the first time she'd rolled over? (I'd run to check *What to Expect the First Year,* hoping she was ahead of the game—and she was.) Somewhere along the line I stopped separating what she did from who she was. I thought her achievements proved her worth. I *did* believe smarter was better.

But I don't anymore.

The sudden thought shocked me. My mind picked it up and turned it over, suspicious. But when I tapped its side, I heard the solid ring of truth. And when I looked at Elizabeth, weeping in the chair, I saw her clearly for the first time in far too long. She was precious. Not because she was intelligent, not because she was *very superior.* Simply because she existed.

Somehow, I had to tell her, without angering her even more. There's nothing more pathetic than a penitent parent trying to suck up.

"Sweetie, let's talk about this," I began.

She raised her head and glared at me. "You just want me to be perfect!"

Yes. Up until ten seconds before, I *had* wanted her to be perfect. I wanted her to get the best grades and keep her room clean and never talk back and do everything right—everything. She'd accused me of this before, and I always denied it, but that's exactly what my response had been: denial.

"You're right," I said, "but you're also wrong."

She rolled her eyes and looked away.

"You may not believe me, and I won't blame you if you don't. But this is the truth: I used to want you to be perfect, but I don't anymore. And I'm so sorry I didn't realize that sooner."

She was quiet. Probably hoping I'd forgotten about the progress report.

"You want to go to college, and I want to help you get there. But this isn't about me anymore, Elizabeth. It's about you. It'll make no difference in my life if you get As or Cs, although it may make a difference in yours. But even if you never go to college, I won't love you any less."

I left her sitting in front of the computer, staring at her lap. Maybe she believed me; maybe she didn't. But *I* did. And that was no small thing.

The parents' waiting area of the same-day surgery unit hadn't changed: same padded vinyl chairs, same worn magazines, same looks on the parents' faces. Five months had passed since the dark January morning when Thomas had his first ABR hearing exam, the morning I read Annie Dillard's essay about polar explorers, not realizing the ice would soon shift under my very feet. This time I knew we were on the brink of something—hopefully something good, but possibly something bad, or even something terrible. The Celexa kept the worst of my anxiety backstage, but even so, I couldn't relax.

I'd brought Jane Austen to read, a good choice for the middle of May, but (as I found out) a poor choice for a waiting room. My jumpy brain couldn't tolerate her long-winded sentences. To wit: Each of them seemed to have, although this may very well be an exaggeration, at least a dozen commas each, making it exceedingly difficult reading for a woman like myself, who loved Austen and had nothing against commas, but who knew that, in the very moment, a key variable in her son's future was being deciphered, and that her life might get easier as a result, or harder, or perhaps remain the same, which could be a relief or a disappointment, depending on what she compared it to.

After reading the same sentence four or five times, I closed the book and looked around. Right in front of me was an open door that led to a small, windowless room. Inside were a floral loveseat, a matching armchair, and a table holding a telephone and a box of Kleenex. A room to receive Bad News. How bad did it need to be to merit privacy? If Thomas's hearing loss was found to be progressive, dooming him to eventual deafness, would the ENT direct me to the floral loveseat?

I was flipping through an old *People* magazine and trying to keep my foot from tapping the floor incessantly when the doctor appeared.

"Everything went fine," he said, sitting down next to me. "You'll be pleased to know that both of Thomas's ears showed some improvement."

He opened his notepad and drew a graph, like he had the first time. "The right ear registered sound at twenty-five decibels. This is considered normal for adults. Children typically register sound at twenty decibels, but twenty-five is still within normal range." He drew another line on the graph. "The left ear still has some hearing loss, but the degree has changed from moderate to mild for all but one of the frequencies we tested."

I tried to keep calm, but it was tough. "So would you consider hearing aids necessary?"

He shook his head. "Completely optional."

Yes! Instantly I felt twenty pounds lighter. I couldn't hold back a huge grin.

The doctor smiled back, but his eyes were sober. "Mrs. Soper, Thomas still has the central auditory dysfunction we detected in January. We'd hoped it was simply a function of his immature nervous system, since he was only a few weeks past his due date at the time. But since the abnormality hasn't resolved itself, it's important that we explore some possible causes."

I stopped smiling. "Like what?"

"Sometimes CAD is caused by pressure on the auditory nerve." He paused. "I recommend an MRI exam to look for growths in the brain that might be causing such pressure."

"Wait—you mean tumors?"

He nodded. "It's important to rule this out before considering other possible causes."

Brain cancer. My body went numb, as if flooded with lidocaine. My eyes strayed to the open door, and the floral couch, and the windowless wall that absorbed unspeakable words.

Dawn broke with the pink light of May as we arrived at Radiology. A nurse directed us to an exam room, where we waited in the chilly silence. Thomas was wide awake. I dangled toys to distract him from his empty stomach—his favorite was the bright turquoise Whoozit, with its wide, red smile.

Ever since the ABR two weeks before, Reed and I had been in a holding pattern, unable to think much or feel anything. We didn't talk about what the MRI might reveal or what the results might mean. When I left for the hospital he stayed home with the other kids, at my suggestion—I wanted them to have the security of a parent in the house, and I wanted to focus solely on Thomas. But even so, I strictly regulated my thoughts. I wouldn't let myself relive the death scenarios still lurking in my consciousness. I wouldn't let myself consider that our time with Thomas might be running out already.

The nurse entered to give Thomas a physical. As she checked his blood pressure, the only sound in the room was Thomas's wheezy breathing. The nurse looked at me with concern. "His breathing is noisy," she said.

"Yes, I made that clear when we scheduled the procedure. His breathing is always noisy. It's normal for him."

"We can't sedate him if he's ill."

My voice sharpened. "He's not ill. He always sounds like this." We'd already waited two unbearable weeks for this appointment—further delay meant more time for problems to escalate, more time for Reed and me to wait in hellish limbo.

The nurse looked skeptical as she left the room, but she returned fifteen minutes later to insert an IV. Strange to say I was relieved to see the IV kit, but I was. It meant the show would go on.

The nurse jabbed Thomas's wrist. He yelled. She jabbed again and looked at me apologetically. "His veins are like rubber—they bend and move away when the needle touches them. I'll have to keep trying."

I nodded and bent close to Thomas's ear. "Hang on, buddy. Hang in there. We'll be done soon." I held him still as he screamed.

The nurse sighed and shook her head. "I'll be right back." She returned with another nurse, wielding a tiny blue flashlight like the one from the NICU. I closed my eyes and stiffened every muscle as I gripped Thomas's shoulders and held them down. An accomplice to the crime. It took all six of our hands to get the job done.

Once the nurses left I rocked Thomas in the glider and sang in his little ear, swinging swiftly back and forth, trying to move as far away from the moment as we could. In an hour it would all be over. The exam would be done, the IV removed, the truth known.

The door opened. My eyes opened, expecting a nurse summoning us to the MRI room. But it was a doctor. Without saying anything he lifted his stethoscope and started listening to Thomas's heart and lungs.

"I'm the radiologist on call today," he said. "Given the noisiness of Thomas's breathing, I recommend rescheduling the procedure for a date when we can have a respiratory therapist on hand. That way we can use a ventilator for breathing support."

I shook my head. "I told the scheduling nurse about the breathing noise. She didn't say anything about needing a ventilator. I can't believe I'm hearing about this *now*."

"I'm sorry about that. But Thomas's safety is what matters here."

I glared at him. "And that's exactly what I'm concerned about. When's your next appointment?"

"Well, we only have a respiratory therapist in the unit once a month. If this month's date is already booked, you'll need to wait until the following month."

A month or more? "You've *got* to be kidding me. We're here to check for brain tumors—there's no way we're going to wait that long." I'd never been so blunt with a doctor before. It felt amazingly good.

His eyes narrowed. "Mrs. Soper, if Thomas goes into respiratory distress while under sedation, he will be in intensive care overnight, and perhaps for several days. I'm giving my professional recommendation that you reschedule the procedure. If you decide to proceed with the sedation, you'll be doing so at your own risk. The hospital will not be held liable for any consequences."

Of course. That's what mattered to them—liability. Thomas's safety was *their* safety. This guy didn't care about Thomas, only himself.

He waited for my decision. Risk pressed on me from both sides. If we went ahead, Thomas might end up hospitalized for days, and there might even be long-term consequences for his lungs. Yet if we waited and Thomas did have a tumor, it could grow larger and more dangerous before the MRI appointment. This could be a life-or-death choice.

The answer was clear to me, and I knew Reed would agree. I looked straight at the doctor. "We're doing the test today. I accept responsibility for the outcome."

He gave a curt nod. "We'll have you sign a release form."

"Fine." He left the room, and I tried to settle myself down. I didn't want to freak Thomas out with my angry vibes.

Five minutes later I followed the nurse to the imaging room, with Thomas in my arms. The MRI machine waited like a beast with a huge, round mouth. The technician helped me position Thomas on its flat, protruding tongue while the nurse connected a syringe to his IV line. "This should knock him out," she said as she pushed the plunger.

Within seconds Thomas's eyes closed. He turned his head to the side and grew still. "There he goes," the tech said. But just as she began strapping him down, he turned his head again, and then again. He lifted one arm and waved it, as if in protest. Then his eyelids fluttered.

"We can give him a few more ccs," the nurse said. "We wanted to stick to the minimum dose, but it doesn't seem to be working."

I nodded. Another syringe, another push. We waited. The low, rumbling growl of the machine drowned out all other sound in the room. After a few minutes Thomas was still partly conscious.

The nurses caught my eye. "There's a second anesthetic we can give, but we'd hoped to avoid it because it suppresses respiration rate. Do you want him to have it?"

"If he's not completely still, you can't do the test, right?"

The tech nodded.

"Then there's no question here. Give him the other drug."

After the third injection Thomas finally passed out. I checked the monitors: His numbers looked good. The tech fastened the straps, and I watched the machine's tongue slide slowly into its hungry mouth. "We'll let you know when he's finished," she said.

As I walked away from the imaging room I heard the machine's growl become a loud roar.

"Can I get you anything?" the nurse asked. "Some juice or soda?"

I shook my head. I was incredibly thirsty, but if I drank something I'd eventually have to use the restroom, and I didn't want to leave Thomas, not even for a few minutes. He was sleeping off the anesthesia. He'd had no problems during the MRI, and so far his oxygen saturation looked great, but the biggest hurdle remained.

"When will I know the test results?" I asked.

"The radiologist has to read the imaging. It might take a couple of days. He'll call your pediatrician with the results."

A couple of days. I didn't know how Reed and I could bear it. "But if the tech saw something really scary, she would've told the radiologist immediately, right? And he'd come and tell me?"

"Probably. I can't make any guarantees, though."

"I understand." I called Reed and gave him an update, then sat down to wait. An hour passed. I was telling myself we were out of the woods when someone appeared in the doorway—the radiologist. He walked straight toward me, his face blank.

I pulled back, sinking deep into the chair, so deep I nearly fell through the bottom, through the floor, into the waiting void. *Thomas will be leaving us.*

He stopped a few feet from my chair. "I read the scan," he said. Then suddenly, miraculously, he smiled. "It looks pretty good. No tumors. No growths."

I exhaled.

"Thomas does have some excess cerebral-spinal fluid around his brain. But at this point, I don't think it's a cause for concern. It might just be extra fluid to compensate for his smaller-than-normal brain size."

I flinched as I pictured a shrunken brain, but then relaxed again. *It doesn't matter. He's okay. Everything's okay.*

"In any case," the doctor continued, "I consider the findings benign. We'll do a neurology follow-up, but I don't expect any problems."

"Thank you. Thank you very much for letting me know so quickly."

He smiled again and walked away. I'd been wrong—he did care about Thomas. And me.

I sat with my hand on Thomas's chest, feeling it rise and fall in perfect rhythm. We'd be going home within hours. No overnight stay, no week in the hospital. The odds had fallen in our favor. But what if they hadn't? What if Thomas had ended up in the ICU, with damaged lungs and no tumor? Would that mean I'd made the wrong choice?

No. The validity of my decision wouldn't have changed. *Thomas might have a brain tumor*—that's what I'd known when we arrived in Radiology. And based on that knowledge, I needed to act.

I called Reed again to tell him the happy news. Then, with the nurse's help, I lifted Thomas from the bed and settled back into the chair. The nurse brought a warm blanket and tucked it around us, leaving an opening for the various tubes and wires still attached to Thomas. I closed my eyes and held him tight.

Summer

From my bedroom I heard the sliding door in the kitchen open, followed by little feet running into the house. "Shut the door!" I called. June heat and summer vacation were upon us. I didn't know which was harder: getting the kids to do a few pages in their workbooks every day, or making sure the cooled air stayed inside the house.

Ben stuck his head through the doorway. "Someone's here."

"Hello?" said a voice from the hall. Melody.

I'd never been so excited for a therapy visit. After saving the document I was working on, I picked Thomas up and went to greet her.

"Thomas's MRI was normal," I reported as she took off her shoes and sat on the living room floor.

"Fantastic! You must be *so* relieved."

I nodded. "And guess what? His ABR showed that his hearing has improved."

"That's great news." Melody got out her clipboard. "What were the numbers?"

"On the right, twenty-five decibels across the board. On the left, two thirties and one forty."

She wrote the results down. "Nice progress."

"Yeah—it's been so great not having to deal with the hearing aids."

She looked up in surprise. "What do you mean?"

Uh-oh. "Well, after the ENT gave me the test results he said aids were no longer necessary."

She cleared her throat. "Your doctor might not be taking into account that Thomas will already have some challenges with developing language because of the T21. For kids like Thomas a little boost in hearing can make a big difference."

My stomach sank. "So you think he still needs them?"

"If you want to optimize his language development, then yes, I recommend that you continue using them."

Crap.

She hesitated a moment. "I'm sorry—I can tell that wasn't what you wanted to hear."

That was putting it mildly. I already had the aids packed up in their red-and-yellow foam bag. I already had the whole issue scratched off the list. Silly me—I thought we'd finally gotten a break.

From his blanket on the floor, Thomas banged a rattle on the leg of my chair. Waves of heat came from the computer, tempting me to turn it off and head for the cool basement. But I needed information.

My Google search for *hearing loss Down syndrome* brought up links to clinical data and abstracts from medical journals. I scanned through a few pages, then moved on—what I wanted to find was a double-blind study showing whether kids just like

Thomas would really benefit from wearing aids, and if so, how much. Wishful thinking. The sites about hearing loss were geared toward typical children, so they did me no good—I already knew a kid without Down syndrome wouldn't need the aids to function normally. Finally, I clicked over to Downsyn.com and scanned the lists of topics under discussion. Nothing about hearing loss. I searched the archives—nothing helpful.

The forum had thousands of members. If I posted a question asking for advice or insight, I'd probably get at least a few replies. In order to do that, though, I'd have to register as a member of the forum. That meant choosing a username and password. Making myself known.

I wasn't ready.

That realization brought me up short. I'd been lurking at this site for months—why, after all this time and all this change, did I still want to stay invisible? These people didn't bite. In fact, they seemed awfully nice. In the current batch of posts on the main forum page, one mom reported on her daughter's ear tube procedure, another shared a link to a recent article about Down syndrome, another asked a question about potty training, another told a cute story about her kid—and in every case, at least a dozen other moms had chimed in with encouragement or advice. There were a half dozen congratulatory posts for kids who were celebrating birthdays. And a new member who introduced herself received a long trail of warm hellos.

But that was part of the problem. All the positive energy on the forum stirred up my unresolved questions about stereotypes and made me wonder where and how I fit into the picture. Friendly, caring, helpful—there had to be a reason for so much goodwill at this forum. Were these women *special* moms? I knew I wasn't. If anything, my reaction to Thomas's diagnosis proved my *un*-specialness. Maybe I was some kind of freak.

There was a pink cherub at the top of the forum home page; I wasn't sure what to make of that, either. Several of the members referred to their kids as angels. I doubted they meant it literally—from what I could tell, they used "angel" as a euphemism for "happy and loving." I wouldn't call Thomas an angel in any case; in my opinion, the word carried too much baggage. Yet sappy clichés were certainly better than ugly ones. If someone insisted on labeling Thomas, I'd take *angel* over *retard* any day.

But what about *special?* The kids' photos on the forum were pretty convincing. Lots of warm eyes and big grins, lots of unmistakable joy. But calling Thomas special seemed right and wrong at the same time. For one thing, he was so *normal.* He got dirty and stinky, hungry and tired. He smiled and laughed and played. He cried and raged. Sure, he had slanty eyes, and noisy breathing, and lower cognitive prospects. Yet he didn't seem to be essentially different than my other babies.

And then again, he did. There's something magical about any baby, but as Thomas grew his remarkable presence remained, obvious yet inscrutable. With my brain finally working again I was hungry for answers, and not just about hearing aids. But that meant talking with people. That meant coming out of the closet.

Alright then. I clicked "register" on the forum index page and filled in the blanks. Freak or not, I was a member of the club.

The backyard buzzed with the voices of a dozen preschoolers. It was day one of the playgroup Elizabeth and her best friend had set up for neighborhood kids. For $1 per kid per day, I had Matt and Sam out of my hair. I didn't tell Elizabeth that I would've paid three times that much.

From the front window I saw a familiar minivan pull up. Its door slid open, and a towheaded toddler streaked toward the house. I waved to his mom, a friend I hadn't seen for a year. She waved back, then got out of the van and headed for the house.

I opened the door as she approached. "Hey, long time no see!"

"I know! I thought I'd come in and say hi for a few minutes, if that's okay."

I was glad she'd showed up. I had a lot on my mind, and this friend was the philosophical type—perfect for a soul-searching chat.

"Sounds like Elizabeth has quite a crowd," she said as her son followed the noise to the backyard. I'm not sure where Elizabeth got her patience from. As a teenager you couldn't have paid me enough to run a playschool.

We sat down in the living room, where Thomas was playing on the floor with his baby gym. "You had a baby! I forgot you were even pregnant," my friend said.

"Yeah, and he's eight months old already. Well, six months, if you go by the preemie charts. Want to hear the crazy tale?"

She settled into her seat. "Go for it."

Bingo. I told her about Thomas's early arrival and how hard the winter had been, with the diagnosis and the feeding tube and the oxygen. And then the spring, with the hearing aids and the MRI. "So much has happened this year," I summed up. "Everything is finally calming down, as far as daily life goes, but I feel like I'm still in a state of flux. Like I'm becoming something different than I was. I don't know how to describe it, though."

My friend looked thoughtful. "You might be interested in something I've been reading about. Have you ever seen a Native American medicine wheel?"

I shook my head.

"It's a paradigm for the human life cycle. Each major stage of development is represented by a different animal, and the progression from one to the other symbolizes how people change over time."

I knew she'd have something for me.

"You start out as a mouse, because as a baby and child you're so small and vulnerable."

Cute. I loved mice, especially the poor little field mice our cat liked to mangle.

"Then, when you hit puberty you become a bear."

I rolled my eyes. "No explanation needed."

She grinned. "And once you have children, you're a bison. You're caring for the young and the elderly, so you need to be solid and sturdy."

Good metaphor. After seven pregnancies I pretty much looked like a bison.

"Then, when you're finally free of primary responsibility for others, you become an eagle, and you get to fly off and explore the world."

Cool. I had a recurring dream about flying that always left me exhilarated—maybe it would come true someday. "So, that's it? We die as eagles?"

She shook her head. "When you get really old you become a mouse again, because you need to be cared for, like a child. But this time, you're a mouse with wings."

"Wings?" I pictured a tiny brown field mouse, wrinkled and furry, with white butterfly wings.

"Yeah. After a lifetime of experience you've gained wisdom, so you're not tied to the earth like you used to be. The wings represent the transcendence of your spirit."

Transcendence.

I stared at my friend, suddenly unable to speak, though I had no clue what a flying mouse had to do with anything. The room grew still, except for Thomas chewing on a board book. From the backyard I heard Elizabeth leading a game of Red Light, Green Light. My friend watched my face, waiting.

"Wow," I finally said.

She nodded, as if she knew what I meant but couldn't explain it either.

Transcendence—that's what I sensed in Thomas. That ethereal presence in his slanty little eyes. A magnetism that drew us to him. Same, yet different. Special, yet not. He was just as small, as needy, as demanding, and as loveable as any little mouse. But somehow, he had his wings already.

We loaded the van assembly-line style with duffel bags, sacks of road-trip snacks, and Harry Potter books on tape (our ancient van had no CD player). The kids clambered in and started squabbling over window seats. I put Thomas in his car seat and buckled the straps tight. Eight hundred miles stretched between Salt Lake City and Portland, Oregon, where my in-laws lived. That meant fourteen hours of driving with seven children aged twelve and under.

But as we pulled out of the driveway I had to smile. Back in the fall and winter I wouldn't have guessed that, come July, we'd be heading off for vacation just like a normal family, with no unusual preparations and no medical equipment. I'd left the hearing aids at home because I couldn't bear the thought of fiddling with them on vacation. Everything in Thomas's duffel bag—diapers, bottles, formula, onesies, toys—was typical baby stuff. (Although I'd never brought formula on road trips with my other babies. I would just lean over the car seat at feeding time, providing free entertainment for the truckers peering through the van windows.)

Once the kids had settled down with pillows and snacks and the first story tape had begun, I relaxed in my seat next to Thomas and thought about my big new idea: a book. I'd been reading a beautiful anthology titled *You Will Dream New Dreams*, a collection of personal essays written by parents of children with disabilities, and I wanted to create something similar that focused solely on Down syndrome. The parenting guides out there were hardly encouraging, and while they might offer some useful clinical information, they couldn't shed much light on what it was like to raise a child with Down syndrome, what it meant, how it felt. Doctors and therapists couldn't know those things. Only parents could.

Moving north along the Wasatch front, I handed Thomas toys to play with until his eyelids drooped. Once he was asleep I climbed over the piles of stuff and into the passenger seat. Reed reached for my hand. "Think we'll make it in one piece?" I asked.

"I don't like our chances," he said with a wry smile. We'd made the drive several times before, and something always seemed to go wrong—car trouble, or weather trouble, or kids who wouldn't use the stinky toilets at the rest stops.

It didn't take long to find out what this trip's mishap would be. We stopped for dinner at McDonald's in Boise, Idaho; I was distributing Happy Meals to the little kids when Andrew came up to me, looking pale. "I'm cold," he said.

I ignored the little red flag that popped up in my head. The air-conditioning was blasting, and I had goose bumps myself. "Why don't you eat out front? That's where Ben and Elizabeth are," I said. He took his food outside—the chicken tenders he'd been begging for over the past hundred miles—but after a few minutes he came back in. "I'm not hungry. I don't feel well," he said. He was shivering. I touched his forehead: warm.

Reed and I looked at each other, silently conferring about whether we should keep driving. "I've got some Tylenol in the car," I finally said, and he nodded.

We drove until it got dark and then pulled into the parking lot of the nearest motel. Reed walked in the office to pay but walked out a few seconds later. "They're full," he said.

There were three other motels in the same area, connected by parking lots. When he walked out of the second office, shaking his head, I was confused. It was a Friday night, so crowds were to be expected, but we'd never had trouble getting rooms before. Then again, the Fourth of July was fast approaching. We'd never traveled on a holiday weekend before.

"We should've made reservations," I told Reed when he got back in the van.

"Well, hopefully we'll find a vacancy somewhere," he said, looking doubtful.

It soon became a game. We'd pull up to a motel and the kids would cheer Reed on as he headed to the office. When he'd walk out again we'd all groan. Other places had NO VACANCY signs in the office windows, and we'd boo as we drove past.

After a dozen tries Andrew got worried. "Will we ever find a place to sleep?"

"Of course we will," I said, although I was beginning to worry, too. Reed turned on the radio and found a station playing Latino rap. (In Idaho. Who knew?) He cranked up the volume and the kids all started dancing in their seats, laughing along with the rapid-fire Spanish. But half an hour later, we still hadn't found a room, and we'd reached the end of the commercial area in the city.

"Next town's only twenty miles," Reed said. "Let's keep moving." The kids kept dancing until the radio station turned to static. Then everyone got quiet. Andrew was moaning in the backseat. I felt his forehead: hot.

There were no vacancies in the next town, or the next. Christine started to cry. Reed was tense. Matt and Sam fell asleep in their car seats, heads lolling at sharp angles. Finally, at 2 a.m. we found a couple of vacant rooms in a battered old building somewhere over the Oregon-Idaho border. The two rooms, joined by a door, were worn and smelly. But they had beds.

The big kids took one room, and Reed and I took the other with the little boys. After settling Thomas into a nest of blankets on the floor, I collapsed next to Reed on one of the lumpy mattresses. Matt and Sam, who'd had a good nap, started bouncing on the other.

Reed groaned and turned on his side, pulling a pillow over his head. My temples pounded with stress—we had one problem solved, but Andrew was burning up in the other room, and chances were the kids would start falling like dominoes. Actually, that's exactly what I wished Matt and Sam would do.

"Guys, cool it," I warned.

But they only bounced harder, giggling like maniacs. "Mom!" Sam called. "We're in the show-and-tell!"

Reed started shaking with laughter under the pillow. I covered my mouth and laughed hard (the last thing we needed was Thomas waking up to join the party). It was just too ridiculous, Sam's uncanny terminology. This trip. Our family. Life in general. Especially the months since Thomas was born, which began with a slumber party even more absurd than this one. As Sam bounced off the bed to explore the minifridge in the corner, I lay back on the scratchy pillow and closed my eyes, glad to know that even the craziest rides eventually come to a resting place.

When we reached Portland the following afternoon, Andrew was still running a fever, and Matt and Sam had the chills. My mother-in-law, Nancy, got the boys comfortable while Reed unpacked the van. I tried putting Thomas on the floor to play, thinking he'd like to stretch after all that time in the car, but he started crying immediately. I picked him up and pressed my cheek against his.

"Thomas has it, too," I said to Reed when he came in.

He shook his head. "Let's just hope you're not next." Yeah, he'd better hope, or he'd be the one playing nurse.

The next morning I felt fine—my mom-immunity was holding firm. Andrew's fever was gone. But Christine wrapped herself in a thick fleece blanket and curled up on the couch. Nancy and I stayed behind with her and Thomas while everyone else headed for the water park.

As Christine slept I sat in the rocking chair, cradling Thomas's hot body against my shoulder and reading the *Dreams* anthology. So far I'd read stories about children with cerebral palsy, autism, and Down syndrome, as well as relatively rare genetic disorders like cri-du-chat syndrome, Angleman's syndrome, and Trisomy 18. The authors spoke with candor, sharing experiences and emotions both wrenching and uplifting. No trite platitudes to be found.

Nancy came in and asked me what I was reading. I held the book up so she could see the cover. "These stories are amazing," I said. "So many parents are dealing with extreme challenges, and for the most part nobody knows. I had no idea, until Thomas came along. It reminds me of being sick during pregnancy, all day, every day, and suddenly realizing there are thousands of people out there with chronic pain or health problems."

Nancy nodded. "Until something similar happens to you, it's easy to overlook the struggles of others. That really impressed me when we were taking care of the boys." She and my father-in-law had cared for two of their grandsons, Reed's sister's children, for nine years. At an age when she should've been flying eagle-style,

Nancy had begun the bison years all over again, nurturing two young children with various emotional and cognitive challenges while also teaching full-time *and* completing graduate school so she could keep her job.

"I don't know how you did it," I said.

She shrugged. "I don't know either, but I'm so glad Don and I made it work. It changed us both. We learned a lot about acceptance, a lot about compassion."

My throat tightened. "When Thomas was born I realized how prejudiced I was toward people with disabilities," I confessed. "Even kids. I can't believe how small and hard my heart was."

"I know what you mean," she said. "I've felt the same way. I'm a lot more sensitive now to kids in my classrooms who have learning disabilities, or behavior problems." She thought for a moment. "It's especially hard for kids whose disabilities are hidden. They look like average kids, but they're not, and people expect them to meet impossible standards of performance." She paused again. "At least with Down syndrome, there are visual cues. People will cut Thomas some slack, and cut you some slack, too."

I'd been thinking the opposite—at least kids who looked "normal" weren't slammed with stereotypes at first glance. But I thought of all the stares Jen had to deal with during Jake's outbursts. Sometimes she got so fed up she stared right back and said, *He's autistic, okay?* Nancy was right—people would automatically have lower expectations for Thomas. That could be a blessing *and* a curse.

Christine stirred under her blanket. "Looks like she might wake up soon," Nancy said. "Would you like me to get another dose of Tylenol ready?"

"That would be great. Thanks." Thomas was fast asleep on my shoulder. Slowly I stood up, then laid him on a quilt Nancy had spread on the floor.

After covering his legs with a corner of the quilt, I sat down and picked up my book again. I'd reached the middle of the anthology, a chapter called "Dreams." I read about a first-time mother who, at age twenty-eight, gave birth to a daughter with a rare genetic condition. When the doctor told her there was a chromosomal abnormality, she asked if it was Down syndrome.

No, the doctor said. *It's something much more serious.*

I started crying as I imagined the scene—chilly hospital room, nervous parents, solemn doctor with devastating news. It wasn't just a story. It *really happened* to a living, breathing couple. The wife, devastated, sobbed in her own mother's arms, recounting all the dreams she'd had for this daughter. College. Marriage. Children. Things I'd wished for all of my children without even realizing.

Then came the grandmother's gentle response. "I know that thinking about all these things is very painful right now, but you have to remember that those are your dreams, sweetheart, not hers. Jesse will have dreams of her own. They might not be like those of other children, but they will be hers, just the same."

I was a mess when Nancy returned. "Read this," I said.

She set the syringe of medicine down. When she finished the story she was crying, too.

We were both quiet. I rocked myself in the chair, watching Thomas sleep. All this time I'd been thinking about myself: What did I want for Thomas? What should I want? What was the best way to get what I wanted? I'd never considered what *Thomas* might want. Worse, I'd never even considered that he'd be capable of wanting.

Thomas was better the next day. Reed stayed with Christine while the rest of us went to church. After we arranged ourselves on a long pew I took Thomas out of his car seat, knowing people would be looking at us because we were visitors. I felt as if I were walking into school with a new haircut.

Once Thomas was settled on my lap, I noticed the ward members sitting on the row in front of ours: two men and a woman. Both of the men appeared to have mental disabilities. One had dark hair that was parted and carefully combed, yet greasy. The other had red hair and a malformed face. He hunched on the pew, rocking himself slightly. As we sang the opening hymn I studied the woman. Fiftyish, floral dress, pink lipstick. I figured she was a kindly volunteer who brought these men to church each week, like the caretakers who shepherd small groups of adults with disabilities through the shopping mall.

When the deacons stood to pass the sacrament, a hush fell over the chapel. Everyone was quiet except Thomas. Dressed in the tiny Ralph Lauren oxford that Kate had sent him, he lounged on my lap and studied his hands with rapt fascination, making periodic squeals of delight. Casually I looked around to see if anyone seemed annoyed. Nobody did. Then I looked straight ahead at the red-haired man, who was examining *his* hands. His fingers were pale, soft, and twisted; his wrists bent at odd angles. He wiggled his fingers in front of his face and made a sound somewhere between a laugh and a moan that split the silence in the chapel.

Birds of a feather. He and Thomas were decades apart in age, but their behavior was the same. It was cute coming from a baby, but not from an adult. What if Thomas still acted like an infant in twenty years? What if he needed me to comb his hair for him every morning, tie his shoes, help him eat breakfast? What if he depended on me for the rest of my life?

The thought didn't terrify me the way it used to. But it made me sad. I might be a bison forever, or an eagle who couldn't fly. And what would Thomas be—an overgrown mouse?

The red-haired man let out a loud squeal. The woman put her arm around his shoulder, leaned close . . . and kissed his cheek.

She wasn't some charitable volunteer. She was his mother.

Ben vomited a huge quantity of root beer all over Nancy's white wool carpet right before we got in the van to drive home. My mind churned along with his stomach as we crossed Oregon and Idaho and finally the Utah border. I knew I had to start compiling the Down syndrome anthology as soon as possible. I felt the same creative urge that had sparked each of my pregnancies, except the medium would be words rather than cells. I even had a title in mind: Gifts.

What a wonderful gift you've been given.

As soon as we unloaded the van and the kids were joyfully reunited with their toys and video games, I booted up the computer and drafted submission guidelines. I had no clue how to compile an anthology. I'd edited dozens of personal essays for *Segullah,* but a book would be a whole different animal. I really wanted to do it, though. More than that—I *needed* to do it. Watching that mother kiss her squealing red-haired son had clinched the deal.

I packed the diaper bag and loaded Thomas into his car seat for our trip to the pediatrician (thankfully, I could leave the little boys home with Elizabeth). July was almost over, and Thomas needed his nine-month checkup. Nine months—they seemed more like years. So much had changed.

Like Thomas's size, for one thing. He was getting harder and harder to lug around. As I made my way down the concrete steps from our kitchen into the garage, the car seat full of Thomas shifted on my arm, pulling me to the side, and I nearly fell. I didn't remember the other kids being so heavy and cumbersome when I carried them in their car seats.

Then I realized why. I didn't carry my other nine-month-olds in their car seats, because they could sit up by then. On shopping trips I carried them on my hip and plopped them in the child seat of the cart without a second thought. But Thomas couldn't sit up on his own yet—when I tried propping him in the cart, all it took was a curve around the end of the aisle to knock him sideways.

He'll be slow. I knew that. But at the same time, I didn't. It was one thing to hear, or read, or talk about future delays. It was another thing to see them happening.

My friend Jen had warned me. *Just when you think you're over the diagnosis, it hits you again*, she said. Kate had warned me, too: *There will be other steps.* I hadn't really believed them; I thought I didn't care anymore whether Thomas was delayed. But I did care. Standing in the stifling heat of my garage, halfway between the door to the kitchen and the door to the van, I cared very much.

A wave of emotion welled up in my chest and broke, flooding me with sadness. *Thomas has Down syndrome. He can't sit up yet. He's slow, he's slow, he's slow.* The thoughts caught me in their heady swirl, threatening to knock me over and pull me under. But then a different thought escaped from the tumble and popped to the surface. *So what?*

I stood very still as the words echoed through my mind. *So what? So what? So what?* And as quickly as the wave had come it moved on, leaving me dripping wet but okay. Relieved, I opened the van door and heaved Thomas's seat into place.

At the pediatrician's office the doctor walked into the exam room with yet another med student in tow. "I have a medical student working with me today—"

"Fine," I sighed, before he asked. The parade of observers was annoying, but I vowed not to take it personally. We would pay our debt to practical medicine, as long as it didn't get out of hand.

The student stood deferentially in the corner during the physical exam. Thomas, on the other hand, kept rolling over right when the doctor needed him to be still.

"He's a wiggly one, isn't he?" the doctor said, surprised. "Down's kids are usually pretty relaxed."

Down's kids. I hated the term—it reminded me of "Jerry's kids." I cringed as I pictured a bunch of almond-eyed children gathered adoringly around John Langdon Down, the syndrome's namesake. Thomas wasn't Down's kid. He was *my* kid.

So much for not taking things personally.

I seethed silently as the doctor finished the exam. "Well, medically, he looks great. Really great." He picked up Thomas's file. "Is he sitting up yet?"

I shook my head.

"Eating from a spoon?"

"No. We're going to try soon, though."

As he kept asking questions I felt worse and worse. Suzanne was always so enthusiastic and encouraging about Thomas's development. I hadn't realized he was so far behind.

He's slow, slow, slow.

So what, what, what?

After the doctor finished making notes, he handed me some photocopied handouts. "These will tell you what typical nine-month-olds are doing. Thomas's development is right around six months, so these will let you know what to look for in the future."

Whatever. I took the papers and turned to stuff them into the diaper bag. When I turned back, the student was standing close to the exam table, and the doctor was gesturing toward Thomas's face. Then he turned Thomas over to expose the back of his neck.

Thomas started to cry, tired and hungry and sick of being handled. The men ignored him. "Excuse me," I said as I edged between them and picked Thomas up. They looked at me in surprise. "He's done," I said.

Thomas was agitated all afternoon from the poking and prodding. I spread his quilt on the floor, but he didn't want to roll around. Christine brought him his favorite toy—a plastic fishbowl that lit up and played music when he put things inside it—but he didn't want to play. His favorite Raffi CD helped, but he still wanted to be held. I cuddled him and stroked his hair, sang to him, carried him on my shoulder while I made dinner. Poor kid. It wasn't fair.

But by bedtime I was maxed out. Putting seven children to bed is like playing that whack-a-mole game, where you hit one critter on the head with a mallet and three more pop up. It's hard even with two parents playing. But Reed had a community meeting about some transportation project, and Thomas was so heavy, and I was so tired. And the kids kept yammering (why do they always have everything to say in their last five minutes of consciousness?). Somewhere around nine o'clock, I stopped feeling sorry for Thomas and started feeling sorry for myself.

By the time Reed came home I'd moved from whiny to angry to livid. As soon as he sat down I plunked Thomas on his lap and escaped downstairs to switch some laundry. The wet jeans in the washer snagged on the edges of the agitator. I yanked them loose and shoved them in the dryer, my mind burning with resentment. Being a mom was hard enough without Thomas's extra issues.

I could hear him crying through the floorboards.

Major guilt. I'd never gotten mad at him before, and that was one milestone I'd hoped to avoid. It happened sooner or later with each of my babies, that terrible, stomach-sinking moment when I lost my temper for the first time, but it felt even worse with Thomas. I'd already failed him in so many other ways. And the pity factor was still in play—don't get mad at the disabled baby! And besides, weren't moms of kids with Down syndrome supposed to be above petty things like resentment?

I breathed for a few minutes before going back upstairs, sobered and penitent. But as I drew closer to the noise my teeth clenched hard. *Why can't he just chill out on his blanket like he usually does?*

I stopped cold. So that's why I was mad at him: I expected him to be easy.

Happy.

Angelic.

I couldn't believe it. I'd bought into the very stereotype I claimed to shun. And even worse—I did so because I wanted compensation. *If he won't be smart, he'd better be happy.*

My anger dissolved. I walked straight to the bedroom, where Reed was rocking Thomas. "I don't know what to do," Reed said. "I can't calm him down."

"Here." I held out my arms. Thomas turned toward my voice, still crying. As soon as he saw me he chuckled with relief, *heh heh heh*, hiccupping the last few sobs in his throat.

Reed laughed. "He sure knows his mom."

Oh, yes. He will know you.

Tears came, swift and smooth. I lifted Thomas from Reed's lap and snuggled him against my shoulder. Then I closed my eyes and swayed him back and forth, whispering apologies in his ear until his body relaxed against mine.

Christine pulled open the sliding door and stuck her head through. "Mom, come outside!"

I hesitated. Whenever I played in the yard with the kids, I got suckered into piggyback rides and rough-and-tumble games until I was completely worn out. It was always fun once I got out there, but I usually resisted at first, as if the kids were trying to pull me out of my very skin.

"We haven't done workbooks yet," I said, like a true party pooper.

She sighed. "Do we *have* to?"

"Yep. Go get your brothers." The more resistant they got, the more determined I got. The program had room for only one-third of the students who qualified, so placement was pretty competitive. I wasn't going to drop the ball again.

A minute later Christine and the boys shuffled into the kitchen, looking glum. "Have a seat," I said with fake cheeriness. I handed out the workbooks and pencils while Thomas watched from his bouncy seat on the floor.

"Mom, *why*?" Ben groaned, as if we'd never discussed it.

"You know why."

"But it's *summer.* It'd be better to practice right before the test, not *now.*"

Arguments lined up in my mind. *The more you practice, the better your chances of making it. You've got to beat hundreds of other kids. You've got to work hard to get what you really want.* But when I opened my mouth, the words wouldn't come.

"Don't talk back," I finally said. "Just do what you're supposed to do."

He looked straight at me. "This is *dumb.*"

I looked down so he couldn't read my face. I felt four pairs of eyes were watching me.

"You guys can go outside for now," I said, needing space to think.

They bolted out the sliding door. I handed Thomas a different toy and sighed. Of course Ben was right. Doing math drills in July was dumb—period. So what should be my next step? It seemed stupid to make them study, but if I gave in, Ben would have the satisfaction of outwitting me. I'd lose major face as the omnipotent mom. And besides, sometimes kids need to do things they don't want to do, for their own benefit.

But was this workbook business really for *their* benefit?

The answer sat plainly on the kitchen table, next to the #2 pencils. *I* was the one who wanted the kids in that program. I wanted them to be labeled as gifted. This was all about *my* dream, not theirs—my dream to have really smart kids.

The dream Thomas had compromised.

I turned away from his bouncy seat, stung by truth: I thought it was okay for him to be delayed, as long as all the other kids were advanced. More compensation.

Christine knocked on the sliding door. "Come play!" she called. "And bring Thomas out, too!"

I couldn't refuse. I lifted Thomas in his seat and carried him out the door, across the deck, and onto the grass. Usually our lawn is yellowish by midsummer; even daily watering can't combat the July heat that sucks the ground dry. But unusual summer rains, which had come the previous few days, had turned it rich green.

"Will you push me on the swing?" Matt asked.

"Me too!" Sam said.

"Okay." I set Thomas's seat next to the swing set.

"Hey, I want a turn!" protested Christine as Matt and Sam claimed both swings.

My hackles rose as the three of them started to bicker and push each other out of the way. But once I calmed Christine down and started swinging the boys, I felt better. I pushed one, then the other, alternating arms. They laughed and shouted as they swung higher and higher, their feet seeming to touch the mountain peaks that stretched across the eastern horizon.

Once Christine got her turn she was in a jolly mood. "Let's play ring-around-the-rosy!" she said. Thomas watched as we held hands and began circling and singing. Elizabeth joined us, then Matt and Sam. We circled again and again, making up nonsense versions of the nursery rhyme until it muddled beyond recognition. Then we dropped the words altogether. *La la la la la,* we sang loudly, still circling.

Ben and Andrew busted into the middle, forcing our arms apart. "Come on, guys, if you want to play then hold hands and follow along," I said. The circle stretched wider. As we started moving again a light rain began to fall.

"Keep dancing!" Elizabeth shouted.

"Wait," I said, letting go of hands so that I could move Thomas's seat under the Japanese plum bush. We joined hands again and circled, faster and faster, still singing, probably scaring the neighbors. The rain pelted our scalps with nickel-size drops. We slipped on the wet grass, and the circle collapsed. Thomas was nice and dry under the bushy boughs of the shrub, but we were completely drenched.

"Sprinklers!" Christine shrieked, pointing at the spraying water that had begun to fan from the sprinkler heads at the bottom of the grassy slope, mixing with the shower from the skies.

"Mom, watch me!" Andrew shouted as he barreled down the incline, jumping over a sprinkler head and dousing himself with its spray. The others laughed and followed. I looked at Thomas, still dry and happy in his cozy spot, and decided it was a perfect time to call uncle and head inside for a change of clothes.

"C'mon, Mom!" Ben said as he kicked off his flip-flops and ran down the hill.

I paused for a long moment, standing on the brink of change. Move forward or shrink backward—the choice was mine, and the consequences would reach far beyond our backyard game.

I unstrapped my sandals and stepped gingerly onto the grass, as if I was setting foot on earth for the first time. My toes curled from the cool wetness. Elizabeth and Andrew and Christine started chanting. "Mom! Mom! Mom!"

I started to run, not caring if I looked like a stoned elephant. Downward momentum boosted my speed. I was flying. The sprinkler head jutted up before me; I pushed with my foot and hurtled over it, landing clumsily on the other side.

All the kids cheered. I took a deep bow. Then I trudged back up the hill toward Thomas, my clothes dripping wet, my skin washed clean.

A perfect summer evening: The sun drew close to the Oquirrh Mountains on the west side of the valley. Shadows fell across the softball diamond. A light breeze blew, dry and mild.

The diamond held about twenty men and women from our ward, all wearing baseball caps with brims pulled low against the sinking sun. Reed stood in center field. I sat in the aluminum bleachers behind the backstop with a few other women who had little ones to tend, or didn't want to huff and puff from one base to the next. Matt and Sam scampered around the park's play area; Christine rested in the grass, picking clover. The big kids had opted to stay home. Thomas stood on my lap, facing me—a favorite pastime of his these days. I had to hold his armpits tightly, though, because without warning he'd bend his knees and topple over.

My two companions on the bleachers had rounded pregnant bellies. Within minutes of sitting down together, we started swapping stories. One told us about her recent adventures at the hospital, where she received IV fluids and drug infusions to treat severe nausea and vomiting. The other told her wild tale of almost giving birth in her car last time she was pregnant. We sounded like a bunch of crusty old veterans telling war tales.

The softball teams switched positions for a new inning. Reed picked up a bat and started swinging to warm up for his turn. All of a sudden he looked fifteen years younger—the wiry, quick guy I had fallen in love with. I hooted something about his backside just to rankle him. My seatmates laughed, and a couple of the men on Reed's team turned and looked over their shoulders.

Over the next few innings we kept chatting about the crazy things mothers go through. "You'd think it would get easier with practice, but Thomas's birth was the worst," I said. "From the way the doctors talked, I figured he was so small he'd slip right out with the first strong contraction. But he was positioned posterior. I thought I'd never be able to get him out. And the nurse kept yelling at me to push." Without warning my eyes got teary. The memory felt so fresh. "I'd never felt so desperate. After he came out I just couldn't stop crying. I knew right then that I would never have a baby again. I could never put myself through that again."

The women sat quietly as I sniffled the tears back. I felt more than a little silly, crying at a softball game, but also relieved. All year I'd wondered if my baby-hunger would return after Thomas's traumatic birth slipped into the past. But as I spoke the memory aloud, I knew I would never bear a child again. It was over.

Thomas squirmed on my lap, tired of standing up but not interested in sitting still. "Good thing you got such a cute one, since he's your last," one of the women said.

I smiled and stood, needing some space. Christine had joined Matt and Sam on the play structure. I walked to the side of the softball diamond and squinted to see Reed chasing a fly ball way back in center field.

I turned around, sensing someone approaching from behind. "Hi, there," one of my neighbors said as she walked up. I didn't know her very well—her kids were college-age, so we didn't have a lot in common—but she was always friendly during our brief interactions.

For a while we made small talk about the game. As we talked she kept glancing at Thomas, then looking away. I wondered what she was thinking.

"Can I hold him?" she asked suddenly.

"Sure." I handed him over, and the woman lifted him to her shoulder. She bounced him gently and patted his back. "It's been a while since I've done this," she said, looking nervous.

"Oh, you're an old pro. It's like riding a bike."

"I hope so, because I'm going to have grandkids before long. This is good for me, in more ways than one."

Curious. I hoped she'd explain.

She waited a minute before speaking. "I haven't wanted to be near someone with Down syndrome for a long time. When I was young, a man with Down's assaulted me."

I clapped my hand to my mouth.

"I was walking home from school, and I had to pass this facility on the way. An institution. You know, back then, they locked people like that up."

I nodded, barely.

"Well, this guy got out somehow, and he jumped me when I was walking past. I'll never forget it."

"Did he rape you?" I whispered.

She shook her head. "Almost. He would've, but I kicked him real hard and ran away."

My skin crawled. As a kid I'd sometimes pictured Eddie forcing himself on me, trying to kiss me.

I put my hand on my neighbor's shoulder. "I'm so, so sorry."

She smiled a little. "It's funny. Ever since, I haven't been able to look at people like him." She nodded toward Thomas. "I couldn't stand seeing that face, you know? But it feels good to hold your little guy."

That face. I'd feared it, too, even my own son's face. And suddenly I knew one of the reasons why: I worried Thomas would grow up to be sexually aggressive. I worried he'd harass women, like Eddie did, or insist on touching them, like that Latino man at the care center. Or worse. Looking at Thomas, the fear seemed ridiculous—he was only nine months old, for Pete's sake—but even the man who attacked my neighbor was once a cute little baby. How did he come to be such an animal?

Because he was treated like one.

Yes. The horrors of institutional life were legendary. How desperate that man must've been, held prisoner, deprived of family life and normal social interaction. No wonder his sexuality and sense of boundaries were warped. By locking him up, and thousands of others like him, society created the very thing it feared.

Thomas squirmed in my neighbor's arms, wanting me again. "Thank you," she said as she handed him back.

"Thank *you*," I replied. "Thank you for confiding in me. And thank you for trying again." I bounced Thomas on my hip to show her what I meant.

She smiled wider, and nodded. Then she walked away through the lengthening shadows.

I hurried the kids down the hallway toward the chapel. We were running late, and I hated walking in after the service had started— besides the embarrassment, it was hard to find an open seat wide enough for all the Soper bottoms. Thankfully, one of the center pews was empty. As we sat down, one of the sisters leaned over from the row behind.

"Well, hello there, Thomas!" she said, reaching for his hand. He glanced at her and turned away.

"He's feeling shy today," I said apologetically. Clearly she'd been hoping for some enthusiastic response. This happened often: People approached Thomas with big smiles, as if he were a sure bet, but got only a cool glance in return.

To my relief, the sister took the snub in stride. "They're so sweet," she said, stroking Thomas's head. "I've known several Down's children over the years, and they're just full of love."

Just then, the chapel quieted as the bishop stood to begin the service. Good thing, because I didn't know how to respond to this sister. I knew she meant well—her words were sincere, her affection genuine—but it bugged me when someone referred to Thomas as "they," as if all people with Down syndrome shared one identity and consciousness, like the Borg on *Star Trek*. At least she didn't call him a "special spirit," like others did. Of course the label was meant as a compliment, but I couldn't see how it benefitted Thomas. His body and mind were already different—why did we have to include his soul? Putting him on a spiritual pedestal only separated him from the rest of us even more.

After the sacrament meeting another sister approached me. "Would you mind sitting with Matt's class during Primary?" she asked. Primary was the Sunday school for kids, which she helped coordinate. "The teacher had to take one of her children home sick."

That sounded good to me. Reed said he'd keep Thomas with him for the rest of church, so my hands would be free. Plus, although I was feeling more and more comfortable interacting with the adults in Sunday school, I preferred to sit with the kids. Especially when I had so much on my mind. I didn't want some well-meaning sister to make another comment that rankled me. (This time, I really didn't want to be rude.)

Summer

The folding chairs in the Primary room were arranged by age group. Matt was already seated with a few girls; I sat next to him at the end of the row. He smiled in surprise.

Aaron's mom pushed his wheelchair right next to me. "Hi, Aaron!" I whispered. He gave me a shy grin.

Guilt again. At the end of our playdate all those weeks ago, his mom and I had talked about maybe getting the boys together at our house or hers, but I'd never followed through. To be fair, she hadn't called me, either. Summer was a busy time. But I was also reluctant to force a friendship between Matt and Aaron. I wasn't entirely sure I should've set that first playdate to begin with, given my self-serving intent. Still, I wondered if Aaron felt hurt that we hadn't called again.

Most of the Primary hour was spent singing. I had to laugh as I listened to the kids try to carry a tune, particularly the littlest ones. A few were on-key, a few mumbled words in a tone-deaf monotone, and a few shouted, as if they were trying to wake God from a long nap. With all my tangled thoughts I really wasn't in the mood to sing along, but I did anyway. And as I sang my heart grew lighter and lighter, full of simple words about God and love, families and faith. When the final song of the hour drew to a close, Aaron leaned over in his wheelchair and rested the side of his head against my arm.

Four weeks after posting submission guidelines for *Gifts,* I had fifty submissions in hand and enough emotional energy to power several major appliances. That initial spark of creative desire had become a furnace, fed by the earnest, poignant stories that showed up in my inbox.

Mothers' stories. Each was different, and the same. Different family situations, different religious beliefs and political views, different financial and educational backgrounds, yet the same overwhelming love for a child with Down syndrome. But love wasn't all these mothers felt—at least, not at first. In story after story I read about fear, guilt, doubt, panic, anger, grief. Apparently I wasn't a freak after all, because contrary to popular belief, these women packed no halos. And for that matter, neither did their children.

So what was the deal? Ordinary moms, ordinary kids—yet there was something extraordinary happening in their families. I could see it in every story I reviewed, in every photograph I collected. And I could feel it in my own home. I felt it when Sam and Thomas lay side by side on my bed, patting each other's cheeks, and when Elizabeth fed Thomas spoonfuls of rice cereal like a proud mother, and when Christine draped a blanket over his sleeping body. I felt it when Ben and Andrew cuddled Thomas on their laps and sang to him. And when Matt jiggled his plastic fishbowl, triggering the lights and music that made him smile.

Love, yes. But a kind of sibling love I hadn't noticed with the other babies. I saw more than affection on the kids' faces. I saw peace, and wholeness, and marrow-deep contentment, as if the universe gone wrong had suddenly been set aright again.

That's how I felt, too.

Strange—peeling back all those layers of depression had released vitality within myself that I never knew existed, and yet I'd never been so calm, either. The Celexa played a part, of course; I'd been swallowing the bitter pills every morning for over three months. But I could tell the difference between the effects of the medication and the effects of living with Thomas. The pills afforded equilibrium: a clean, neutral room safe from the black drag of despair. Thomas provided a doorway from neutral into beautiful.

Summer

And so did the mothers' stories I read every day. Working at the computer, with Thomas playing on his blanket beside me, I was often filled with a sense of buoyancy, as if a strong yet gentle wind had carried me above myself. It reminded me of the flying dream I had every so often. The details changed slightly each time, but the basic scenario remained the same: I'm standing outside, looking up at the sky, wishing I could leave the earth behind. All of a sudden I realize I can. In fact, I always could—I just didn't know it. My faith ignites. Feet pressed against the earth, I push hard and lift into the air, borne by some unseen power. As I soar into the stratosphere, finally free, I wonder why I waited so long.

"There's Eric!" Matt said as I pushed the shopping cart toward the produce section. "Hi-ii!"

Eric waved as he walked past us, heading in the opposite direction. "Hi-ii!"

Matt and Sam giggled. Over our past few trips to the grocery store, they'd struck up a friendship of sorts with Eric. I was so glad their first memories of an adult with Down syndrome would be positive. And I was secretly proud of our little human-interest story: "Woman has baby with Down syndrome; kids befriend local bag boy."

Once our cart was full I stopped by the book table, where bestsellers were stacked in tidy rows. One title caught my eye: *The Year of Magical Thinking,* by Joan Didion, the renowned novelist and essayist. I flipped it over to find a black-and-white photo of a family: mother, father, child. From the jacket copy I learned that the author's husband had died suddenly at the very time their only child was critically ill. The author said the book described the "weeks and then months that cut loose any fixed idea I ever had about death, about illness . . . about marriage and children and memory . . . about the shallowness of sanity, about life itself."

I put the book in the cart, quickly, before I second-guessed myself. I didn't usually buy books at the grocery store. With nine people to feed, the budget was tight. But it wasn't every day I read a cover blurb that summed up my recent life in fewer than fifty words. I put my purse on top of the book—whether to hide it or hold it captive, I didn't know.

I'd been looking forward to seeing Eric at the registers, but when we got in line I didn't see him anywhere. Disappointed, I let a pimply adolescent boy bag the groceries but declined his offer of help out to the car. Then, on our way out of the store, we saw Eric gathering carts in the parking lot, just a few spaces away from our van. The boys called his name, and he turned and waved. When we reached our van he walked over to say hello.

"Hii-ii!" he said to Thomas.

Thomas smiled. "How old?" Eric asked, pointing at him.

"Nine months."

"I was really little, like that," he said. "My mom has pictures!"

"I'll bet you were pretty cute."

"Yeah, I was! I looked like him." He pointed at Thomas again. "I looked like him."

My breath caught for the slightest moment. "Yes. Just like him." I wondered if he knew why.

The little boys wanted to keep playing. "Hii-ii!" they shouted. Eric stepped closer, reached down, and started tickling the boys. They shrieked with glee. Eric beamed. He tickled them again and again. Matt looked panicky—he was laughing so hard he couldn't breathe. Eric kept tickling. With a flash of horror, I pictured myself in that plastic car with Eric's ruddy face looming over me, his hands tickling me.

"Eric, that's enough." I put my hand on his shoulder. He stopped immediately.

Matt looked like he was about to cry. "I don't *like* that."

My heart sank. Things had been going so well—I didn't want the boys to be scared of Eric. Then I got mad. We were trying to do the right thing here. Why did Eric have to screw it up?

Then I saw his face: anxious, and a bit confused. He didn't mean to cause any harm. Clearly he'd been taught about boundaries—he stopped right when I told him to. And Matt *had* been laughing.

I took a deep breath. "It's okay, Matt. Sometimes when we're having fun we don't notice when it's time to stop, but Eric understands now."

Matt nodded. Then he waved to Eric. "By-yye!"

Eric waved back. As he walked away I shook my head at myself: All that time I'd been thinking we were doing him a favor, when really it was the other way around.

I couldn't put the book down.

The night before New Year's Eve, Joan Didion was preparing dinner for herself and her husband of forty years. They'd just returned from visiting their adult daughter at the hospital—she was in a coma, induced in an attempt to save her life during complete septic shock. While the author mixed the dinner salad, a massive coronary took her husband's life. These were the first words she wrote after it happened:

> *Life changes fast.*
> *Life changes in the instant.*
> *You sit down to dinner and life as you know it ends.*
> *The question of self-pity.*

After reading half the book in one sitting, I walked around the house in a daze. I couldn't imagine losing Reed—and then postponing his funeral because our child was in a coma. I couldn't feel what the author felt. But I knew it was real. Just like the essays in the *Dreams* book, her experience didn't read like a sad newspaper article that tugged at my sympathies but remained, in the end, a story. I knew she had really lived this nightmare. She'd walked the hospital corridors; she'd breathed the oppressive air of the ICU. She'd lost a forty-year marriage in the middle of a dinnertime conversation, somewhere between a question and an answer. She'd left her husband's clothing in his closet for months, because when he returned—as he surely would—he'd need something to wear.

"Magical thinking" came from a mind bent by a blow, a mind so bent it couldn't absorb reality.

I went to the refrigerator to get Thomas a bottle. As I grasped the handle I looked at the rows of calendar squares, with their lines and numbers. Months before, I couldn't make any sense of them. I couldn't complete a simple phone call. Joan Didion wrote the wrong address on her husband's autopsy forms; because of the error, she didn't receive the report until he had been dead for eleven months. "Cognitive deficits," her doctor explained. Blankness, confusion, inability to think or speak clearly. A common byproduct of grief.

Grief.

It welled up so strong and fast I gasped aloud. All the grief I'd been holding captive since way back in October. It pulled me backward through days and weeks and months, back through summer's brightness, back through spring's awakening, back to that horrid room with walls papered in darkness and doubt. I cried, braced against the refrigerator door, feeling its cool surface against my forehead, awash in pain so keen I thought I might collapse. As the wave moved past, another began, and another, coming hard and fast like labor contractions, pulling me farther back in time. The NICU, with the too-small babies screaming, or silent. My hospital room, where I made desperate phone calls, trying to rid myself of reality. And finally, the delivery bed where it all started. A baby I didn't see, and two doctors with solemn eyes, and seven short words ending life as I knew it:

We think your son has Down syndrome.

I felt calm and quiet in the days that followed. For a short while grief had flowed so strong and pungent I could still taste it. But it had passed, at least for the time being. I felt like I'd vomited and vomited until my gut was blessedly empty, and only clean truth remained.

I wished I'd seen the truth sooner. I wished I'd known that mourning didn't mean failure of my faith or my mother-love. I wish I'd known that locking away grief made it dangerous. That trying to be strong would only make me weak. That no matter how hard I tried to be, I wasn't my mother.

My mother.

I found the phone and called her, my heart pounding. "Mom, I need to ask you something."

"Of course. What's on your mind?"

"It's about you. And it's personal."

She paused. "Kathy, you're my daughter. You can ask me anything."

I took a deep breath. "How did you stand it, all those years when we were struggling at home? I never saw you break down. I never even saw you cry. Where were your feelings?"

After a moment she spoke. "Where were my feelings? They were inside of me, sweetie, where they belonged."

"So you were sad, too? And mad, and scared? Because you never seemed that way, not even once."

"Yes, I felt all of those things." Her voice wavered. "But I had to be careful—I couldn't let myself fall apart. That's why I walked around like a zombie all the time."

"But it hurt so much," I said, crying again. The divorce with my father, the conflicts I had with my stepfather, the stress of our blended family—it hurt me so badly, and I'd thought it didn't hurt her. "All those times I was sad, and you were so calm. I thought you didn't care."

Mom started to weep. "Of course I cared. Of *course* I did. That's why I kept my feelings private—to protect you. I didn't want to burden you with *my* pain, Kathy. You had enough of your own."

I wiped my eyes and nodded to myself. I'd done the same thing for the same reason. But it backfired. *I'm sorry, Mom*—that was Ben's apology, and the quiver in Andrew's voice, and the defeat in Elizabeth's shoulders, and Christine's tears. By hiding my feelings, I made them ashamed of their own.

"I'm so, so sorry," Mom said. "I didn't mean to hurt you by keeping things to myself. That's the last thing I wanted."

"I know. And I'm sorry, too. I really am." More crying.

"Please, honey. Please don't apologize. It wasn't your fault."

"But it wasn't yours, either. You did the best you could—I know you did. You always did."

She didn't speak for a minute. I could hear her sniffling. "Thank you. That means the world to me." She cleared her throat. "And Kathy, I want you to listen. *You're* doing the best *you* can. That's all any mother can do. It's taken me a long, long time to accept that. I hope you'll believe it sooner than I did."

As we hung up, I wondered if I *could* believe it. I'd mishandled my children's emotions all year. Maybe I didn't know any better, but I *should* have. By trying to prevent suffering, I only caused more. By trying to prevent failure, I failed more miserably. And by trying to be selfless, I made myself center stage while seven children waited in the wings, including one very small, very vulnerable baby.

The question of self-pity.

My unraveling mind stopped midturn, realizing that I faced another trap. I could pity myself for pitying myself and be sucked again into a downward spiral of self-blame. Or I could forgive myself. I could step out of that suffocating room and into another—a sane place, a wise place. A place where I had done my best, and my best was enough.

"Mom, when are you going to be done?" Ben groaned. He and Andrew had been waiting all afternoon for me to come watch a "hilarious" SpongeBob episode on the DVD we'd rented from the library.

I didn't even take my eyes off the computer monitor. "I just need a little while longer."

"You keep saying that," Andrew complained.

True. The submissions deadline for *Gifts* had passed, and I had sixty-three personal essays to edit. I felt compelled to finish the manuscript as quickly as possible. I worked all day, every day, taking breaks to fix meals and change diapers. The dishes and laundry piled up, unnoticed. But Thomas rolled around happily on my bedroom floor, although sometimes I had to rescue him when he got wedged against the wall or under the furniture. And the other kids were cooperative—most of the time.

"A few more minutes," I said. The boys rolled their eyes and left the room.

I couldn't resist the sense of urgency hovering over my

shoulders. The more essays I read, the more I understood the need for them to be heard. I was horrified to read about obstetricians and perinatologists giving subtle or not-so-subtle pressure to terminate pregnancy. And I was even more horrified when I learned the abortion rate for fetuses prenatally diagnosed with Down syndrome: 90 percent.

It hurt just to think about that number. It hurt to imagine those mothers, so frightened, even desperate. It hurt to imagine the would-be babies.

I glanced at Thomas, who had rolled over to his fishbowl and put his hand inside, trying to feel the mysterious glittery water sandwiched between two layers of plastic. It had been a terrible thing to know about his problems before I knew *him.* His scrunched-up face and rose-petal fingers were my only consolation. Women who received a diagnosis during the early trimesters of pregnancy had much less to go on. Some faced a life-or-not decision even before they saw an ultrasound photo or felt a little foot kick their bladder. Add the insidious social conditioning against the disabled and the chilly clinical climate regarding Down syndrome, and sadly, high abortion rates didn't seem so mysterious.

"Are you done *now*?" Ben asked from my doorway. When I shook my head, he and Andrew gave me one of their mom-you-tax-my-patience sighs. They were frustrated, and so was I. With so much to think about, so much work to get done, I had no interest in watching banal cartoons about pants-wearing sponges. The boys didn't get it. But then again, how could they?

I stopped typing and faced them. "This is really important to me, guys. And I think it will be important to other people, too. Do you remember how scared we were when Thomas was first born?"

Their eyes softened, and they nodded.

"Did you ever think we'd love him this much?"

They glanced at Thomas, who was trying to put his face inside the fishbowl, and laughed.

"This is exactly what I'm talking about. There are so many people out there who are scared just like we were scared, and there are all these stories from moms about how much better their lives are because of their kids with Down syndrome. Maybe if we could've read stories like that, we would've felt a little less scared. That's why I'm so busy."

They thought for a moment. Then Ben spoke up. "Keep working, Mom."

The classroom was crowded with five-year-olds and their parents. Some of the kids looked nervous, some excited, some both. Same with the moms and dads. Starting kindergarten was a big deal for everyone involved.

In our district the school schedule ran year-round, starting at the end of July. It felt strange to be in a classroom in the middle of the summer.

With Sam by my side and Thomas's carrier over my arm, I guided Matt toward the name-tag table. He was wearing his trying-to-look-cool face, which he'd perfected after years of being at the mercy of four older siblings. Then we approached the teacher, who wore a plaid jumper and a schoolmarm hairstyle, streaked gray. She glanced at his name tag. "Welcome, Matthew!" she said. "Or do you prefer to be called Matt?"

He looked at the floor and mumbled something.

She bent her knees so she could see his face better. "What would you like to be called in class?" she asked again.

He looked up with a gleam in his eye. "Who cares?"

So much for making a good first impression.

I scanned the room for familiar faces. My eyes rested on the far corner, where a mom and dad stood with their children. The mom reached down to pick up her daughter and swung the child onto her hip: a little girl with a blond ponytail, almond-shaped eyes, and a teeny tiny nose. The little girl I'd seen at Christine's musical.

I quickly turned around before the mom caught me staring (again). My pulse raced. I wanted to talk to her, but for some reason I felt tongue-tied.

Thomas starting yelling in his car seat. As I unbuckled the straps and lifted him out, I had an idea—maybe if that family noticed Thomas, they would approach me.

Matt and Sam were roaming the room, peeking at the different stations: painting, dress-up, reading, counting, writing, listening. I casually moved closer to the mom, a few steps at a time. When I got within a few feet, I stopped and turned so Thomas's face would be visible over my shoulder. Then I waited, feeling stupid, but hopeful.

"Excuse me," a voice said.

I turned around with feigned surprise. It was the mom, still holding the blond girl. "I noticed your cute little boy, and I thought I'd introduce myself."

I smiled. If only she knew.

We chatted for ten minutes or so. I told her a bit about Thomas's early months and she responded with empathetic nods and exclamations. Then she told me about her daughter, who was three years old and learning to walk. Suzanne had been their first early intervention therapist, too. I hadn't felt so comfortable in ages. Although we'd barely met, we already knew each other somehow, and we already cared about each other's children.

Matt and Sam tugged on my hands, ready to go.

"I'm sure we'll be seeing each other around," the mom said.

I waved to the little girl. "Bye!" She looked at me for a moment, then ducked her head against her mother's shoulder.

I followed the boys out of the room, pleased by serendipity. My first face-to-face chat with another Down syndrome mom. After the fact, it seemed silly of me to have been so shy. Our conversation held no resemblance to the awkward encounters I'd envisioned way back in the fall. But then again, nothing was the way I'd thought it would be at the bitter start.

I opened the door for Suzanne and Melody for the first time in months. At the beginning of the summer I'd scaled Melody's visits down to once a month and requested that she and Suzanne come together, so that I didn't have to deal with two appointments. Then we skipped the July visit because of vacations.

"He's gotten so big!" Suzanne said as she settled on the floor next to Thomas.

"I know. And watch this." I turned on the stereo, and immediately he got up on all fours and started rocking to the beat.

Both ladies cracked up. "That's fantastic that he's responding to music so well," Melody said.

"Yeah, he does it every time he hears music." He had pretty good taste, too. Raffi got heavy play, but so did indie rock from the eighties and nineties, and even some grungy punk tunes. When we played The Clash he rocked so hard and fast it looked like he might launch.

Suzanne scooted closer to Thomas. "Well, Thomas, you're ready to crawl! Let's see what happens if we give you a little boost."

She knelt behind him and grasped his thighs. "I'm showing him how to bring one knee forward," she explained to me. But as soon as she nudged his leg, Thomas lifted one arm and reached behind him, trying to swat her hand away.

"It's okay, buddy. Just give it a try," I said.

Suzanne gently pushed his leg again, and he let out a yell.

She let go immediately. "Still no luck with the practice sessions?"

I shook my head. "He seriously hates to be handled. He refuses to do anything that's not his own idea."

"Yes, he's a stubborn little guy, isn't he?" She sighed. "Well, that can work in his favor. As long as he's self-motivated, he'll keep progressing. I wouldn't worry."

I wasn't worried. Not anymore, that is. For months I'd felt caught between conflicting agendas: Should we maximize sameness or celebrate difference? But I was done setting agendas. Thomas knew what he wanted, and he worked hard to get it—why not let him take the lead?

Melody picked up her clipboard. "How about the hearing aids? That still a struggle, too?"

"Yeah. If anything, it's worse than when we started." I hesitated a second, then took the plunge. "I'm planning on returning the aids at our audiology appointment next week."

The ladies exchanged glances. "How come?" Melody asked.

"It seems like they're doing more harm than good. If he didn't mind wearing them, we'd keep using them, but I've got to take his reaction into account."

Melody dug through her bag and pulled out a Xeroxed handout I'd been studying over the past weeks: a graph showing all the speech sounds in the English language and the decibel levels at which a typical person would hear them. "Tell me his ABR numbers again?" she asked.

I told her, and she marked the numbers on the graph. "So, it looks like Thomas can hear all the phonemes—that's good news. But for a few of the sounds, he's right on the borderline."

I nodded. I'd already figured all this out.

"Technically, his remaining hearing loss shouldn't interfere with his speech development, but the boost he gets from the aids could really help him. It's the same thing with eyeglasses—even a small correction in vision can be a significant change."

"But we don't even know if the aids are helping. And besides, these are $4,000 'glasses' that he can rip off and break easily."

Melody looked uneasy. So did Suzanne. But I felt great, so I kept talking. "If he can hear all the speech sounds without aids, then I say they're just not worth the effort."

Not worth the effort. As I spoke I realized how blasphemous the words sounded. Not worth the effort, when the latest professional approach to Down syndrome was to provide every possible compensation for delays. It sounded like I was being lazy, or apathetic. Like I didn't care about giving Thomas the best possible life.

But that was the whole point of our decision. Reed and I had weighed the risks and benefits, considered the odds, and made a choice that we felt was in Thomas's best interest. His hearing ability was an important factor in "maximizing his potential," but so was his emotional well-being. If we had to fight him constantly in order to save his life, or his health, or perhaps even his hearing, we would. But not for the possibility of slightly enhancing his hearing. That was a lousy deal.

"Well, okay," Melody finally said. "This is your decision. You're the mom."

Exactly.

"Hold his arms," the audiologist said as she tried inserting a probe into Thomas's ear for the tenth time. His protests sounded strangely muffled. We were in a soundproof booth for Thomas's first behavioral hearing exam, and the heavily insulated walls sucked up sound like sponges.

The exam required Thomas to have probes in both of his ears. Once the audiologist got them in, she had me sit with Thomas on my lap facing the booth's window, while she took her place at the soundboard on the other side. Flicking switches and turning dials, she sent tones through the probes into Thomas's ears, one ear at a time. When he turned in the direction of the tone, he was rewarded by flashing lights (on the right side of the booth), or the antics of a drum-banging monkey puppet (on the left side). But within thirty seconds, he'd ripped both probes out.

"Okay, let's try it without the probes," the audiologist said through the soundboard's microphone. She called his name again and again, projecting the sound to the right or left side of the booth. But in order for that approach to work, the booth had to be totally quiet. Fat chance. Thomas banged his hands on the table in front of us, blowing raspberries and yelling happily.

The audiologist opened the door of the booth and handed me a toy. "See if this will distract him," she said. I put it on the table, and Thomas quieted down as he fiddled with it. We got two decent responses out of him before he started banging the toy against the table.

This is dumb.

"I think we're done," I said. The audiologist nodded from the other side. I opened the booth door and carried Thomas out of the stuffy air.

After making some notes on the test form, the audiologist showed me the results. "According to the test, his right ear has moderate loss, and his left has moderate-to-severe loss."

"Yeah, but the test was pretty much worthless, wasn't it? I don't think it could tell us much of anything."

"I'm inclined to agree," she said. On her report she'd checked the box marked "poor" to indicate the accuracy of results. "We'll try this again in six months or so and see if we get more reliable data."

I put Thomas in his car seat. She handed me a copy of the test form, and I handed her the case with the aids.

"These just aren't working for us," I said. "We're turning them in."

She looked surprised as she took the case. "I see. Are you sure?"

"Yes." The ridiculous hearing test only confirmed the decision. Some things just didn't make sense.

She pulled the contract from Thomas's file and signed and dated the line for equipment return. I did the same. The breast pump, the oxygen stuff, and finally the aids: Thomas was attachment-free at last.

I said good-bye and headed out through the halls of the school for the deaf, past the classrooms that Thomas wouldn't be part of. The decision Reed and I had made would likely draw criticism from many professionals, and even from other parents. But that was okay. They could shout their opinions from the studio audience, but at the end of the day, we were the ones who would live with the consequences. And when everything shook down, our peace would come not from how well Thomas could speak, but from the knowledge that we'd honored his multifaceted needs rather than clinging to a narrow goal of "normal." We couldn't know his dreams—not yet. But I was willing to bet he wanted to be treated as a whole person.

The McDonald's Playland buzzed loudly with kids shouting and moms talking. I set our tray of Happy Meals on the table, then lifted Thomas from his carrier and buckled him into a wheeled high chair. He could sit straight for a minute or so at a time, but I shoved some burp cloths in the space just to help him be a bit more secure.

My friend Darlene set her stuff on the table next to mine. Her sons scurried off to the climbing structure, with Matt and Sam following right behind.

"So, how's the book coming?" Darlene asked as we settled into seats opposite each other. She was a writer—a poet—and had been cheering me on all summer.

I leaned back with a sigh of satisfaction. "Just a couple more essays to edit and I'll be done."

"What are you going to do with yourself then? I always feel kinda lost when I finish a big project."

"Me, too. So I've got another one lined up—writing my own book."

She raised her eyebrows. "Wow, good for you! What about?"

I pointed to Thomas, who was starting to slump in the high chair. "Working on all these other moms' stories has made me think a lot about my own."

"I can imagine. You've been through so much this year."

"Yeah, and I'm not sure what to make of it." I rearranged the burp cloths and sat Thomas straight up again. "I sketched an outline at the beginning of the summer, when I started to realize how much things have changed since he was born. I figured writing might help me understand it all."

She looked thoughtful. "This might sound weird, but I'm kind of envious. It seems like parents of kids with disabilities know this big secret that the rest of us don't get to understand. It's like you're all in this club, and you have the key to life or something."

Thomas waved his hands and yelled. "The key to life? Hmmm . . . nobody gave me one of those yet," I joked as I fished his bottle out of the diaper bag. "Seriously, the people I'm meeting are really great, but I can't believe they have a corner on the enlightenment market."

"Well, they'd better not—I want to be enlightened, too, and I can't custom order a kid with Down syndrome."

I laughed. "True. You could adopt one, but there's actually a long waiting list."

"Really?" She paused. "I had no idea. I mean, I knew some people adopted kids with special needs, but I didn't realize there was a line."

"I know. I was surprised, too." It was one of my many discoveries from the online Down syndrome community.

Thomas wanted out of the high chair. As I unbuckled him and lifted him out, I saw a woman staring at us. I sat down and pretended not to notice. But as Darlene and I resumed our conversation, the woman approached our table.

"Your baby is adorable! Would you mind if I held him?"

I hesitated—Thomas usually didn't like strangers, especially when he was cranky. But the woman looked so eager. "Sure, but he might cry," I warned as I handed him over.

"Oh, I doubt it." the woman said, cradling Thomas against her shoulder. "I just love Down's babies. They're always so happy!"

Thomas took one look at her and yelled. Loudly.

People at the nearby tables turned and stared. The woman looked mortified. I took Thomas out of her arms and smiled consolingly. "He's ready for his nap," I explained.

Flustered, she retreated to her table. I sat down again and tried not to laugh. I meant her no ill, but sometimes it's funny when stereotypes collide with reality. I wouldn't be surprised if God had been chuckling at me all year long.

The three of us were in bed: Reed, Thomas, and I. Thomas slept in his crib most nights, but he liked to fall asleep in the crook of Reed's arm, just like I did. Our lounge time together was one of the best parts of the day.

The other children were asleep. Our window was open to the summer night. Above the bed the ceiling fan circled, making a faint vibrating sound. Thomas lay on his back, playing with his hands. Reed and I lay on our sides facing each other, with Thomas between us. Our love child—corny, but true.

"Just think if someone told us before we were married that we'd have seven kids someday, and that one of them would have Down syndrome," I said. "What would you have done?"

"Run away screaming."

I snickered. It was the same for me. Back then, our future would've sounded like a death sentence.

Reed held out his finger for Thomas to grab. "It's weird," he said. "I used to think our lives were pretty much what we made them. But I'm realizing we don't have nearly as much control as I thought. For a long time everything was going our way, and then Sam was born sick. And then we had Thomas. Things just happen, and *boom,* everything changes."

"Yeah." I thought for a minute about what I used to believe. "Do you think those things happened for a reason, though? Do you think God made them happen?"

"I don't know." He paused for a moment. "With Sam, no. I think it was just one of those things. With Thomas, maybe. But maybe not. I think God knew what would happen, but that doesn't mean he *made* it happen. Maybe it was random nature."

Random nature. The concept used to terrify me, but I'd come to find it reassuring in some ways. I couldn't believe that I was divinely appointed to have a child with Down syndrome. I couldn't picture God waving some magic scalpel above my ovary so that my egg would divide abnormally, and then waving it again so that exact egg would be released at just the right time. And while Thomas's disability might serve some grand cosmic purpose, I couldn't call it a blessing any more than I could call it a tragedy. As Reed said, Down syndrome wasn't inherently good or bad, right or wrong—it just *was.* What it meant was up to us.

So why did I resist the fact that it might mean different things to different people. I told Reed what had happened at McDonald's, and he laughed just like I had. But the encounter had been bugging me ever since. "I don't like people thinking Thomas is perfect," I complained, "and I don't like how they give him no credit for his happiness, or lovingness, or whatever. The way they tell it, all the good things about Thomas are due to Down syndrome."

"Well, yeah. But I don't think anyone means it that way. People just want to say something positive, and they haven't considered all the implications of what they say. They haven't had any reason to."

True. Before Thomas came along we didn't have any reason, either. Maybe what bugged me wasn't so much what people said, but the fact that they said it in ignorance. It didn't bother me that other parents of kids with Down syndrome had points of view which differed from mine. What I resented were easy answers from casual observers.

"Do you think the clichés are true, though?" I asked Reed. "Do you think Thomas is special?"

He thought for a moment. "Depends on what you mean. Yeah, he's a really sweet kid, but I don't think he's more capable of love than our other kids. And I don't think he's any more loveable."

"Neither do I. But do you think he'll teach us to love each other, like you said in his blessing?"

"I think he will. I think he already is. But I don't think he was born just for our benefit, or anybody else's. We're learning a lot from him, but he's got his own stuff to learn in life, too."

Yes. He had more to do than sit around and make us feel all warm and fuzzy, like a space heater in a cold room. But I hoped he would stay close no matter what. Funny—after worrying for so long that he'd never leave me, I was worried that he would.

"When you said Thomas had a unique mission on earth, did you have any sense of what that might be?" I asked.

"Not specifically. I just know that he'll be able to do whatever he came here to do." He paused. "But I don't think it really matters what he does. He's valuable even if he never *does* anything. What matters is who he *is*."

After a long pause Reed spoke again. "I didn't tell you this before. But when I was preparing for the blessing, I was thinking a lot and praying a lot. I kept asking, 'What's going to happen?

How severe will his disability be? How can I learn how to be his father?'"

I nodded, although he could barely see me.

"And then I felt an answer. Well, kind of an answer. It didn't resolve my questions, but they didn't seem to matter anymore. I just had this really strong impression. Like I was hearing a voice with my mind instead of my ears."

I hardly dared ask. "What did it say?"

"Thomas is your son."

The words hung like stars in the darkening room, then slowly sank into the sheets. Thomas drifted into sleep. In the stillness I listened to him breathe, as soft as the night.

Planning Christmas cards in August might seem silly, but in our case it was a smart move. Decent Soper family photos were hard to come by, given all the fuss of haircuts, outfits, poses, and at least one kid possessed by at least one demon for the duration of the photo shoot. I wanted the dirty deed done well in advance of holiday chaos, so I was starting early. First task: hair. The boys would get buzzed with clippers (the way my mom used to clip our sheepdog). But I couldn't bring myself to buzz Thomas's head—not yet. So I loaded him in the van and took off for a visit to Peggy, my longtime friend who ran a salon out of her home (and could actually do a decent job with my very weird hair). I knew she'd get a kick out of giving Thomas his first "real" cut.

Peggy lived in our former neighborhood, twenty miles south along the Wasatch front. The mountainsides were burned brown by summer heat. Hard to believe there might be snow on them within a month.

Thomas was nearly one year old. Peggy hadn't seen him since December, when he was only a five-pound scrap of a baby, covered with tubes and wires. When we walked into her salon, she went nuts.

"*Look* at him!" she gushed. "He's gotten so big. I can't believe it!"

"I know. Crazy, huh?"

"A miracle." Thomas grinned at that.

"Yeah, you know we're talking about you, don't you?" Peggy said. "Oh, he's such a cutie. Are we doing him first?"

"No, me first. He might freak out, and I want to make sure I get out of here with presentable hair." I hadn't had a cut since before Thomas was born, and it had grown from a sleek bob to a pleasantly curly mess to a complete disaster.

I settled Thomas on the floor with a colander full of perm curlers to play with and plopped into the swivel chair. Peggy reclined the back so my neck rested against the edge of the sink. I shut my eyes and sighed with pleasure as she scrubbed my scalp with cherry-scented shampoo. If my neck didn't cramp in that position, I would pay her to wash my hair for a full hour.

"So, how *are* you?" she asked as she toweled my hair dry and combed it out. "Tell me everything that's happened since December."

That was another reason why I drove twenty miles for a haircut—free therapy. While Peggy snipped and combed, I started at Christmastime and moved forward, through the cold, hard darkness of January, the gloom of February, the despair of March. Then the relief of spring, and the layers of darkness that had been falling away like scales ever since. An almost-year, summed up in thirty minutes. The condensed story surprised me—had I really lived it?

When I finished, Peggy shook her head. "Incredible. And look at you now."

I studied my face in the mirror, older-looking than I expected (always the case since the year I turned thirty) and awfully pale for summertime, but peaceful. My still-damp hair fell to my shoulders. I looked like my mother.

Peggy put her hands on my shoulders and smiled at me in the mirror. "Nobody would ever guess you've been through one of the hardest things that can happen to a parent."

One of the hardest things? A year before I would've agreed, but sitting in Peggy's chair with Thomas at my feet, I wasn't so sure. Maybe I was feeling modest. Maybe I was already forgetting how hard it had been. Or maybe that assessment just didn't hold true.

I lifted Thomas from the mess of perm rods, then sat with him on the swivel chair. Peggy tried to get a smock around his neck, but he shoved her hands away. She approached with the comb and scissors, and he shoved again.

"You can't fool this kid," she said.

"Yeah, he must think we're about to skewer him." I held his hands down as gently as I could for most of the haircut, but I had to hold his head firmly against my chest so Peggy could get the lines straight around his ears and neckline.

Once she finished, she called for her teenage daughter to bring the camera. "Thomas's first haircut!" Peggy announced as she snapped a photo.

As I wrote her a check she stepped out of the room for a minute, and then returned with a sealed white envelope. "For his baby book," she said.

His hair. I got all teary. "Thank you."

On the way home Thomas snoozed in his car seat, looking so cute with his big-boy haircut. I drove north along the summer-brown mountains, thinking about the hard things and harder things that parents face. Kidnapping. Addiction. Disease. Death.

Disabilities that steal a child's mobility, or emotional stability. Any of those would be much, *much* harder to deal with than Down syndrome. Yet Peggy herself once taught me the limited value of such comparisons. *Knowing other people are in worse pain doesn't erase your own,* she'd said. And mine had been terrible.

But as the pain faded, I was beginning to see how unnecessary most of it had been. Thomas's diagnosis brought some inherent difficulties, like health concerns and education issues, but the stuff that *really* hurt didn't come from Down syndrome. It came from my reaction to Down syndrome. And that reaction was based largely on ignorance and prejudice. How much grief stemmed from my twisted beliefs that faster meant smarter, smarter meant better, and better meant happier? The bulk of my suffering had been self-inflicted, like when I soaked my bloody toe at Christmastime: The injury called for only a tablespoon of salt, yet I dumped in half a cup. Down syndrome didn't need to hurt so much. Neither did depression. And for that matter, neither did motherhood.

The irony just about killed me, but I had to smile. Thomas's disability had enabled me to face my own. And his diagnosis, which once seemed like a burden, had granted the sweetest relief.

The Relief Society president checked her watch. Standing next to the piano at the front of the room, she cleared her throat to get our attention. "Welcome, sisters! It's time to begin."

The sisters were a lively bunch this Sunday—it took a full minute for everyone to quiet down. The president made announcements about upcoming events: a blood drive, a gardening class, a ward social. I used to attend every gathering on the calendar. Maybe I'd be ready to try again before too long. But I needed to take things slow as I adjusted my spiritual bearings. My new landscape of faith was beautiful yet strange, swept by winds of chance as well as by fate, graced by God's will but shaped by my own.

After a hymn and a prayer, the instructor began the week's lesson. I had a hard time paying attention. I kept looking around at the sisters—their profiles, the backs of their heads, the instructor's smiling face. They were women I'd been hiding from all year, women I'd appreciated and resented. Mostly resented. I sheepishly recounted all the ways they'd helped my family: They cooked meals, offered rides, tended kids. They prayed for us. They brought Thomas gifts and gave him the warmest of welcomes. And they would've done even more if I had let them. Instead, I shut them out. My pride got in the way—pride, and vanity. Monogrammed silver, clutched in a frostbitten hand.

The more I thought about it, the more the truth stung. It's normal for a mother of a baby with Down syndrome to grieve, and it's normal for a mother of a premature, medically fragile baby to need help. It's even normal to want painful things to go away. But normal wasn't good enough for me. I wanted to be better than that. Above average.

Gifted.

Angelic.

The Relief Society instructor began wrapping up her lesson. I sat on my padded folding chair, awash in regret. I wished I had been more humble, more gracious. I wished I had been easier to please, even if just a little bit. I wished I had acknowledged my church family's good intentions, both in the things they did and the things they said—clearly, I'd transferred my unfair expectations of myself onto them as well. The last thing the world needed was more contention, more suspicion, more separation between good people doing their level best.

After the instructor ended her lesson, the president invited us to share our testimonies if we desired. As soon as she sat down, I stood up, walked to the front of the room, and turned around.

"A few months ago, when I first came back to church, I thanked you ladies for helping our family after Thomas was born. But I want to thank you again."

I paused to grab some Kleenex from the box on the piano.

"It was a really hard time for me. As much as I appreciated your help, I was pretty cranky about it. I didn't want to need help. I like to be the one giving it, not the one getting it."

Several women nodded in sympathy. Tears rolled as I felt their compassion wash over me, warm and soft.

"I just want to thank you for being so good. You're so good. You might not believe it, but you are."

Half the room was crying. I looked at all their faces and wondered why I'd ever doubted their goodness. They were *so* good—I could feel it. And from their gentle smiles, I knew they saw the same goodness in me, even when I couldn't see it in myself. Which was most of the time.

Week after week, Annie Dillard writes, *Christ washes the disciples' dirty feet, handles their very toes, and repeats, It is all right—believe it or not—to be people. Who can believe it?*

I, for one, had not.

That afternoon we had a family testimony meeting, which meant we gathered in the living room and took turns expressing our faith. It was something we did once a month, usually on the same Sunday as our ward testimony meeting. Theoretically they were solemn spiritual occasions, but more often than not, they turned into giggle fests.

Matt wanted to go first, which was risky. He tended to get goofy when he was the center of attention. Sure enough, when he stood up he pretended he was holding a microphone, like a talk-show host. "I really like Jesus!" he said with a cheesy grin. Of course all the kids cracked up. And of course Sam pulled the same stunt when it was his turn. Reed and I tried, and failed, to put a lid on the hilarity.

Andrew raised his hand, and Reed motioned for him to begin. "I want to share my testimony that I know we're blessed to have Thomas in our family."

Everyone got quiet.

"I know we can help him, and he can help us. I love him so much." His voice trembled, just like it had all those months before when he lay in the dark and spoke his love for his tiny baby brother.

Christine's voice broke the stillness that followed. "Sometimes I wonder what heaven will be like. But I think I already know, because of Thomas."

"Me, too," Elizabeth said. "I feel sorry for families who don't have a baby with Down syndrome."

Thomas was on the floor with his fishbowl, trying again to feel the glittery water, oblivious to all the adoration. He had no idea what he'd done for us, just by being himself. Just by existing. Every day, he reminded us what really mattered—and it had nothing to do with communication methods, or classroom situations, or goal sheets. What mattered was being together. What mattered was love, small and sweet and simple.

We ended our testimony meeting with a prayer. The kids headed to the kitchen for ice cream. But Ben lingered behind, his face drawn, looking at the floor. He stepped close to me and covered his eyes with his hand.

"What's the matter?" I asked.

He couldn't speak at first. "I'm just sad. I love Thomas more than anything, and I don't want life to be hard for him."

I put my arm around him. "What kind of hard?"

"Just that it won't be easy for him at school, because he won't be able to learn as easily as other kids." He started crying. "And people might tease him. They won't know what he's really like."

I wished I could contradict him. I wished I could tell him that everyone would see how funny Thomas was, how quick and clever, how determined and strong. But not everyone would.

"How did you find out what Thomas was really like?" I asked.

He sniffled. "By playing with him. And just being with him."

"Don't you think other people might find out the same way you did?"

"Maybe." His shoulders started to shake. "But Mom, what if they don't?"

I didn't know. Dread gripped me at the very thought.

And that gave me an idea. "Ben, do you feel worried about Thomas all the time, or only when you start thinking about the future?"

He wiped his eyes with the back of his hand. "When I start thinking."

"Sometimes that happens to me, too. And to Dad. When we start imagining what might happen, we get a little scared."

Ben nodded.

"But when we're just hanging out with Thomas, it doesn't seem so scary."

He nodded again.

"Maybe the best way to deal with our worries is to just focus on what's happening here and now. Know what I mean?"

"Yeah." He hugged me for a long minute and wiped his eyes again. Then he went to kiss his baby brother, and to claim his share of rainbow sherbet before it all melted. Smart kid—he knew the here and now didn't last very long.

"I'm finished!" I said when Mom answered the phone.

"With the book? Oh my gosh! Kathy, that's fabulous!"

"I know. I'm totally stoked." No book could fully capture the reality of living with and loving a child with Down syndrome, but *Gifts* came close. I only wished I could've read it when Thomas was first diagnosed.

"What's the next step?" Mom asked.

"Well, one of the contributors volunteered to do the typesetting, and once that's done we'll send it to Amazon." I'd arranged to have the book published through their print-on-demand service.

"I can't wait to see it! When do you think I'll be able to buy some copies?"

"In October. Right around Thomas's birthday, if you can believe it." He looked so grown-up in our new family portrait, which hung above the mantle. Thomas sat on my lap, right in the middle, looking slightly cross-eyed and charming as ever.

Mom kept bubbling over. "I'm so proud of you, my dear. What an accomplishment."

I blushed. The accomplishment wasn't mine alone, but why say no to flattery? "Wait till you read the stories," I said. "They're gorgeous. And the moms are such amazing women. All of them donated their writing with no thought of reward—they just want to help people. We're going to use the royalties to buy books for new moms."

"You know, that doesn't surprise me one bit," she said. "Special babies really do come to special mothers."

My shoulders clenched. "No," I said. "I don't think so."

Mom was quiet. My heart pounded. I didn't mean to get persnickety, but it just wasn't true. I wasn't special. I'd bet none of the other Down syndrome parents considered themselves to be special, either. And what about all the mothers throughout history who were so frightened of Down syndrome that they abandoned their babies to institutions, or left them to die outside village walls? How about the modern-day moms who chose abortion? Nothing special. Just a bunch of scared women.

I had to explain. "I know what you mean," I told Mom, "and when you read the book you'll understand what I mean. None of these moms started out any different from anyone else. They're wonderful people, but I don't think that's why they have kids with Down syndrome. I think it's the opposite. I think having a kid with Down syndrome helps them become wonderful."

Mom stayed silent for a long moment. "I never thought about it that way," she finally said.

Neither had I—the words just came out. They sounded right to me, but even as I spoke I knew they were incomplete. Having a child with Down syndrome didn't automatically grant those women compassion and goodwill. Whether the diagnosis came prenatally or postpartum, each of them had to decide whether to welcome her baby into the family. Each of them had to decide whether to open her heart to change, to difference, to hidden beauty and unsung worth. And each of them, consciously or not, had said yes.

Yes, we will love him. We will love her.

Maybe my friend Darlene was right. Maybe some parents of children with Down syndrome really *do* have the key to life. But if so, the club is hardly exclusive. Everyone who walks the earth faces the same choice: to love, or not. And everyone who chooses love receives the same reward, although it comes in different packages. Mine happened to be the slightly cross-eyed little boy sitting in the center of our family portrait, which hung in the center of the hearth, which stood in the center of our home—right where we wanted him to be.

On Sunday there was a church conference for multiple wards, similar to the "Strengthening the Family" conference I'd avoided earlier in the year. I didn't know the theme, and I didn't really care, either—I just wanted to make it through the two-hour meeting without a major headache from trying to keep the kids quiet.

A room with a video feed was provided for young families who grew restless during the long meeting. Usually it was packed with kids even noisier than ours, so we avoided it. But when we arrived that morning the room was completely empty. A major coup. I had the kids spread out in the first row of chairs next to the video monitor, free from the gaze of tight-lipped elderly church members.

The woman appeared about halfway through the meeting, right when my kids had hit their limit of sitting passively and began to titter, poke, and whine at each other. She was fifty-something, alone, positioned on a chair a few rows behind us. When I first noticed her I was mildly curious, but as my kids got rowdier I got annoyed. *If she wanted peace and quiet, she shouldn't be in here!* I thought, even though she hadn't done or said anything to indicate disapproval.

When the meeting ended and we stood to leave, she approached me from behind. As I caught sight of her from the corner of my eye, I felt a quick touch of panic—was she going to give me a lecture? Or, if I was lucky, give me one of those "What a lovely family you have!" lines we garner from time to time?

I turned with a benign smile, hoping for the best. She looked at me with an expression I couldn't read.

"Could I please hold your baby?" Her voice sounded funny— sort of choked, as if she were trying not to cry. Without hesitation I handed Thomas to her, and she began to weep.

She carried him back to the chair she had been sitting on and settled him on her lap. "Oh," she said, "oh, he has the most beautiful face." She stroked his cheek and cried harder.

Reed distracted the kids while I stood quietly, not sure what to do.

"I had a boy," she said finally. "A boy with . . ." She glanced at Thomas.

She *had* a boy. I steeled myself. "A boy with Down syndrome? And he passed away?"

She nodded. "I don't usually tell other parents, because I don't want to scare them." Sweet lady. She didn't know I'd already scared myself plenty this year.

"How old was he?"

"Five," she whispered.

Five years. I still couldn't picture Thomas any older than that.

"So young," I said. "What was his name?"

"Jason," she answered with a faint smile.

"I'm so, so sorry."

She smiled wider, as if to console me. "This was long ago—he would be thirty-one now."

"You must miss him so much."

She nodded and wept again. I could feel her grief, and her love. And with sudden clarity, I knew the two weren't mutually exclusive. They were two sides to one coin—the coin that had slipped into my pocket the moment I heard Thomas's first gurgled cry. I loved him even as I mourned him. I loved him even when I wished him gone. In truth, love was the very reason I'd wanted him to go—I thought he'd be better off without me.

I didn't think that anymore.

The woman was still crying. Thomas didn't usually let strangers hold him, but he continued to sit calmly on her lap, as if he knew what she needed. With trembling hands she ran her fingers through his hair and hugged him tighter. "His face, his face," she whispered. "It's been so long."

I lugged the bucket into the kitchen from the backyard and set it on the countertop. It was full of peaches from our tree, sun-warmed and golden, firm and fuzzy and heavy with the rich scent of September. Summer was almost over.

I lifted the peaches out of the bucket one by one and held them under running water from the faucet, rubbing their fuzz clean, dreaming of peach jam, peach pie, and peach cobbler (the best breakfast ever—with ice cream, of course). I was excited to make a grand peachy feast. At harvest time the year before I'd been six months swollen, too tired to make or bake anything. Too tired to do anything other than exist.

With a sharp paring knife I halved the fruits and pulled them open, revealing their pitted red-brown stones, whole and hard. I was startled when, splitting one peach, my knife struck the stone right on its crease, cracking it open. The seed clung to one half of the stone. I pried it loose with my finger. A tree in embryo, only a centimeter long. Thomas had been about that size when he began to move within me, a watery dance that I could not yet feel. But his genetic destiny had been set well before then, back when he was two cells, combining and dividing in a miraculous dance of their own. Back when he was only a seed.

So much happens within a mother, without her knowing. When Thomas was conceived, I didn't know that my body was creating a child of change. When I sliced peaches at the kitchen counter, I didn't know that I was on the verge of birth, and of death. The death of old ways. Old values. Old self, packed in a hard shell of protective beliefs.

> *I only produce normal babies.*
> *I can conquer any difficulty through sheer willpower.*
> *I will always give my children what they need.*
> *I am something better than human.*

Strange—I'd clung so tightly to those falsehoods, as if they could keep me safe. Yet I felt safer with them stripped away, safer with the naked truth in full view. I only wished change didn't hurt so much. It hurt to have my mind and heart cracked open. It hurt to be left raw in the open air. It hurt to lose the only life I knew, and to realize that no amount of magical thinking could bring it back.

On my fingertip, the peach seed looked and felt like a soft, damp almond. It seemed so small and so vulnerable. Yet when its time came, it had to leave behind its shell in order to live. Just as a baby must leave behind the womb, and a mother must leave behind her illusions.

Halfway to the NICU, I thought I might collapse. Thomas's car seat hung from the crook of my left arm, which had gone numb. My right shoulder carried the diaper bag, and my right hand carried an overstuffed plastic bag of preemie clothes. I walked—no, shuffled—along the crosswalk that connected the children's hospital, where Thomas had just had a cardiology checkup, and the university hospital where he was born.

Packing the bag of clothes had been bittersweet. I'd gathered all the tiny outfits we'd received as gifts as well as those we'd borrowed from the NICU, except for one: the blue pants and striped shirt with the embroidered tool set. That went into a memory box I'd started for Thomas, along with the inky blue cap with the white star.

His birthday was only three weeks away, and the girls had big plans. Helium balloons were a must. Christine was lobbying for a Thomas the Tank Engine train as one of the gifts. Elizabeth wanted to make the cake. I'd almost cried when I realized Thomas wouldn't be able to eat his own birthday cake—he couldn't manage food with much texture. But Elizabeth had a solution. *I'll make one out of whipped cream,* she said. I pictured Thomas slamming his hands into the fluffy white stuff, sending it flying all over the kitchen—and I smiled. Perfect.

I pushed the square metallic button on the wall to open the unit doors. There was the nurse's desk. The whiteboard, nearly full of patients' names. The bulletin board, ready for a new crop of Penny's photographs. The basket of crocheted caps. I felt like I was walking into a museum exhibit: *Thomas Soper, the NICU period.*

"May I help you?" asked the nurse at the desk.

I set the car seat down and approached with the bag. "I have some clothing to return, and some to donate. We were here last year."

"Thank you very much." She took the bag, smiled, and returned to her charting.

I stood there, feeling a bit silly. I didn't want to leave yet. "I'm wondering if some of the nurses who took care of Thomas are working today." I rattled off several names, but she shook her head.

I picked up the car seat and turned to go. The exit doors swung open. But after I'd stepped through, I turned around again.

"What about Valerie?" The lactation nurse.

"Yes, she's here. Want me to page her?"

I nodded and set down the diaper bag. When I saw Valerie coming down the hall, I held up the car seat. "Hi," I said, suddenly nervous. "I don't know if you remember us, but you were such a big help with Thomas, and I just wanted to show you how well he's doing."

She studied my face for a moment and then peered in the car seat. "What's your last name?"

"Soper."

"Thomas Soper! Of course I remember. He looks so different now." She paused a moment. "And haven't you changed as well?"

The understatement of the year. I could've tried to explain. I could've told her about the flying dream, and the half cup of salt, and the naked peach seed—but if I had, she might've called the social worker.

"Yeah, my hair's longer," I said.

She smiled. "I'm so glad you came in. How long has it been since Thomas was here?"

"Nearly a year. He was born in October."

"That's right. Around Halloween?"

I nodded. She leaned over the car seat. "Hello there, Thomas!" He grinned, and so did she. So did I.

"How is his health?" she said. "Any lingering issues?"

"Well, he's had a couple sets of ear tubes, and he has a bit of hearing loss, but other than that he's fine. We just had his cardiology checkup, and they think his little hole has closed by now. And the enlargement of his heart hasn't caused any problems so far."

"That's wonderful news." She motioned to a couple of nurses passing by. "Do you ladies remember Thomas Soper? Look how much he's grown!"

They stepped close. "Is this little Thomas?" one asked. "I can't believe it!" Before long a small crowd gathered in front of the nurse's desk, cooing and smiling at the celebrity. NICU parents walked past us with curious glances. I could only hope they'd be standing where I was, someday.

Valerie gave me a hug good-bye, and all the nurses wished us well. I lifted Thomas's car seat and walked through the heavy wooden doors for the last time, then stopped and looked behind me. A woman stood in front of the whiteboard, studying the list of names. Her hospital gown was wrinkled, her ponytail ragged, her feet bare. One hand sprouted a capped IV line. The other held a bright flash of gold: a tiny yellow cap from the basket by the sink.

Aspen groves covered the mountainsides with dandelion-yellow, strangely bright against the dark gray sky. The rain turned from sprinkle to drizzle as we took the freeway exit for Murray Park. "Are they going to cancel the Buddy Walk?" Christine asked from the back of the van.

"I don't know, sweetie. I hope not." I'd had to talk the big kids into coming—truth be told, I'd had to talk *myself* into coming, but I didn't want to turn around and go home. I scanned the street signs as we made our way through intersections, looking for the turnoff, then saw a large blue-and-white placard on the corner: BUDDY WALK, with an arrow pointing forward.

More signs led the way to the park entrance. I'd hoped to find a decent parking space so we wouldn't get drenched, but the lots were jammed. Cars were parallel parked on the side of the road.

People streamed toward the covered pavilions in the distance, some with umbrellas, some with jackets over their heads.

After cruising up and down the aisles, I finally found a spot in the far back corner of the lot. I turned to face the kids. "Okay, guys, let's do it."

Ben groaned. "Mom, we're going to get wet."

"Yep. Good thing you're a tough guy. I'm sure you can handle it."

He groaned louder. "What about Thomas? You don't want him getting wet, do you?"

The kid could smell my thoughts like a dog.

"I'll cover him with my jacket. He'll be fine." I hopped out of the van and got the stroller from the back, then loaded it with the diaper bag and my purse while the kids climbed out. Once Thomas was buckled into the stroller, covered with a blanket and my fleece hoodie, I herded everyone forward. "C'mon, it'll be fun!"

The little kids skipped ahead. Ben dragged his feet. But his pace picked up once we got a full view of the gathering, which featured some unusual VIPs: Darth Vader, Boba Fett, and several stormtroopers. As we got closer we saw they were shaking hands with people and posing for photos.

"Wow," I said, oh-so-casually. "Good thing I brought the camera."

The lady at the registration table handed us Buddy Walk T-shirts and told us we'd missed the walk itself, but we were welcome to stay for lunch. Perfect—the kids cared more about food than they did walking. Andrew put his shirt on immediately. The one I got for Thomas looked like it might fit by the time he hit college.

Down the path from the registration table, we passed a row of booths: Cotton candy. Popcorn. Sno-cones. Face painting.

Balloon animals. Behind the booths were carnival games.

"Mom, can we—"

"We'll see." Lunch was included in the registration fee, but I wasn't sure about the extras. At least the rain had slowed to a light sprinkle.

I wondered where all the people were. Small groups mingled here and there, but from the number of cars I'd expected hundreds. At least we wouldn't have to wait in line for a Star Wars photo op. The boys gathered around Darth Vader, close but not too close—he was, after all, the Dark Lord. But when I pushed the shutter button, nothing happened. A little red battery symbol blinked on the view screen. Matt would lynch me when he found out I'd botched the deal.

A sudden sound made me stop and turn—a crowd of people was coming down the path. No, not a crowd, a *parade,* stretching back as far as I could see. The frontrunners held a huge banner framed with blue and yellow balloons: UPTOWN DOWNS BUDDY WALK, 2006. We stepped back just in time. The walkers moved past us in a wave of blue shirts, people of all sizes and shapes. Hundreds and hundreds. Some pushed strollers with balloons attached, some carried signs, many cheered aloud as they crossed the finish line. Every one of them had woken up to rain but came anyway. They didn't want to miss the celebration.

The sky cleared as the last stragglers came along. We followed the masses to the lunch pavilion and then took our loaded plates to a nearby bench. As we ate I watched the families around us. They could pass for any crowd at the mall or the park, completely unremarkable, except in every cluster of people there was a familiar-looking face. Some of those faces belonged to toddlers and preschoolers, some to school-age kids, some to teens and adults. Stepping-stones to our future—a future I no longer dreaded, even though I still couldn't imagine it.

Summer

My friend Jen had told me that Jake's autism meant different things at different ages, and that every time he reached a new stage in development she had to adjust to his disability all over again. I knew we hadn't seen the end to our problems. But so far, Thomas himself had been providing solutions. Sad he wouldn't be smart? Voila—he proved that smart mattered not. Worried he'd crimp our style? Surprise—he was the ultimate in cool. Scared we'd miss out on a good life? Ta-dah—he showed us what a good life really was.

And what about when he grew up? What about my eagle fantasies? I shook my head—instead of holding me captive, like I'd feared, Thomas was setting me free. He granted me a bird's-eye view of what was real, what was true, what was valuable. And I sensed my future with Thomas would be priceless.

It was funny. All along I'd worried about waking up one morning to find an awkward disabled guy eating Froot Loops in my kitchen. But that guy wouldn't be some random man with Down syndrome. He wouldn't be Eric, or the man I hid from on the train, or the red-haired man in my in-laws' ward, or any of the men sitting near me, drinking sodas in the sunshine. He would be Thomas. He would be my son. Of course that being the case, he probably *would* be weird—but so much the better. And he probably would have limitations. But when it came to happiness, the only doors closed to us would be the ones we refused to open.

After lunch we handed out flyers advertising *Gifts*. The Amazon version would be released the following week, and—hooray!—a respected publisher had the manuscript under consideration. The kids were good sports about helping, but after fifteen minutes or so, they started eyeing the cotton candy booth.

After inquiring at the registration table, I turned to the kids with magic words: "Everything is free."

Their eyes lit up. "Seriously?" Ben asked.

Seriously. We hit the games first. Most of the volunteers were leaving for their lunch break, so they let the kids take charge. Drunk on freedom, they threw balls through hoops, ran the obstacle course, and hooked rings over bottle tops. Then they raided the treasure chests, helping themselves to the prizes inside. Most of them showed admirable restraint.

A small crowd was waiting for cotton candy, but there was nobody manning the machine. After a couple of minutes one of the moms took charge. "How hard can it be?" she said as she began spinning the sugar. My kids scurried to get in line. So much sweetness up for the taking, so many treasures to be claimed—all we had to do was step right up.

From one of the pavilions we heard what sounded like a band striking up. When we drew closer, we saw three girls with Down syndrome onstage in matching sailor suits, shaking to "Boogie Woogie Bugle Boy." They were smiling and swaying, wagging their fingers in time to the music on the PA. From the stroller Thomas bobbed his head and wiggled in his seat, moving to the music. When the song ended the crowd erupted with applause. Some people got on their seats and whistled.

Next up was a boy in a Spiderman suit, busting some major dance moves to the Spiderman theme song. My kids cracked up and cheered along with the crowd when he was done. Then came a kid in a motorcycle jacket and sunglasses rocking out to "Greased Lightning." Then three girls who shimmied through their steps in pink feather boas. Halloween had come early this year—and clearly, Down syndrome was nothing but another costume.

After a slight break in the action, four girls in sparkly red jackets hit the stage with a hip-hop routine. Energy streamed from their bodies, filling the air and touching us with glowing fingers, just like Thomas's radiant presence touched us every day. How it happened was still mystery. Maybe that extra chromosome acted like Teflon, preventing anything heavy or dark from sticking to his soul. But I still couldn't believe that his soul was that much different from mine, or Reed's, or Ben's, or anyone else's.

The audience cheered as a track from *High School Musical* boomed through the pavilion. A group of dancers in matching sweatshirts took the stage, raising their arms high and waving their hands to the snappy beat. Their bodies moved fearless and free, bending and twirling and jumping, inspiring us to do the same. *We're all in this together,* the lyrics rang out. And we were. The whole audience was on its feet, grandmas and grandpas, mothers and fathers, brothers and sisters and friends. We clapped and stamped in unison, as if we shared one heart, thumping to the same rhythm. As if the dancers' wild joy had ignited ours, freeing it from heavy layers of social convention.

Look what was hiding in these sorry scraps of bodies.

Maybe that was the answer to the mystery: By sharing his abundance, Thomas helped us rediscover our own. His innate goodness sparked ours. His raw humanity released ours. His unrestrained love awakened ours, calling it forth from deep, heavy sleep. Maybe the heaven we found in Thomas was a long-lost heaven inside ourselves, a sublime Pole within our very skins.

The afternoon was gone. Slowly we pushed the treasure-laden stroller toward the parking lot. Ben held a sno-cone in each hand, clearly amazed by his good fortune. Matt and Sam's shirts were covered with red and blue syrup. Christine and Andrew clutched bags full of popcorn and candy and prizes. Elizabeth tied her blue and yellow balloons to the handle of the stroller, where Thomas lay curled on his side, eyelids fluttering with baby dreams. We could still hear dance music on the breeze.

By the time we reached the van the rain had started again, sprinkling a gentle benediction. "I can't believe all the stuff we got," said Christine as she climbed into her seat, hands full of loot.

"Yeah," said Ben, buckling his seat belt. "This was much cooler than I thought it would be."

Indeed. I lifted Thomas from the stroller and settled him into the car seat, pulling the straps snug. Our little mouse. Our little mouse with wings, carrying the sweet and silent promise that we, too, can learn to fly. That costumes aren't worn forever. That none of us is of this world.

Thomas

A summer plum, pussywillows,
wind chimes.
Eternal dappled afternoon
and the rainbow in the sprinkler.

You'd think he was a kite
snapping in the merry gust,
dancing with the moon.

Million-dollar jackpot grin
that makes you want to stick around and try your luck.

Sweet padded dumpling hands,
like paws with feathered fingers.
Shiny chocolate-puddle eyes
that follow you around and crown you king.

But most of all, that heart—
a heart large and bright enough
for us in all our tiny stinginess
to sit beside and warm our bony hands.

— "For Thomas" by Darlene Young

Acknowledgments

Many people have asked me how a mother of seven can write while keeping the home front intact. Here's my current version of "intact": My laptop nestles on the kitchen table amongst stacks of sticky breakfast dishes (despite the fact that it's 3 p.m.). My kindergartner sits on my lap, jostling my elbow and my concentration. My toddler scrounges a snack from the broken crackers all over the floor. My tenth-grader wants to make zucchini bread from the pile of giant green zeppelins crowding the counter, but the mixing bowl is still crusted with batter from yesterday's pancakes and might require a hammer and chisel.

In short, this book is an unlikely triumph over the second law of thermodynamics.

The triumph is shared by the dozens of people who spent some or all of the past two years putting up with my crazed-writer ways. Those hearty souls include the exceptional women in my writers' group, Sharlee Glenn, Angela Hallstrom, and Darlene Young, who endured multiple drafts and various crises, both literary and personal, and somehow managed to love me all the while. Likewise, I thank Katrina Stonoff, wordsmith extraordinaire, for her extensive investments of time, skill, and care. For their insight and encouragement, I thank my early readers: Rebecca Bingham, Brittney Carman, Jennifer Graf Groneberg, Lisa Hardman, Melanie Jex, Emily Milner, Emily Orton, and Angela Schultz. Special thanks go to Angela Schultz for bearing my growing pains with a generous heart, and to Jennifer Graf Groneberg for blazing the trail I've been privileged to follow.

I thank Patricia Bauer for championing the cause of all people with disabilities, and for gracing my story with a portion of her own.

I thank my brilliant band of *Segullah* sisters, who continually sustain me with their faith and friendship. I also thank my many associates in the dynamic Down syndrome community, which unites parents across the nation and around the world. In particular, I thank Rebecca Phong, who first welcomed me to that community, and the sixty-two other women who made *Gifts* a beautiful reality.

On the professional front I thank Jennifer Enderlin at St. Martin's Press for giving me confidence to venture into the maelstrom known as the national trade. I thank my agent, Kate Epstein, for taking me under her wing and navigating the chaos with patience, skill, and good cheer. And I thank the Globe Pequot Press—particularly my editors, Kaleena Cote and Mary Norris—for providing a clean, well-lighted place for my story to (hopefully) live long and prosper.

For loving and forgiving their distracted, oft-distressed mother, I thank my children: Elizabeth, Benjamin, Andrew, Christine, Matthew, Samuel, and Thomas. They are my story. (And no, Ben, you don't get a cut of the royalties.) I think my caring father, Peter Lynard, for making my education possible and encouraging me to pursue a career in writing. I thank my mother, Carol Petranek, for her extraordinary love and support through all the seasons of my life. I thank my friends, Kate Castle, Jen Erekson, Ellen Reichard, Kerry Spencer, Kylie Turley, and Darlene Young for being a cherished part of my life, and of this memoir. Even more, I thank my husband, Reed, who has shared every aspect of my life with unflagging love and loyalty for the past sixteen-plus years. To his credit, he (almost) never complained about my extended affair with my "second husband" (the laptop) and has yet to utter one word about the ten pounds of stress fat I gained while writing this final draft.

And finally, most of all, I thank Thomas Reed Soper for transforming my life, and my heart.

About the Author

Kathryn Lynard Soper is founder and president of The Segullah Group, a nonprofit organization that produces personal writings. Her publications include *Segullah,* a literary journal for Mormon women, and two anthologies—*Gifts: Mothers Reflect on How Children with Down Syndrome Enrich Their Lives* and *The Mother in Me: Real-World Reflections on Growing Into Motherhood.* Kathryn lives with her husband and seven children in Salt Lake City, Utah. For more information about Kathryn and Thomas, visit www.kathrynlynardsoper.com.